GABRIEL FAURÉ

A Life in Letters

GABRIEL FAURÉ

A Life in Letters

Translated and
edited by

J. Barrie Jones

B.T. BATSFORD LTD · LONDON

To Percy Young

ISBN 0 7134 5467 9 (cased)
    0 7134 5468 7 (limp)

Typeset by Lasertext Ltd., Stretford, Manchester, England.
and printed by Anchor Press, Tiptree, Essex.

for the publishers
B.T. Batsford Ltd.
4 Fitzhardinge Street
London W1H 0AH

Contents

List of letter facsimiles
(between pages 96 and 97)

List of photographs
(between pages 96 and 97)

Acknowledgements

The preparation over several years and eventual completion of a book of this size – involving as it does transcription, translation and commentary – would not have been possible without the co-operation and generous assistance of a large number of people. There often develops a love-hate relationship with any lengthy research topic, resulting in the inevitable attendant fluctuations of enthusiasm. My first debt is to the late Philip Radcliffe for helping to sustain my interest in Fauré's music when acting as supervisor for my doctoral thesis on the composer in the early 1970s. His generous spirit and encyclopedic knowledge of music were and will remain a legend.

In Paris my debt to a number of individuals and institutions is considerable. The late Mme Philippe (Blanche) Fauré-Fremiet, daughter-in-law of the composer, was always most generous and hospitable on the occasions when I visited her home. Not only did she allow me unrestricted access to the extensive correspondence then in her possession, she also presented me with a copy of her husband's *Lettres intimes,* which forms the backbone of the present book, as well as a number of photographs and other documents. I owe a particular debt of thanks to M. Jean-Michel Nectoux who, as explained in the introduction, has been largely responsible for the present state of Fauré scholarship. His publications and his conversations with me have been invaluable. He most generously gave me copies of his early book on Fauré (1972) and of his Fauré-Albéniz correspondence. My overall debt to M. Nectoux will be readily apparent by the end of this book. I offer my cordial thanks to the courteous staff in the music department of the Bibliothèque Nationale and in the library of the Paris Conservatoire. I must acknowledge the permission granted by the Bibliothèque Nationale to quote from manuscript letters in its collection. I am especially grateful to the Société Française de Musicologie, published by Heugel et Cie., and also to the now defunct *Association des amis de Gabriel Fauré*: in both instances I have generously been permitted to quote from their publications free of charge.

I am greatly indebted to various departments, colleagues and friends at the Open University in Milton Keynes. This book could not have been completed in its present form without a number of generous grants from the research budget of the University's Faculty of Arts. It was a great relief to me to be able to draw upon the expertise of Mike Levers of the Open University's graphic design department: his photographic skills made my subsequent work on letter facsimiles a pleasure rather than a drudgery. The staff in the Open University library was invariably cheerful and helpful, and on a number of occasions pointed me in the appropriate direction regarding elusive books and catalogues. John Taylor, of the university's publishing division, has smoothed an often thorny path over the years by scrutinizing my translations; he has made innumerable suggestions which have contributed greatly to the flow and naturalness of my efforts, and I am particularly happy to place this on record. A burden which few authors ever have to carry is the immense labour involved in typing, often from an untidy and illegible script. I offer my deepest thanks to Margaret Curtis, Valerie Moggridge and Hildegard Wright for their exemplary skill and constant enthusiasm for this task. Additionally, Hildegard Wright helped me with Fauré's relatively few but frequently inaccurate attempts to write German. For the reproduction of the acknowledgements, introduction and index I express my cordial thanks to Sandie Smith. Finally, Hilary McLeod transferred, at very short notice, the complete typescript onto a word processor: for this I am deeply grateful.

In conclusion my thanks are due to Timothy Auger of B.T. Batsford Ltd, for his patience, enthusiasm and helpful advice. For other assistance of various kinds I am most grateful to Roger Nichols and Paul Chipchase. I must also express my profound appreciation to Trevor Herbert, Staff Tutor and Senior Lecturer in Music at the Open University in Wales, who has read through the whole typescript immediately prior to publication, and as a result has suggested a number of improvements and corrected several errors. For those which remain I must accept full responsibility. My greatest debt, however, is to Percy Young. From the beginning he has taken a deep interest in this book, and his knowledge and experience have been of inestimable value to me. He has not only read the whole book and made a large number of suggestions but has also given most generously of his time and trouble. Typically, in addition to all this, he has kindly read the proofs with meticulous care. The dedication of this book to him can indeed be merely a small recompense for his labours.

Introduction

Fauré's reputation, outside of France, has depended hitherto on his highly personal songs, a small part of his chamber music, and the *Requiem*. Indeed the *Requiem* has taken a particular hold on the hearts of the British and American public. Yet there are many works by Fauré – the Second Piano Quartet, much of the late chamber music and a great deal of the solo piano music – which are still relatively unknown to the general public. And turning to Fauré's two full-length works for the stage – *Prométhée* and *Pénélope* – to be able to attend a performance of either is indeed an event in one's life.

Fauré's correspondence has attracted even less attention than his music. As is so often the case with a famous figure who died as recently as 1924, much of this correspondence is widely scattered, despite important collections of letters preserved in various departments of the Bibliothèque Nationale in Paris and smaller collections in Europe and the United States. Although Fauré was in his early thirties when the telephone was invented, he lived in an age when letter writing was not merely an act of communication but might even be described as an artistic pursuit in its own right. Certainly Fauré's correspondence was voluminous, and although there may one day be a 'complete' edition of his letters it can reasonably be assumed that the day in question has to be in the distant future.

Pending that arrival, there is a pressing need for the publication of as much relevant material as can conveniently be contained in a single volume. The present book is an attempt to paint a portrait of Fauré by means of his own and his correspondents' letters, complemented by linking biographical material. As far as is practicable, it should be possible to read the whole book as a biography and in many places as an autobiography. I have made no attempt to discuss Fauré's music, except briefly where remarks in the letters themselves seemed to invite such discussion. The most recent large-scale book on Fauré's music in English, one which is particularly authoritative on the composer's sketches and musical techniques, is that by Robert Orledge, published by Eulenburg in 1979. The reader is referred to this work for such information as may be required.

Recent research on and publication of Fauré's letters have been confined almost exclusively to France and almost single-handedly to one musicologist, Jean-Michel Nectoux. Since the early 1970s he has written several books and numerous articles on Fauré and his music. His many achievements include complete reassessments over the dating of a number of Fauré's compositions. Equally impressive is his scholarly and painstaking research on Fauré's letters, many of which he has edited for publication. His *Correspondance Saint-Saëns – Fauré*, published in a second edition in 1978 by the Société Française de Musicologie (Heugel), and the correspondence between Fauré and Albéniz, printed in the *Travaux de l'Institut d'études ibériques et latino-américaines* at Strasbourg in 1977 both paved the way for his masterly *Gabriel Fauré: Correspondance*. This appeared in an English translation by J.A. Underwood in 1984, published by Marion Boyars. It comprises a collection of 212 letters, mostly by Fauré, and also includes much interesting material on Fauré's relationship with Marcel Proust, the Princess de Polignac and other Parisian society figures.

The present book can be regarded as complementary to Nectoux's volume. (Out of a total of 312 letters, only 15 overlap.) I have selected my material from five sources of which one is the collection of *Lettres intimes*, edited by Fauré's younger son Philippe, originally published by Grasset in 1951 and long out of print. There are two collections of manuscript sources on which I have drawn. The first, described unofficially as the *Fauré Archives*, was housed originally at the composer's last home in Paris, 32 Rue des Vignes in the Passy *arrondissement*. This was also the home of Fauré's younger daughter-in-law Mme Philippe Fauré-Fremiet, who most generously allowed me to photograph over 100 letters in her collection. Before her death in 1983 this collection was transferred to the Bibliothèque Nationale. This institution now houses by far the largest assemblage of unpublished material relating to Fauré. Out of this vast collection I have selected 22 letters originally in the Département de Musique. The last two sources are again from published material. Among the most interesting letters are those between Saint-Saëns and Fauré: interesting because of the frank exchange of views between two great musicians. I have taken 24 letters from Nectoux's edition of these composers' complete correspondence, referred to above. Finally, I have quoted six letters from various issues of the *Association des amis de Gabriel Fauré*, an organization which formally disbanded in 1983 on the death of its president, Mme Philippe Fauré-Fremiet.

There are five sections to the book. Three convenient events in Fauré's life were his marriage in 1883, the production of his open-air lyric drama *Prométhée* in 1900, and that of his opera *Pénélope* in 1913. The Great War forms an obvious self-contained area, a period when in his letters Fauré voiced quite strong views as to the way the war was being conducted, and was himself greatly distressed by the fact that one of his sons and many of his pupils and friends were on active service. The sections thus correspond to the years 1845–83, 1884–1900, 1901–13, 1914–18 and 1919–24. Relatively few letters survive from the time of Fauré's youth, and our knowledge of his courtship with Marie Fremiet and of the years immediately succeeding their marriage is scanty. For this reason the linking material is more substantial in the first two sections than it is subsequently. The terrible siege conditions in Paris during the Franco-Prussian War represented an ideal opportunity to flesh out the material at this point by means of relevant quotations from Parisian newspapers and journals. Similarly, not many letters survive from Fauré to his wife during the first ten years or so of their marriage: with the exception of brief foreign visits undertaken to propagate his music and to pay visits to Bayreuth, this was a period when Fauré tended to remain in Paris. When in 1892 he was appointed inspector of music in the provincial conservatories, this marked the start of a period which was to entail a considerable amount of travel, resulting in more numerous letters to his wife than previously.

Short extracts from a few of the *Lettres intimes* have appeared previously in print, but the book has long needed an English translation as it is the principle source of information on Fauré's travels, on his views of music and musicians, and on the genesis and progress of his own music, in particular that of *Pénélope* and the late chamber music and songs. Sometimes these letters are somewhat sparse and occasionally telegraphic in certain details; this is partly due to Marie Fauré's replies, many of which have not survived. Any ambiguities or obscurities in the letters are frequently a direct result of this. In addition, Philippe Fauré-Fremiet made occasional cuts in the letters where certain matters of minor interest were being discussed. However, these cuts rarely result in an impairment of the narrative thread.

By 1900 Marie Fauré had become the principal confidante of her husband. The increasingly protracted periods of separation between them may have occasioned a conscious move away from those close friends at the time of Fauré's bachelorhood and early married life: Marie Clerc and the Princess de Polignac, for example. Perhaps Fauré felt guilty on the frequent occasions when he left his wife behind in Paris, particularly as it seems likely that the numerous concert tours which he undertook he thoroughly enjoyed because of, rather than despite, Marie's absence. For whatever reason, when away from Paris Fauré wrote to his wife almost daily. It is certainly instructive to compare these letters with the ones he wrote to his first fiancée Marianne Viardot, a representative selection of which appears in the first section of the book.

More will be said of Marie Fauré in the first two sections, and it must be stressed that relatively little is known of the more intimate details of the Faurés' married life. It seems certain, however, that Marie eventually came almost to resent her husband's success, not so much out of jealousy, but because she seemed never to take any part in it. She did not, for example, attend the triumphant first performances either of *Prométhée* at Béziers in 1900 or of *Pénélope* at Monte Carlo in 1913: performances which represented two of the greatest successes of Fauré's career, the more so as he had always been associated almost exclusively with the composition of music in the smaller forms. It is difficult to escape the conclusion that Fauré, despite the fondness he undoubtedly felt for his wife, never seemed at his happiest in her company. For all the painted fans she worked in order to supplement her husband's modest income, she was concerned essentially with the upbringing of their two sons and with domestic matters in general. The everyday problems of family life easily upset her, as is shown by the letters she sent her husband in 1896 when he was paying one of his many visits to England. These letters, trivial enough in themselves, go a long way towards revealing Marie Fauré in her true colours. Nonetheless, the letters from Fauré to his wife reveal him as a superb depictor of fine scenery, a shrewd observer of human nature and a witty and lively commentator on both the important and the more humdrum aspects of everyday life.

Regarding the unpublished material in the *Fauré Archives* and Biblio-thèque Nationale, the greatest problems were, as might be expected, those of decipherment and dating. Fauré's own handwriting is not generally difficult to read, and inevitably becomes clearer as more letters are read. More obvious difficulties arose with Fauré's correspondents, with the appearance of new styles of handwriting each requiring a return to square one with the perusal of new and quirky graphic styles. A few – Richard Strauss, Debussy and Queen Elisabeth of the Belgians – were exemplary in their neatness and legibility, but many letters posed well-nigh insuperable problems of transcription. Some of the letters from these two sources are, as far as I am aware, here published for the first time.

Fauré rarely dated his letters fully until his old age. The edition of the *Correspondance Saint-Saëns – Fauré* by Jean-Michel Nectoux, noted above, was invaluable to me regarding innumerable problems of dating and its frequent footnotes. The letters in the *Association des amis de Gabriel Fauré* periodicals were also edited by Nectoux.

On those occasions when I had to fall back on my own resources, the Easy Reference Calendar was helpful. Square brackets around a complete date is usually that of postmark; if not, a note is supplied or an explanation given immediately preceding the letter in question. A date such as 'Friday [21 Jan.]' can obviously be inferred from the date of postmark where it exists, and in such cases I have not commented further. Square brackets around a year where the original writer supplied only the day and month, for example '4 July [1887]' indicates that the year has been added by another hand acting on information from the postmark on the original envelope. Where the latter was no longer extant, I have indicated the method of dating.

A number of letters display a curious quirk whereby, for example, '31. x.^bre 11' is not 31 October, but 31 *December*, 1911. I am unable to say how widespread the practice was in regarding the months from September to December as the Romans did: i.e. as the seventh, eighth, ninth and tenth months of the year. In any event, this foible is certainly a trap for the unwary.

There are occasional situations where the original French gives a characteristic flavour to the letter, by means of the familiar *tu* rather than the more formal *vous* for the second person, which is difficult to convey by means of the simple English 'you'. English is in fact the only European language where the familiar forms of 'thou' and 'thee' have, except in the Bible, disappeared completely from the written form and have very nearly done so from the spoken tongue, except in remoter areas where dialect is still occasionally in use. I have identified those letters which originally employed the *tu* form by adding an asterisk to the letter number. (It will be noticed that quite a number of letters from Fauré to his wife do not refer to the second person at all! I have not, in these cases, added an asterisk to such communications.) Now and again Fauré uses *vous* in letters to Marie, where obviously 'you' means 'you and the boys'. Similarly, when a letter begins 'Cher Monsieur' without a surname following, the meaning is not always as formal as the English 'Dear Sir'. In such cases Monsieur has been left in the original French.

It is sometimes difficult to be consistent with titles and proper names. Ideally one ought perhaps to translate all foreign titles of songs and operas into English. In practice this is a cumbersome procedure. In many cases it is usually unnecessary since many French compositions, at least, are universally known in the English-speaking world by their original titles. Additionally, a song such as Fauré's *Les berceaux* will be found in that form in the library catalogues; this will not usually be the case with 'The cradles'. The title of the song cycle *La Bonne Chanson* – as in a number of Messiaen's organ pieces – is impossible to translate satisfactorily into English. 'The good song', in the translation of Nectoux's *Gabriel Fauré: Correspondance*, is a totally inadequate realization of the meaning. It may seem perverse to retain the form of *Pénélope* when the English version of the name is almost identical. It is however consistent with the usual practice of retaining a title in its original form. On the other hand I have translated the names of individual characters in this opera, since it seemed more sensible to refer to Eumaeus and Ulysses rather than Eumée and Ulysse. Hence the inconsistency – more apparent than real – of *Pénélope* the opera, and Penelope, the principal character in that opera.

I have decided against providing a map of France to indicate the extent of Fauré's travels: the towns and villages he visited are so numerous that it would have been impossible to indicate them all. Smaller places are usually given some indication of their proximity to a well-known town or region, either in a note or in the text. I have given this information in miles, although the letters use, naturally enough, the metric system. The large numbers of personal names in these letters are identified (where it has been possible to do so) and commented on both in the notes and in the linking material, so as to provide some semblance of variety.

Paragraphing and punctuation in the manuscript sources have been left as in the original, even where this may at times seem to result in some eccentricities. The only exception to this practice has been the occasional addition of a comma or the substitution of a colon for a semicolon (or vice versa) in order to clarify the meaning.

Although the letters are arranged chronologically there may at times seem to be an inordinately extended interval between one letter and the next; and at other times a large number of letters within a relatively brief period. This is easily explained. When Fauré was in Paris his life was, for the most part, relatively uneventful. His absences from Paris seemed to coincide, not altogether surprisingly, with events of a more colourful and interesting nature. One thus finds frequently a whole batch of letters within a concentrated period: the letters to Marianne Viardot (August– September 1877) and those to Marie Fauré describing the events leading up to the first production of *Prométhée* (August 1900), for example. Such bursts of concentrated letter writing are seen vividly during the brief summer months of most years after 1900, when Fauré left his family in Paris in order to compose, free from the distractions not only of family life but also of his Conservatoire responsibilities. His favourite places were the Haute Savoie region of south-eastern France, the Riviera and Switzerland.

Finally, there follows a brief summary of the abbreviations used for the five provenances of source material and a reminder of the meaning of the asterisk employed throughout the text.

LI   *Lettres intimes*, ed. Philippe Fauré-Fremiet

FA   *Fauré Archives:* material originally at the home of the late Mme Philippe Fauré-Fremiet, and now in the Bibliothèque Nationale

BN   Bibliothèque Nationale (Department of Music)

SSF   *Correspondance Saint-Saëns – Fauré,* ed. Jean-Michel Nectoux

AAGF *Association des amis de Gabriel Fauré,* issues ed. Jean-Michel Nectoux

★   Indicates original letter employs the familiar *tu* form for the second person

1

The apprentice composer
1845–83

Not untypically for a composer, Gabriel Fauré was not born into a musical family, but one which originated in the southern *département* of Ariège. On his father's side, both his grandfather and great-grandfather had been butchers; on his mother's, the family had some pretensions to nobility. However, Fauré's father, Toussaint-Honoré (1810–85), was a schoolmaster in Gailhac-Toulza, the town where Gabriel's maternal grandfather was born. At the age of 19 Toussaint-Honoré married Marie-Antoinette-Hélène de Lalène (1809–87). By 1839 he had been promoted to duties of a more administrative nature as an Assistant Inspector of the primary schools at Pamiers. Gabriel, born on 12 May 1845, was the youngest of six children, having a sister Rose, and four brothers, Amand, Paul, Fernand and Albert. He was put out to nurse at a neighbouring village until he was four, by which time his father had received further promotion as director of the Montgauzy Teachers' Training College (*École normale*).

Having returned to his own family circle, Gabriel's life assumed some semblance of normality. However, as his siblings were all somewhat older than he, and as his natural inclination was to be taciturn and thoughtful, it is hardly surprising that throughout his life Gabriel Fauré was a man somewhat difficult to know intimately. His more extrovert brothers seem to have had little in common with him; his sister was 15 years his senior. Still, his wanderings into an old chapel, which had formed part of the ruined convent at Montgauzy, brought him into his first contact with music. He discovered a harmonium there, and one day was heard playing by a blind elderly woman who directed Toussaint-Honoré's attention to Gabriel's skilful musicianship. Toussaint-Honoré sought the advice of Dufaur de Saubiac, parliamentary deputy for the *département,* and it was on his recommendation in 1854 that Gabriel was sent to the Ecole Niedermeyer in Paris.

Louis Niedermeyer (1802–61), a Swiss composer and teacher, had established his 'Ecole de musique religieuse et classique' in 1853. The broader scope of the curriculum and the more liberal attitudes of the teaching staff had already indicated to knowledgeable musicians its superiority over the more traditionally-based Conservatoire. Moreover, Gabriel's obvious musicianship was so pronounced that Niedermeyer offered to take him without payment. Despite the excellence of the courses of study, certain conditions at the school were far from ideal. The rooms were gloomy, the food mediocre. Yet because of the enlightened nature of the teaching and the companionship of the kindred spirits he found there, Fauré in later life always spoke of the school with fond recollection and gratitude. Dufaur de Saubiac did more than merely attempt to gain Niedermeyer's interest in Gabriel at the outset. Fauré's earliest surviving letter indicates how de Saubiac helped his young protégé in more prosaic ways: this letter, despite its grammatical errors and a frequently-found childish tendency towards needless repetition, remains both respectful and poised.

1   GABRIEL FAURÉ to M. DUFAUR DE SAUBIAC

Paris
7 March 1855

Sir, I am writing a couple of words to you so as to advise you not to take the trouble of fetching me in a fortnight, as my aunt has promised to fetch me. I am advising you of this in order that you will not take the trouble of fetching me. I can say quite truthfully that they are quite happy with me on the piano. Has it been a long time since you had any news from Foix? How is your family? I've written 3 letters, no replies, don't know why.

Goodbye, Sir
Your very devoted
FAURÉ G
Paris 7 March 55

Even without knowing that at the Ecole Niedermeyer a special interest was taken in musical history, chamber music, Gregorian chant and sixteenth-century music, one could guess its musical catholicity from the numerous prizes awarded to Fauré during his years there. They consisted of: Handel's *Judas Maccabaeus*, sole prize for musical rudiments in 1857; Haydn's *Seven Last Words*, equal second prize for harmony, 1860; a volume of John Field's concertos, first prize for piano, 1860; and the full scores of Mozart's *Don Giovanni* and *The Magic Flute*, first prize for composition, 1865[1].

Niedermeyer died in 1861, and providentially for Fauré this resulted in the arrival at the school of Camille Saint-Saëns (1835–1921) as professor of pianoforte. However, as César Franck was to do at the Conservatoire in the succeeding decade, Saint-Saëns complemented his classes by playing the music of Liszt and Wagner to his students. More significantly, he examined the youthful compositions of those same students, and as Fauré remarked in an article written towards the end of his life:

> He read them with a curiosity and a care which only masterpieces would have deserved.[2]

A strong friendship was established between the 15-year-old Fauré and the 25-year-old Saint Saëns almost from the beginning, and was to last until Saint-Saëns's death 60 years later. During the summer of 1862 Saint-Saëns had been to visit Fauré's parents, who were by this time living in Tarbes in the *département* of the Hautes Pyrénées, not far from Lourdes. Toussaint-Honoré was now a director of the Ecole Normale in Tarbes, a branch of the Académie de Toulouse. From time to time Fauré's parents would send parcels of food to Saint-Saëns's home in Paris. (*See* letter 6). After Saint-Saëns's departure from Tarbes, Gabriel Fauré wrote him a number of letters in which it is clearly evident that he was already suffering from the headaches and dizziness which were to trouble him for much of his life. Most of the personal names mentioned in these letters were friends of the Fauré family. The letters also make reference to various beauty spots, such as Gavarnie and Bagnères de Bigorre. Fauré erroneously dated the next letter 12 August instead of 12 September, and the succeeding letter 1863 for 1862.

2 GABRIEL FAURÉ to CAMILLE SAINT-SAËNS

Académie de Toulouse
Ecole Normale de Tarbes
Tarbes
12 August 1862

At last I think I am starting to get better... The incessant headaches have ceased, and people no longer fear that my illness might be serious. This will be equally welcome news for you, I know, it is for this reason that I am telling you about it. What will please you more is the great pleasure your letter has given me, and there are those people who convey their thanks to you in return for your kind greetings: my parents first of all, M. Caron and finally the ladies of his family.

People talk to me about you to such an extent that it might become boring if ever it were within my power to get tired of hearing your praises sung, and of singing them myself... This is the first time I have said something nice to you, so don't think I'm being too flattering.

Everyone is sorry you have left though it isn't stopping everybody from enjoying themselves now and again. In the circumstances I am playing a somewhat dreary role, given the state of my health.

Mlle Henriette is still charming (as to whether she is beautiful, that's another matter), and as for the ill-wind towards you she isn't being such a nuisance any more. You have removed a terrible thorn from my flesh and I owe you more than I can say!

As soon as I am better I shall flounder as best I can in what you deign to call your little 'nastiness'. Do you know why I shall play it? Because of its major key which is extremely fond of me, and which I love very much myself.[3]

Mlle Léon is leaving here: this is to inform you that she is well. The Cabanel ladies arrived today too: I have paid them your compliments, and they received them enthusiastically.

I was re-reading just now a descriptive guide to Gavarnie: it talks of the climb up to the Roland breccia – it appears to be very easy and really splendid: we must consider doing it next year.

In anticipation of this epoch which will, I hope, recall for you our true friendship in every respect and also my mother's tender concern – she is sorry she can no longer scold you – all affectionate greetings,

Your devoted friend
GABRIEL FAURÉ

My parents also send you their good wishes, and along with me pay their compliments to the ladies.[4]

In front of me I see a picture showing an elephant... and this elephant... was... so much the better then.

Your letters are so charming, affectionate and entertaining that were it not for fear of being a bore I would ask you for myself and my parents to give us your news sometime. Would you?

The squirrel is well. The ducks are forever splashing about in the stream, and Fernand is still rehearsing. To keep himself amused he is repeating to himself... In 1293... Burgundy was fortunate and... the silken ladder... etc... etc.

It was my mother!!!!!

3 GABRIEL FAURÉ to CAMILLE SAINT-SAËNS

Académie de Toulouse
Ecole Normale de Tarbes
Tarbes
18 September 1863

O Rifleman,[5] Are you in London or Paris? If you are in London, more's the pity; if you are in Paris, even more's the pity, but if you were here I would say to you: So much the better then!!!

We are still having a good time, as we did when we were lucky enough to have you here; however you, thankless wretch... well, *you* have deserted us, you have fled! Already our recollection of you is fading into oblivion!

O, the wretched so and so!... and why was it so wretched? etc... etc... (My memory of Gavarni[e].) The Pierrefitte gorge is always finer than the other one... You remember? What is your recollection of it? It is always charming, but always coquettish too...

As regards news, it might be worth your knowing that every [day] they're rehearsing a very funny little vaudeville – performed by Mme Cabanel and Henriette Sourrieu, and by M. Albert and my brother... It will be very entertaining. You are hereby invited. It's on Monday evening... By taking the 8 pm train on Sunday, you arrive on Monday at four... but in your case, death would be preferable than to return to this ghastly hole Tarbes... You prefer the eagles in Veau beau Square... *Ingrrrrat*!!!

Farewell, my good friend and teacher; all my relations send their best wishes, and have fondest memories of the ladies – as for me I cling for ever to your neck.

Your devoted and affectionate
GABRIEL FAURÉ

Lafforest's son, smoking a cigarette quite close to me, sends his best wishes to you. Poor Lasserre[6] is very upset, for his father still gets worse and worse... Yesterday they gave him the Viaticum[7]... So you can tell how serious his illness is.

I have entrusted your gaiter to the Morgans, who will bring it up to you. The handkerchief and shirt are at the laundry, I'll bring them back for you myself.

Do please write back to me, we await all your news impatiently.

G

4   GABRIEL FAURÉ to CAMILLE SAINT-SAËNS

Académie de Toulouse
Ecole Normale de Tarbes
Tarbes
21 September 1862

I am writing a few words in haste to inform you of a sad piece of news: poor Lasserre, your friend, a friend to all of us, has just lost his father: we have just accompanied him to the cemetery. His sorrow is great, but it has been so for a long time as he has been expecting to see his father die at any moment; he himself has asked me to write to you.

Farewell, I'm being called to dinner and here we don't joke about that.

Your limping friend, for I *am* limping
GABRIEL FAURÉ

I've just finished my meal where we've been discussing the following matter. I have spoken about the organist's job in the Senate. I think I might be able to fill this post? In that case would you please tell me if the post is still vacant? Then my father could write to M. Pietri, a Senator and ex-Police-Prefect, whom he knows very well and he could also talk about it to Mr de Bourjolly[8], a Senator living in Tarbes whom you know, ah-ha! Yes, you certainly do.

I think if I got this post – since the organ has only to be played on Sundays – Mr Niedermeyer[9] would no longer have second thoughts about granting me the Sunday in question.

Farewell again.

All affectionate greetings. My parents send you their best wishes, and along with me have fond memories of the ladies.

I am still not quite up to the mark for at the moment I have a pain in my leg which is making me both limp and suffer at the same time... I am like a Cauterets[10] horse limping on three legs, the fourth being out of action. You should have found a few words from me when you got to Paris. Your letter from London [lost] gave all of us the greatest pleasure, your continuing love for us gives us the greatest pleasure... Your promised eight-page letter will be the very best of all.

My brother Fernand has come in just as I was about to finish my letter, he sends a kiss for your left eye.

5 GABRIEL FAURÉ to CAMILLE SAINT-SAËNS

Académie de Toulouse
Ecole Normale de Tarbes
Tarbes
7 pm 16 October 1862

I have just received your nice letter [lost], and thank you most sincerely. It gave me a great deal of pleasure by proving that in Paris I shall find once again a friend who from time to time will supplant those strong ties of affection which I am leaving behind here. I am sad to be leaving: do forgive me.

I shall arrive on Saturday night: on Sunday morning I shall come to wake you up at 11 o'clock. I have been invited to the Morgands for lunch: if you will allow me to do so I shall bring him and Louis de Lafforest to Vespers.

Many affectionate greetings, my parents send their best wishes; we talk of you very frequently, I can assure you. They are longing for the holidays to come so as to be with you again.

Please convey my compliments to the ladies.

Your very devoted
GABRIEL FAURÉ

.   .   .

Not a great deal is known about Fauré's activities in the 1860s. Some of the songs published in the next decade date from his student days at the Ecole Niedermeyer. Almost certainly the *Trois romances sans paroles* for piano were composed in the 1860s though they were not published till 1880 as op. 17. In July 1865 Fauré finally left the Ecole Niedermeyer with his 'Maître de Chapelle' (i.e. choirmaster) diploma, and in January 1866 embarked upon his first organist's post at the Church of Saint-Sauveur at Rennes, in Brittany. This appointment was due mainly to the efforts of Gustave Lefèvre (1831–1910), Louis Niedermeyer's son-in-law, who had succeeded Alfred Niedermeyer as Director of the school in 1865. Fauré disliked the four years he spent at Rennes, finding life there provincial and boring. Writing to his wife from the town 30 years later, he recalled his mood:

> *I look back on what I used to think at that time, and remember that it was* nothing, *having a mediocre view of myself, absolute total indifference, except for things of beauty and sublimated thoughts, but without a shadow of ambition. What a character!...*[11]

His disillusionment was probably one reason why his normally tactful behaviour failed on one occasion, causing the master–pupil relationship between Saint-Saëns and himself to be underlined somewhat heavily in the following New Year's greeting.

6 CAMILLE SAINT-SAËNS to GABRIEL FAURÉ

[Paris]
1 January 1867

Old chap, apparently you have not written to M. Lefebvre [*sic*] since you came to Rennes, and it seems that it was he who got you your post. You have committed a serious offence there which you really must rectify as fast as you can.

The butter is exquisite, and I feasted on it again just now. You really deserve to be scolded!

I am not entirely in agreement with you on the vocal piece; it is perfectly possible to have several pieces published with the same words: since the publisher[12] I have in mind for you is particularly noted for religious music, this might be excellent bait, but I do not know how I can make him swallow the songs to begin with.

Laussel[13] has been ill; he is now very well. Yesterday we made a real racket in the house with my piece which was surprisingly successful; Brayer was in it, why weren't you there?[14]

My surprise is still not ready: that one is turning out to be a real mystery.[15] Meanwhile, a thousand kisses! But kisses on paper are not the same thing at all.

C. SAINT-SAËNS

In 1868 Saint-Saëns arranged for Fauré to act as accompanist for the soprano Marie Miolan-Carvalho (1827–95), who was undertaking a concert tour of Brittany. As a compliment to her young accompanist, she consented to sing his early song *Le papillon et la fleur*, composed seven years previously, which brought Fauré's name before a wider public. In 1869 he entered into his first publishing contract with the house of Choudens in Paris, resulting in the publication of most of his early songs throughout the 1870s. Fauré and Rennes parted company early in 1870 when he was asked to resign his organist's post by the priest of Saint-Sauveur. Fauré had frequently been seen smoking cigarettes in the porch during sermons; the last straw was to appear in his organ loft one Sunday morning still wearing evening dress after having spent the previous night at a ball in the town.

Fauré was not sorry to leave, the more so as his next appointment was at the church of Notre Dame de Clignancourt in northern Paris, a move which brought him into the musical, artistic and social capital of the country. The next letter is an interesting one. Jules Tannery (1848–1910) was a mathematician, and later was to teach mechanics at the Sorbonne and to be director of the Ecole Normale supérieure in Paris. The church authorities at Rennes had suspected that Fauré was in no way an ardent Catholic, and it is easy to see that the young composer found in Tannery a kindred spirit.

7* JULES TANNERY to GABRIEL FAURÉ

Rennes
12 April [1870] (St Jules)

My dear and wonderful friend, I saw M. Le Roy this afternoon and we are dining together this evening; truly you are so right to complain about me and I am quite ashamed about it. Fortunately you know my incurable laziness, and that in spite of not writing to them I do not forget my friends, especially those like you. Moreover I have to say in addition, as my last excuse, that the dreadfully cold weather which has come back this last month had made me quite stupid. I began to return to that state of stupefaction which we once went through, by virtue of the theory of the Evolution of the Species. Having got back to my hovel I put the smallest possible distance between me and my fire which I hastily relit. And there, doing nothing, meditating lengthily and deeply over absolutely nothing, I spent all my time: wincing when the accursed school bell summoned me to my boring duties.

Now I am beginning once more to live, to breathe, to get excited: the sky is blue; such heaven! I go out and walk as far as I possibly can, fleeing the hateful town, my worries and my dreams: my delight is to notice buds turning green, or to look in the water at small fish, really small ones, which wriggle about and disappear at the slightest noise I make: my pleasures are certainly innocent enough, the Lord knows! Moreover it's such a long time since I did any serious work – I rest, or rather I allow myself to rest. In the evening when I get back, I read a little, I work for half-an-hour, and I joke with the ubiquitous Langlais whom I have converted completely to my furious hatred of Napoleon. Every evening I undermine his reputation a little: he became mad, he disseminated his theories around the world and stirred up ferments. From time to time I go to the home of that splendid M. Guyor, where I smoke a cigar by the fireside, and together we say as many good things about you as we can. That comforts me a little. (I have made him aware of the evil aspects of the inept comedy with which you are familiar.)

And so I have gone through a moral crisis which is still perhaps not quite over. These latest incidents have got through to the Council,[16] and the decisions which it will certainly take have just about induced me to stop being a practising Catholic. If this continues as it has begun, the union between Society and Church will become a dream that is an absolute chimera – barring a radical revolution in the last-named. There are two alternatives: one, either this revolution will take place through the very excesses of ultramontanism – and this is what I hope – or, catholicism will destroy itself, and I do not *want* to believe that yet. In any case, the communing of ideas for me is impossible with a society which enters upon a path of that sort, and which professes doctrines of that sort: compromises I had held dear up till now can no longer satisfy me: there are times when one must make up one's mind, when contradictions become glaring to such a degree that one must make one's choice; not in the long run that my ideas have changed very much. Apart from a greater freedom of thought, a freer interpretation of doctrines, I think and feel as before; but I refuse to go along the way followed by the Council fathers: such intolerance, such violation of language, when allied to doctrines so despotic, does not suit me. As for practising the faith under such conditions, this would be an act of hypocrisy *vis à vis* the officiating priest – or in every respect an impossible compromise in matters of conscience. My God forgive me if I am deceiving myself.

It gives me pleasure to think I shall be shaking both your hands in a few days; I leave tomorrow evening for Mondeville, and from there I shall write to you to warn you of my arrival. This will be towards the end of Easter week, either Thursday or Friday.

Until then, many many handclasps
JULES TANNERY

8★ JULES TANNERY to GABRIEL FAURÉ

Rennes
17 June 1870
Bang, Bangbangbang!
To be damned and loved
You call me an old so-and-so to the world; you yourself are an old so-and-so if you think that you are forgotten, when I am merely being lazy: well, that's how it is, one seeks relaxation from one's weariness. After having written a speech on distributors – a sublime tome – by which time the administration has asked you to make corrections so that one is not called by the population of Rennes an atheist of materialist inclinations, a pantheist, a chemist, a humbug, (this adventure suits me down to the ground doesn't it?),[17] when one has made these concessions, when the heat is so intense you sweat like a baker's oven, when one is compelled to take up one's post again and take off in succession one's boots, socks, trousers, shirt, flannel vest, in order to write to you; can you believe that one still has in one's heart sufficient courage to do it, do you believe that my friendship for you is sufficiently strong to perspire a litre and more, do you believe that I, in this scanty costume, who again hardly has the courage to light my pipe, I can still make my pen run over the paper?

Fortunately it is a little less warm today. For my guard leave, I went with my brother to St Malo and Jersey where I could spend only 24 hours and was horribly bitten by bugs from England. All the same, I have returned full of enthusiasm, my eyes quite overwhelmed with that light blue sky and my heart overflowing with happiness. I still see the sea bathed in sunlight, and the venerable dark rocks breaking the views up and preventing the beauty of the landscape from becoming monotonous. And then Jersey! What everlasting happiness this land [has] – verdure, flowers, gaiety everywhere: and if you go upwards, the sea. This promenade has a festive spirit at every moment – what pretty little corners, all graceful with their small streams coming out from under the leaves, sheltered, warm and cosy like a good fire. How I should like to live there and never die.

And the return to St Malo! The white-coloured steeples and dark rocks which rise up in the centre of the luminous mist which sea and sun help to make at the same time; the great walls which close up the town, almost stifling it; and the water – blue, clear, and sparkling which still separates you from it and rocks you to sleep as it goes past.

But I think I am beginning to make up these idylls. My enthusiasm, you understand, hasn't cooled yet. It's difficult with the weather so hot, but all the same it will happen soon enough.

It was my first real sea voyage and it was an entirely pleasurable experience; it is true that the sea was very calm; all the same I felt great pride in having lunch on the *Warder* in the midst of people doing just the opposite: I have never eaten better ham seasoned with better 'pickles' (I don't know if that is quite right – I haven't got my English dictionary.)

See you soon, since you must come in July. Meanwhile then, give me your hand and that of your splendid brother.

JULES TANNERY

The Franco-Prussian War was soon to change the lives of many. Relations between France and Prussia had been strained for some time when France declared war on 19 July 1870. Fauré was soon engaged in the conflict, serving as a liaison agent when Paris was besieged. He must have been heartened a great deal by the encouraging letters he received from family and friends, such as this from one of the families he had known in Rennes. (Yves Gigout was not related to the composer Eugène Gigout (1844–1925), who had been one of Fauré's closest friends when a fellow pupil at the Ecole Niedermeyer, where later he was a professor.)

9   YVES GIGOUT to GABRIEL FAURÉ

Rennes
18 August 1870

My dear M. Fauré, I cannot thank you enough for your kindness in sending me the interesting newspapers. This morning I received two from the 17th and two from the 18th. There seems to have been some delay in despatching the first. You cannot imagine, my dear friend, the army's impetuous spirit everywhere. Our town normally so quiet is full of activity; you see nothing but the Mobile Guard all the time. Yes — they are all infused with a truly patriotic ardour which brings tears to the eyes; it's wonderful! Surely with all this fervour the Prussians will be driven back. From the very first we must give our thanks to God that we are living in this area; if we were surrounded on all sides by innumerable hordes of Prussians, how many of us would have returned to France! And who would have defended our country? For a long time now they say the beggars have been within the walls of Paris; but, thank the Lord, we appear to be directing operations impeccably; one is becoming more aware of this, and it is – let us hope – only the prelude to a brilliant, crushing victory against our enemies. May my prediction be true and speedy. Albert is at Châlons: his sister, who is in Rennes, has just told me so. Matters of grave import are going to happen in these parts; may he see his poor mother once again! I do hope so.

Your defence operations must proceed apace. Old Loison after all his exploits is a good example. Léon is in the National Guard: a sedentary post, so he writes to me. And will you be staying in Paris! I hope you will. Send us some of your news. The newspapers you have kindly sent tell us what's happening; your handwriting on the wrapper itself tells us about you. The two sons are in the New Mobile Guard, every day they go to the walls to get some experience. They are playing a little at being soldiers; but at last they seem to be consumed with a fighting spirit too. Down with the Prussians. Long live France. My wife, my daughter and I – we all offer you a cordial handshake.

All good wishes to you
YVES GIGOUT

The next letter was sent to Fauré by his brother Albert, a naval officer then stationed at Brest. Albert was eventually compelled to take early retirement on account of a fever contracted in China. He died in 1908.

10★ ALBERT FAURÉ to GABRIEL FAURÉ

Préfecture Maritime
du 2mè Arrondissement
Cabinet du Préfet
Brest
1 September 1870

My dear Gabriel, Let me congratulate you, I haven't had time to do it so far. The momentous decision you have taken has not surprised me, knowing you. You strike your blows in a quiet way, but you are not a man of half measures. You did not relish the Mobile Guard: I can understand this. You would risk being bored by doing exercises there for two months with no opportunity for active service. In your militia regiment you will soon be engaged in driving out this pack of northern savages. This will be tough: and all honour to those men who undertake this risk. Honour above all to those who, like yourself, have left a secure job to take up their rifles and march to the frontier. You will probably be the only one from our family to march against the enemy: we all have every confidence in your lucky star which will bring you back safe and sound, and covered in glory. I am worried over my not being able to follow you: the Navy is an absurd occupation, there's no doubt about it. Here we have the third serious war in which its role is quite insignificant. We must give it up as lost: is it therefore our job to strike up a superior posture by always applauding those who have just been into battle? I fear so.

I should very much love to embrace you before you go. Do not forget us in your warlike enthusiasm; and remember that Louise and I love you very much, we are extremely proud of your determination, and we send you our sincerest good wishes. Louise has sent you 100 francs; tell me, or have Amand tell me, if you need *more money*. It really is a great blessing for me and for all of us to have Amand close to you. We feel certain that as long as you are over there, that fine fellow's kindly attentions will not be lacking as far as you are concerned. Once again don't forget: Brest is not far from Paris, and we can send you everything you ask, either in cash or in kind. My poor friend – I am more distressed than ever at not having been sent to Paris: I could have been present at your début. But Amand is there, and we know what a capable fellow he is.

Farewell, my fine Pista, good luck; we kiss you as heartily as ever we have before.

Your brother
FAURÉ ALB
Rue du Château 38
Brest

The siege of Paris soon resulted in the rationing of foodstuffs and shortages of other commodities. Contemporary newspapers and periodicals indicate all too clearly the rapidly deteriorating situation in the capital. On 8 October *Le Figaro* reported that

> By fresh meat they mean ox, sheep, pig and horse. Those who want horsemeat are allowed a double ration. Butchers, delicatessens and tripe-shops will receive no more meat from the city abattoirs.

Full meat rationing was introduced on 15 October, and food shortages of all kinds were now clearly evident. On 16 October, *Le Figaro* remarked

> That Paris is deprived of oysters and truffles is doubtless a misfortune, but a misfortune which touches only upon certain persons: those who are able to procure numerous other comforts. But that Paris has no cheese is more than a misfortune, it is a public disaster where the victims are every class of society.

Still, music remained. *Le Soir* reported on 3 November that after a performance of Cherubini's *Requiem* (with the funeral march from Beethoven's 'Eroica' Symphony at the offertory)

> M. Saint-Saëns, organist at the Madeleine, presided at the organ. As his concluding voluntary he played the Triumphal March by Beethoven. May this fine composition be the prelude to the impending success of our armies!

With the continuing food shortages it is hardly surprising to read in *Le Figaro* of 30 November

> Butcher's Shop Open
> DOGS, CATS & RATS

Inside you can see through the window pane heaps of fresh meat, which probably came from these animals whose slaughter has, as yet, not been sanctioned by the government.

My God! To think we have come to this —

The situation obviously posed problems for hotels and restaurants; culinary expertise of an unusual kind was now called for. Henri Cozic, writing in the weekly periodical, *L'Illustration*, on 10 December quotes a hotel menu which, like opera libretti, is more appetizing when *not* translated:

Soup – *Consommé of horse, with millet*
Removes – *Skewers of dog liver,* à la maître d'hôtel
    Minced saddle of cat, with mayonnaise
Entrées – *Shoulder and fillet of braised dog, with tomato sauce*
    Jugged cat with mushrooms
    Dog cutlets with young peas
    Ragoût of rats à la Robert
Roasts – *Leg of dog, garnished with young rats*
    Endive salad
Vegetables – *Begonias with their juice*
    Plum pudding with sauce and marrow bone of horse
Dessert and Wine

The populace must have been somewhat alarmed by having to eat these unusual animals; a paragraph from *Le Soir* on 20 December reads

The men of science have recently kept themselves busy by eating the meat of dogs, cats and rats; and they have agreed to recognize that the flesh of these animals, when it is prepared correctly, can be eaten without the slightest drawback. However, regarding rat meat, the recommended treatment is to cook it by raising the temperature and keeping it for a certain length of time at that of boiling water in order to destroy the germs of trichadic worms which have sometimes been observed in these animals.

However, this state of affairs, and indeed the war itself, were not to last much longer. On 28 January 1871 Paris surrendered with the agreement reached between Bismarck and Thiers,[18] and Fauré's activities resumed a more musical course. He was employed for a short while as organist at Saint-Honoré d'Eylau, but was compelled to flee from Paris to Rambouillet, using a false passport, during the troubled but mercifully brief Commune period. The Ecole Niedermeyer had been transferred temporarily to the Niedermeyer estate, Champ d'asile, at Cours-sous-Lausanne in Switzerland. Fauré was invited to teach composition there, and as a result spent most of the summer in those congenial surroundings. One of his earliest pupils was the composer and conductor André Messager (1853–1929).

Fauré returned to Paris in the autumn, and in October was appointed choirmaster at the church of Saint-Sulpice, under the composer and organist Charles-Marie Widor (1845–1937). An undated poem sent by Saint-Saëns to Fauré is extant, and is dated by Jean-Michel Nectoux 'about 1871', though it could probably be ascribed to any year in the early 1870s. It demonstrates in gloriously poetic terms how the friendship between the two composers was by this time very close – this is the first surviving document in which Saint-Saëns uses the familiar *tu* and not the more formal *vous* – and in addition shows that Fauré's mother was obviously still delighting in the despatch of rural goodies to the famous composer in sophisticated Paris.

11*   CAMILLE SAINT-SAËNS to GABRIEL FAURÉ

O thou whose perfumed fingers press with harmonious rhythm those
  keys of ivory!
With grace and charm thy mother, living in sunshine
  at the foot of the mountains blue,
Has sent me some paté whose yellow sides enclose
  one thousand ravishments:

A paté akin to the golden robes of the glorious
  Emperor of China
The robe that covers the bosom of the son of the
  heavens, the bosom that covers those thoughts so divine.
On Monday, the golden robe will open up, releasing
  its divine thoughts;

But should your presence be missing at this
  effulgent unveiling
The paté would be as the butterfly which leaves its
  cocoon on a showery day, denied its vision of the sun,
And my cheeks, shrunken with sorrow, would droop
  towards my breast,
Like a forgotten peony in a waterless vase.   [original text p. 208]

In November 1871 there occurred the foundation of the Société Nationale de
musique française, a momentous occasion in the history of French music. The
joint founders were Saint-Saëns and Romain Bussine (1830–99), a professor of
singing at the Paris Conservatoire and minor poet; two of his translations of
anonymous Italian poems Fauré was later to set to music.[19] Fauré was also
closely associated with the Society, along with Franck, Bizet, Duparc and
Massenet. The motto *Ars Gallica*, and the avowed aim 'to make known those
works, published or otherwise, of French composers connected with the
Society, to help the production and dissemination of all serious musical
works', emphasized the surge of nationalist feeling in France after the
disastrous defeat by Prussia earlier that year. The first secretary of the society
was Alexis de Castillon (1838–73), one of César Franck's earliest pupils who
was to survive the foundation of the Society by less than eighteen months.
Fauré took over the secretaryship in 1874.

    Many of Fauré's songs and chamber pieces were first performed in public at
Société Nationale concerts, and it must have been gratifying that certain
artistic circles were now admitting him to their company. In 1872 Saint-Saëns
had introduced him to the wealthy and artistic Viardot family, which exuded
such warmth, friendship, appreciation of his musical gifts and genuine artistic
understanding that he felt much more at ease there than in the loving but
provincial and uncomprehending atmosphere of his own distant family circle.
Pauline Viardot (1821–1910) was the celebrated Spanish contralto who knew
intimately many of the great artists of the day: Gustave Flaubert, George
Sand, Ivan Turgenev. Her son Paul and her three daughters Louise, Claudie
and Marianne were all musical. The fact that all three sisters sang undoubtedly
spurred on Fauré's interest in song-writing throughout the 1870s, and most

members of the Viardot family had at least one composition by Fauré dedicated to them.

From January 1874 Fauré started to deputize at the organ of the Madeleine for Saint-Saëns, who began to be called away more often from his duties by his increasingly numerous concert tours. The Madeleine was one of the most fashionable churches in Paris, and so once more Saint-Saëns was responsible for bringing the name of his friend and celebrated former pupil before a wider section of the Parisian public.

During the 1870s Fauré found yet another 'spiritual home' in his close friendship with the wealthy industrialist Camille Clerc and his wife Marie. Like the Viardots, the Clercs held soirées at their home in Paris, which were attended by Saint-Saëns, Bussine, Messager and many others. They also had two country residences, at Villerville and Sainte-Adresse on the Normandy coast. Fauré was as likely to be found at Sainte-Adresse as he was at his own flat in Paris, as his father guessed when he sent the following letter to his son, requesting his assistance in a family matter.

12★ TOUSSAINT-HONORÉ FAURÉ to GABRIEL FAURÉ

Tarbes

2 September 1874

My dear Gabriel, We returned to Tarbes yesterday, in reasonable health. Would my letter find you at Ste-Adresse? I do hope so very much, because of your brother Fernand whom Father Grasset, headmaster in Algiers, would like to have as his Vice-Principal. But while he himself wants him, this worthy man has written to us to have Fernand's application strongly supported in the first instance by the Vice Chancellor of the Toulouse Academy. This will come about, but as always political influences abound with the Minister, or with the ministry committees. We thought that you could make use of your 48 hours' stay in Paris by seeing to this application: Fernand Fauré, 35 years of age, instructor at the College of Further Education, graduate in science and mathematics, 17 years' service, *second form* teacher of mathematics at Tarbes High School for 11 years. He wants to go into administration and for preference is seeking the Algiers High School, because the climate of this city would suit his wife, whose health is delicate – these are the facts which it is imperative to make the most of to acquire the title of Vice-Principal in a school which is not one's first – it's up to you to do the rest.

We did not have one week's good weather in the month we spent at Bagnères where it rained almost continuously during August. Your mother was trying to get warm last Sunday – and in Tarbes the heat was overwhelming. It seems that the dogs were howling in the middle of the day when they went across the Place du Maubourque in Tarbes. Yesterday, old chap, suffocated by the heat in a railway coach arriving at Tarbes, there was a young man who had come from a pilgrimage to the Virgin at Lourdes.[20] As for you, my dear Gabriel, do not tire yourself, do not hurry unduly to come to see us, since we shall be happy to remain until mid-October. Stop with Amand and do give him a hearty kiss for us, as well as my elder brother, his wife and the children. Victorine awaits your arrival: the whole family, as she must have written to you, will not be coming to us before 10 September.

Farewell, my friend, and good-bye,
Your father,
FAURÉ

Our affectionate greetings to M. Saint-Saëns, and our compliments to his worthy mother.

You can bring us some news of the ladies.

The next letter is really a series of detailed instructions by Saint-Saëns for the music and order of service at Sunday offices in the Madeleine at Easter. Saint-Saëns's clever sketch of a man at the console, the organ pipes replaced by a large rocket, heads the letter and is omitted here, but a facsimile of the first page is reproduced between pages 96 and 97.

13   CAMILLE SAINT-SAËNS to GABRIEL FAURÉ

[Undated, *c.* 1874?]

For the gradual (when there is a sequence) after the first 'Alleluia' intoned by the choir, the organ plays a short prelude. The choir carries on and takes up the initial intonation to complete the 'Alleluia'. The organ intones the sequence. After the *Credo* and the priest's intoning, the organ plays the Offertory. At the *Orate fratres*, the organist thinks seriously of finishing. When the children in the choir fidget, the organ stops.

The organist wipes his hands. After Communion, the organ plays the *Domine salvum* – in B flat. At the *Ite missa est* the organ replies with a prelude *of a few notes* (pianissimo).
After the benediction: exit.

The organist goes to lunch at Richard Lucas.[21]

At 2.13 Vespers. Verset for each psalm. Hymn.
Magnificat.
Benedicamus in F

Recreation
At 3.43 you go back for the *Salut Regina coeli* in G. The choir gives the intonation sequence (if there is one) between the two motets *Domine s.* after the *Deus meminerit* followed by the verset for the prayer. After the final psalm, definitive exit.

An interesting description of Fauré at this time comes from his young friend Camille Bellaigue (1858–1930), who was later to edit a disastrously abridged publication of the letters from Fauré to Marianne Viardot. This thumbnail sketch, written many years later, appeared in Bellaigue's introduction to these letters which were published in the *Revue des Deux Mondes* on 15 August 1928.

> *Very brown in the face, with dark eyes and hair. His personality seemed a little dreamy and melancholy, but at times it was enlivened by a fit of youthful, even somewhat child-like, mirth.*

14* TOUSSAINT-HONORÉ FAURÉ to GABRIEL FAURÉ

Tarbes
18 May 1876

My dear Gabriel, Thank you for remembering me, thank you for your kind letter, finally thank you for the good wishes you send for my birthday, and for the improvement in your mother's health and mine. You are all of you my own dear children, and in the love you have for us we find the greatest consolation for the troubles which in fact we have had to bear for some years. Victorine has returned to us so your mother is happy, and I am glad to see her surrounded by her children as far as is possible. I am glad too at the prospect of being able to see that school once again, a school which I had completely enlarged and improved, and to which I had happily dedicated the last years of my active service. Yes, the joy we can see on all sides is all the greater when we can attribute the happy outcome of this affair to the course of action and intervention of Amand.

A telegram from the Vice Chancellor of Toulouse orders the inspector at Auch[22] Academy not to keep on M. Fontes and to have him leave for Tarbes without delay: no doubt it will be tomorrow when these good Auch people get to us. Thank goodness for that!

We are writing to Amand as soon as he has informed us of his return to Chateauroux for, like you, we will not be hoping to see your brother included in this the first of M. Marcène's undertakings. If the job were better I would have him ask for the consultancy post of the *Préfecture*, which on account of the resignation of your friend M. de Lafforest, is vacant in Tarbes at the moment.

Except for Fernand, who has been plagued by facial neuralgia for ten days, everyone is fine in the Rue de l'Enclos des Capucines where the Baby is the centre of attraction for all. This precious child is a great comfort to us, and you won't begrudge him any kisses when you are in our midst, something we want very much as long as we are here.

Goodbye, dear son, and all our very affectionate wishes to you.

Your father and friend,
FAURÉ

Mother has come in to get me to add to my prose that you will be able to take your little beasties into the school grounds during the next holidays. You will be able to do gymnastics with them.

It was in the country homes of the Clerc family that Fauré wrote most of his first two chamber works (the A Major Violin Sonata, op.13 and the C Minor Piano Quartet, op.15) and his Ballade, op.19 for piano. Indeed, it was due to the diplomatic efforts of Camille Clerc that the sonata was published. No publisher in Paris would take it, since its classical serenity allied to romantic warmth was regarded as something altogether new in French music. Clerc had strong links with the publishing firm of Breitkopf and Härtel in Leipzig, but even he could not perform miracles, as letter 15 demonstrates.

15   CAMILLE CLERC to GABRIEL FAURÉ

Paris
5 November 1876

My dear Fauré, To all appearances I am treating you badly by being silent, but I wanted to have something to say to you regarding Leipzig. Despite all possible haste, I was able to write only on the 13th, because I wanted to tell you definitely about the Borrewald subscription in order to get a good *start* to my letter. I am sending you as *pieces* my Breitkopf letter and their reply which I received yesterday – I do not need to tell you that my letter of the 13th, where I do not appear to be doing too badly by *making a fuss*, has been written solely to bring about the result in your favour.

To sum up, these people offer to publish the work at their expense on condition that they retain the copyright. I believe that from your point of view this result is a flattering one by their proposition, and it is obvious that your work has been appreciated by them.

Now it is up to you as to what suits you in seeing what there is to be done. Léonard,[23] to whom I went so I could show him the letters (as I had shown him mine), is of the opinion that you should accept. Publication will not be a problem since it is merely a question of expenses, and you know that, as with other people, we are genuinely and completely at your service. But the fact that you are being printed by such a publishing house is worth the trouble of being looked over, although it is certainly tough to *give away* a work like that. On the other hand Léonard believes it would be difficult to divide the copyright, and give it away just for Germany.

I have tried to see Bussine to get his opinion, but he was out and I did not want to delay writing to you....

So there you are, my dear friend, that is how things stand; I hasten to let you know about them, and it is *you* who must decide. For the time being I will say nothing to Leipzig.

I hope you will bring us back your quartet[24] – if there's a chance of its being as fine as your sonata!

My wife joins with me in sending you every good wish – please convey my respects to your family.

Yours sincerely,
CAMILLE CLERC

The year 1877 was a crucial one in Fauré's life. It began well, when to enthusiastic applause, the A Major Sonata was performed at the Société Nationale on 27 January. The composer himself accompanied Marie Tayau and the occasion marked a turning-point in Fauré's career as a composer. Saint-Saëns, who was to write an enthusiastic article on the sonata in April, resigned the organistship at the Madeleine in March, to be replaced by Théodore Dubois (1837–1924), a professor at the Conservatoire and later to be Fauré's predecessor as director of that institution. Fauré stepped into Dubois's former role as the official *Maître de chapelle* at the Madeleine.

Having been attracted to Marianne Viardot (1854–1919) from the time he first visited the Viardot family circle in 1872, and she presumably to him, Gabriel and Marianne finally became engaged in July 1877. There can be no doubt that Fauré was deeply in love with her, and for a short while Marianne may well have been in love with him. During that summer they were separated, as Fauré decided to visit the spa town of Cauterets in his native *département*, close to the Spanish frontier. In addition to his customary headaches Fauré was suffering from a serious throat infection which he hoped would be alleviated by the various treatments that Cauterets could provide. Marianne herself spent the same period on a convalescent holiday at Luc-sur-Mer and Cabourg in Normandy, and during the three weeks they were apart Fauré wrote her 35 letters. A heavily abridged version of these letters was published in 1928.[25]

Philippe Fauré-Fremiet considered that his father's letters to Marianne Viardot displayed 'a vein of innocence surprising in a man of 32',[26] which seems a curious judgement. They certainly begin most respectfully, but some of the subsequent letters demonstrate Fauré's passion for her. A few are the products of a hypochondriac in their wealth of lurid details regarding sulphur baths and other spa treatments; others are full of extremely quaint and unidentifiable allusions to friends, incidents, gossip and so on. The almost untranslatable silly poems and made-up words make these letters some of the most wayward and curious that Fauré ever wrote, although the sense of humour in some of them was a characteristic which Fauré often displayed in the company of close friends. Unfortunately there are few musical remarks of interest; probably the letters as a whole would prove more interesting to a psychologist than a musician. Eleven have been selected as being of sufficient interest to justify inclusion here. The names of various friends of Fauré in the Cauterets district appear in them, but it has not been possible to identify them.

16   GABRIEL FAURÉ to MARIANNE VIARDOT

Tarbes,
11 o'clock Sunday evening [19 August]

My dear Marianne, When I reached Tarbes at two o'clock my parents and friends immediately took possession of me, and only now can I take refuge near to you. I have had to respond to their numerous questions, urgent and all motivated by the most affectionate concern. I cannot describe their happiness, and how everything my brothers have said about you to them, everything which Mme Clerc has written to them, has paved the way for them so they are able to take pleasure in my happiness. They are all aware of that cherished prize which belongs entirely to me: they know the extent of my deep love for you; and if they were already predisposed to love you, their affection for you and their respect for your parents are, as from today, sentiments which are both absolutely profound and genuine. My niece, Marguerite, who is very anxious to make the acquaintance of her future aunt, has asked me if you would object to her writing to you? I have taken the liberty of sanctioning this, and have asked her to tell you of the hubbub which developed this evening around the maternal table – where we had the rare pleasure of all being together in great numbers – and where your beloved name was fused with my mother's as far as best wishes were concerned – it was her birthday.

Early tomorrow morning I shall be on my way and will arrive at Cauterets sufficiently early to make myself at home, see the doctor and begin immediately the treatment he is to prescribe – and I promise you to follow it most punctiliously. Will there be a letter from you? I dare not live in hope, bearing in mind the enormous distance between us and the lackadaisical dilatoriness on the part of the postal service. However I am *desperate* to know how you all are, and to hear whether those first whiffs of sea air have produced favourable results: *I am anxious for your assurance that you have forgotten how turbulent and touchy my love for you has been these last few days!* The more I carry on, the less clearly do I understand this inexplicable agitation that comes from deep within me! I can no longer sleep because of it!

I should make a poor start if you were to take any notice of the tone of this first letter: the migraine which started yesterday at that sorrowful moment of parting has intensified and absolutely enveloped me during the course of the day: I've made the long journey from Paris to Tarbes with this all-too-loyal companion, I haven't closed my eyes, I've been somewhat overwhelmed by the welcome awaiting me here: in short, I am *done for* tonight! However I should never have slept if I hadn't written to you: I preferred to do so badly rather than not write at all. Regard this letter, then, merely as a simple preface!

I beg you to kiss your mother on my behalf, and I beg her to agree to kiss you for me! Give my affectionate greetings to your sister and Mlle Charlotte, as for you, my dearest Marianne, allow me to thank you once more for all the happiness you are giving me – rest assured that I love you with all my heart, now and always.

Your *distant* fiancé
GABRIEL FAURÉ

My parents remain captivated by your delightful letter. I have read it with feelings of deep emotion, and I feel a boundless love for you when you show such affection for them. They are very appreciative.

17 GABRIEL FAURÉ to MARIANNE VIARDOT

Cauterets,
Sunday [26 August]

Dear Marianne, I received a very affectionate letter today from your mother. She corroborates all the splendid news you have told me about your health and plans, and these I keenly encourage so that you can get as much benefit as you can from that splendid air you are taking. She adds that they are thinking of me very, very much, and for that I am most grateful to my *darling Marianne*. I am most anxious to take up yesterday's letter which may have made you fear that I was going to do something stupid. No trace remains of my compulsory bath at Gavarnie,[27] and the old cold in the head was driven off when I was near those old rock pinnacles. I have kept just an impression of the most imposing views you can imagine – I remain very impressed by them. Today I've had two woollen shawls sent to your sister and yourself – I beg you both to wrap yourselves up in them in the evenings. The shopkeeper showed me how to wear them, but any demonstration will not be easy. Let's try: you have to place a small part of the shawl over one shoulder in such a way as to cover only the shoulder and arm, then wrap yourself up in it, and throw it back over the same shoulder. What a stupid fool I am! I should have told you plainly straightaway that you must wear it like the Spaniards wear their wraps – or better still, as your fancy takes you. What a business for an insignificant parcel of wool! I have beads of perspiration on my forehead!

I have spent the day at the piano, and have been disturbed only by a long visit from M. Höskier. The poor man is here without his wife; he maintains that my position is somewhat analogous to his, and he is taking advantage of it. I have agreed to go and dine with him tomorrow at Argèles, along with Bonnat and M. Trélat. The latter overwhelms me with the most friendly attentions, he declares that his wife worships me (hm!) and that she has been distressed at not having seen me at her house for three years. I took a sly delight in my reply to him! If she had not seen me it was simply because she had not invited me – you get that sort of thing *here*!

Do you remember the name of a famous barrister, *Maître* Nicolet – the one Gounod wanted to introduce me to so that I could put myself in the picture over the law which authorized me to see that Choudens brought out my songs? M. Höskier has made use of his presence here by talking to him about me and my present difficulties. He has done this so charmingly that *Maître* Nicolet has taken an interest in this matter to the extent of allowing himself to bring the business up again when we have both returned to Paris – and, of course, *gratis pro Deo*, which means in Belgian, for the love of art. You can see that it is a good thing to search out such friends, even so.

Here one lives out in the open to such an extent that the seclusion I am experiencing brings real happiness to me, which is alarming to those who know me. They come to see how I am as if I were beginning my death agony. Never before have I felt such desire to live, and never have I been closer to feeling extremely well.

To give you a few minutes' mirth I have parcelled up the Cauterets local paper. I suggest you read the first article which improves my status, as far as I can see. I also recommend the combined music and theatre article, together with Gounod's *Ave Maria*, finally the panegyric on gargling, gargling places and garglers! I'm adding to this package a pen-and-ink sketch by one of my friends – of a distressing accuracy. Multiply these people by one hundred and you will have some idea of the sight that the Raillère [a stream two miles from Cauterets] presents before ten o'clock in the morning. This very moment that I'm writing to you, M. Charles Dauclo is performing the Mendelssohn Concerto in the Casino with the accompaniment (!) of an orchestra (!?!) – Good Lord! *I* am quite happy *not* to hear them – him, the concerto and the orchestra!

Do you realize, my dear Marianne, that I have only one more Sunday to spend here – this one is now returning its fine soul to the Lord? With what delight tomorrow shall I say the same thing on Monday – and so on until the termination of my *sorrow*.

You cannot suspect that it is all I can do to prevent myself sobbing fit to split the rocks open every time I write to you. That would only stupefy you to the point of boredom and I should be failing considerably in the objective which I am offering you. I have every confidence that you are fully aware of the very real sorrow which our separation causes me; and I intend to speak of it no longer, but to emulate your philosophical acquiescence. Your mother has promised me a letter from you tomorrow. I am aware of someone whose importunities will be superfluous when the clock strikes two!

Do forgive my handwriting which is becoming more and more *microscopic* daily – I must be tiring your sweet and beautiful eyes! As from tomorrow I will try to be more easily decipherable. Farewell, dearest Marianne, let me imagine that both of us are at that moment when they close 500,000 doors and windows at Bougival;[28] let me pretend that I am not well-behaved and that you are scolding me just a little. So, I kiss you very tenderly, as indeed I love you and will continue to love you for ever.

GABRIEL TOTO

I am going to write to your sister.

18 GABRIEL FAURÉ to MARIANNE VIARDOT

Cauterets,
Tuesday 28 August

Dear Marianne, I was very sorry when I asked you yesterday for a letter every day: your letter today has removed those regrets. You had nothing to tell me since the day before, so you said; and yet you have written four pages, full of interesting things where every line reveals your incomparable self and your desire to alleviate the distress I cannot dispel at being separated from you. How I should love to see you then, to thank you with all my heart, to say to you yet again: you are a *pearl which you yourself do not realize* and *I am determined to worship you*! I'm very happy that sweet little Jeanne, whom you love as much as if you were her mother, is by your side.

It is most moving, the way you look after her. When you hold her in your arms you are beautiful, as beautiful as the most beautiful of illustrious Maidens; also *you* are too quietly-spoken to shout at me again, and *I* esteem you too highly to take back what I said.

I saw in one of the sporadic newspapers which take off round here that the shores of the English Channel had been attacked by a fierce storm. I almost rejoiced in it because of the mighty spectacle on which your eyes could gaze, but I grew somewhat cold at the thought of those poor devils who have lost either their lives or their boats, or both at the same time. Ill-fated folk, and a cruel occupation! Better to beat time under the watchful noses, stuffed with tobacco, of the priests at the Madeleine.

I hope that the hurricane has ceased, that the angry billows are putting some colour in your cheeks, that you have now been able to take your baths and begin your constitutionals again. How could you let your good friend Charlotte go away? She was such a kind companion for you. Will you find her when you return to Les Frênes? And when are you going back there? Don't scold me too much for the confession I am about to make. I am plotting to leave Cauterets soon (either Saturday or Sunday) so that I can go to Tarbes where I shall beg my mother to fatten me up – by mechanical means if necessary. My two table companions are about to go away now, and I am thinking (not without dread) about the daily menu and the way it feeds me its unchanging poison. If however you insist on my continued immersion in warm water I will give in; but I think I can assure you that four days either more or less spent in this place will not give me back my high chest C – not that I've ever had it! My voice is naturally weak, nothing can change it and the hoarseness I was suffering from has more or less cleared up. I shall await your permission before deciding anything.

I've been strumming my harpsichord[29] for quite a long time today. It's a running battle with my next-door-neighbour – she is stumbling through the *Beautiful Blue Danube*. Both of us, you and I, have to bear our Calvary, our cross, our bitter chalice: you the *Il Trovatore* fantasy; I the *Beautiful Blue Danube*.

Talking of the Danube, nothing but distressing news of the Russo-Turkish war comes from the hustings. It grieves me because of the distress our *good Uncle*[30] must be feeling over his compatriots' defeat. And he no longer has you to console him! How many people must be missing you, dearest Marianne! Will there be a letter tomorrow? Once again, only you know. I am really thankful that you seem to be so happy when you receive my letters. If I were able, I would send you two a day so that I could thank you for yours and for the *brownish pistol* I've received straight in the heart! How Toto would love to kiss you! Farewell, my dear betrothed, *fairest treasure!* Think of me.

GABRIEL

My best wishes to everyone

19 GABRIEL FAURÉ to MARIANNE VIARDOT

Cauterets

2 September, Sunday

My dearest and *beautiful* Marianella, yes *beautiful! Most beautiful!*... *I am leaving for Tarbes!*... Hold on to the furniture so as not to succumb to a violent attack of indigestion. I shall leave quite soon, at five o'clock; I shall be in Tarbes at eight o'clock. I shall dine with my own folk, indulge in a bit of gossip, and at seven o'clock tomorrow morning, I shall clear off to *Cabourg!*[31] *Don't rush to change your address.* A *slip* of the pen. I meant that tomorrow morning at seven o'clock I shall return to Cauterets – my treatment for today and tomorrow will not be affected.

On a more serious note this is why I am sleeping at Tarbes tonight: I have still not received a line from my parents since I've been here; two letters from me remain unanswered, and I'm beginning to be really worried. I solemnly swear to you that I will not remain with my parents one minute longer than I've said, and my transplantation will result in my sleeping tonight in a different bedroom from this one. So do try to be as easy-going as I am, and do not scold me.

I have written to our uncle and told him that I wished you loved me only a quarter as much as you do him. Obviously you consider me incapable of ever having one quarter of his fine qualities, since when I ask you how I can conquer your affections completely, you laugh prettily at Toto's dark snout! In short, it is necessary to give in to your wishes, and one has to admit that in scolding me and prescribing a longer stay in Cauterets, you are showing your true affection for me. Do understand that I am not deceiving myself over this, and that each day I love you more dearly.

Please tell lazy old Georges,[32] who is unable to complete a letter in one day, that I have written to M. Dufaure to beg him to send me 500 francs which I need to settle the bill for my sumptuous stay in Cauterets. Next, take careful stock of this, namely: I shall leave this delightful spot on *Friday*, will sleep in Tarbes and set off on *Saturday* for Paris, where I shall fall into the arms of the Madeleine on Sunday. Please, therefore, send your *Wednesday* letter to my Tarbes address (Rue Péré), and your *Thursday* letter to Paris. *I* shall write to you from all the places where I shall be stopping, until you say 'Enough, we've reached Paris!' Your letter dated Friday, the day I received the despatch telling me of your unfaithfulness to Luc,[33] says not a single word about your plans. So they seem to have been fixed up very quickly. I hope you have not been too bored, and I am anxious to know that you have settled in well at Cabourg. There are some things which do help you when you're writing to me, since they provide you with incidents of which the most trivial in fact interest me to the highest degree. In any case I am not very well provided for in this place. Dead as a doornail from morning till night. It's true that if I probe the recesses of my mind for some sort of letter you accuse me of *flattering* you! To be serious, is this fair? So let me rest secure in the knowledge that I am in love with everything to do with you, and do not complain that you are loved in an *extravagant* manner . . . if you don't, I will put *absinthe* and *brandy* in my gargling mixture! . . . God forbid! Farewell until tomorrow, dear, dear, dear, dearest Marianne. I kiss you most tenderly.

GABRIEL

Many good wishes to your sister and Georges – my regards to Jeannette's little upset stomach.

20   GABRIEL FAURÉ to MARIANNE VIARDOT

Cauterets
Monday evening 3 September

A thousand thanks, dear Marianne, for your letter in which you regret so touchingly that you are not receiving my two each day on a regular basis. It has not always been possible to write to you in the morning, not even a few lines, however I shall attempt not to fail you in future, since you give me your assurance so prettily that this gives you pleasure.

I have already told you about the rituals which accompany the *numerous* readings of your letters. When, as today's did, they speak of the Place Vintimille and our all too distant home,[34] *I learn them off by heart!* Certainly I miss the Loges fair and those distant memories of four years ago, which I would have been very happy to reminisce over with you. When you want me to talk *about the past* I shall have to go back beyond that period; for at the time of our *supernal idyll*, already the present had begun – already my heart was filled with thoughts of you, and that swaying motion of ours rocked a dream to which I did not dare admit! Four years have passed since then, four years of lost happiness for me – which we shall endeavour to recapture, shall we?

I shuddered with horror at the account of your mishaps in the hotel at Luc, and I'm sorry that you did not leave this inn sooner, an inn more hospitable to wind and rain than travellers. I hope that tomorrow you will tell me about the wonders of Cabourg and the weather there. Here we are enveloped in severe wintry weather: for the last three days cold and dampness have been our hosts. Try to captivate the sun! . . . I was going to add that this would be easy for you, but I suppose you would rap my knuckles! Can you guess what my sister talked to me about yesterday evening? *A cook!* A maid and cook; accomplished, honest, clean, obliging, who has been in service with her, who lives in Paris at the moment, and who would like to leave the house where she is in service. I will let you have more details of this *Josephine* – in any case it will be easy for us to see and interview her on our return.

Thank Georges very much for me, both for his letter and for the walks he is having you take. He is a very fine brother to take care of you like that, and I like him more and more. Tell him I shall still go and meet him off the 8 o'clock train!! In your sister and Georges I've certainly got serious-minded allies, haven't I? My other ally, that prodigious 'Muse of Les Frênes',[35] will always make me blush though! Yet another overture? And me, nothing. Confound her!

This afternoon I saw going by and took by the roots of its hair something which might have looked like a romance for a violin. I have pulled too hard, and a spurious lock of hair remains in my hands. If the something in question comes along to claim it tomorrow, *whatever it is*, I will apprehend it and bring it to you in Bougival.[36] As for my *piano piece* (!!!) I know it less and less. It's the warm water which has made me a numbskull. I asked you yesterday to write to me on *Wednesday* at Tarbes and on *Thursday* in Paris. It would be better, if you can, to still write to me at Tarbes on *Thursday*, since the postman gets here before the departure of the train I shall be taking on Saturday to return to Paris. Paris, oh joy, oh happiness, oh rapture! To leave Cauterets at midday on Friday with one's conscience admittedly clearer than one's voice. To be in Paris on Sunday! Oh, those vistas!

I'm very glad I followed your instructions, in the first place because I hope that I have pleased you – and also because it will perhaps do me some good. All those silly sauces from the restaurant I offer you as a burnt-offering! Ah! If only Jeannette were here so that I could revel in her piquant remarks – there are no topics she would be short of, such as absurd ways of making a pile of money. Fortunately let's hope that once this period is over it will be quickly forgotten, that only your enchanting letters will remain, letters which all prove that you are taking pity on me somewhat, and that you love your Toto. If on Sunday I fall into your arms a little roughly, just blame these mountain slopes, which are determined to throw me off balance!

Farewell, till tomorrow *morning!* While your head is leaning over my letter I want very much to kiss you on your neck! *However*, that makes you cold! Do you remember? Farewell, I will kiss you when you are asleep!

GABRIEL

Fauré's use of German words and phrases in some of the following letters is an allusion to the fact that Marianne was teaching him the language.

21 GABRIEL FAURÉ to MARIANNE VIARDOT

Cauterets
Tuesday evening 4 September

With the help of this beautiful paper,[37] dear Marianne, I attempt to gain forgiveness for this morning's letter: its *fatuous mood* covers me in confusion! It was the happy thought of leaving which made me lose at one and the same time both my head and the most elementary notions of *propriety*! I have languished here as I should have languished wherever you were not, and I salute my deliverance less than the next hours and days when you will be restored to me: for ever, is that not so? My pen is therefore like me – distracted. This evening I shall try to make it more reasonable and more worldly!

Your enthusiasm for Cabourg has made me very happy, and I hope you will find some compensation for all the inconvenience of the water supply – it was so primitive in Luc, and you should not have had to put up with it for so long.

So enjoy this Paradise and your soul-walks; and tell me whether the mirrors *in which you look at yourself* are truly reflecting your real state of health.

Mine warns me that I have put on weight and gone *brown* again, what a fright I am. Fortunately negroes are fashionable just now, ever since [those] nations have been admitted into the Zoological Gardens.

I have received today a letter from Mme Clerc, funny and enjoyable as usual. I've also had a line from Joel, with a newspaper cutting which I have tried to translate by looking up every word in the dictionary – without success. ('*Sprach*' leads me astray completely.) On the other hand I know how they say 'I am going to have a little nap!'

Ich gehe machen jetzt kleines Schläfchen! [sic]

Through her bald husband Mme Höskier sent for me to go and dine with them this evening. On completion of this exercise, we took three strolls in front of the casino, and – shivering – we all returned home. Apart from this uneventful incident, I have seen nothing, said nothing, nor heard anything which deserves the honour of being brought before your *wondrously beautiful* eyes! (Oh! Only once by accident, so do not scold me!)

Tomorrow there is, irrevocably, my last visit to the doctor; the day after tomorrow, no less irrevocably, my clothes to be packed away in my trunk; and the day after, the supportive glass of warm water. The latter I will drink without flinching. Then, Bougival! That is to say, my adored Marianne and her family, with all of whom I am truly in love. How kind and affectionate everyone is to me! What have I done to deserve it, and what beautiful, good fairy was present at my birth? I still cannot get used to all this good fortune, and wherever it comes from I give thanks to the great unknown Manitou,[38] who sent it to me. Farewell, dear Marianne, dream no more that *you are being assassinated*, I beg you, but on the contrary dream that you are alone – happy, loved by everyone, and cherished by me. I kiss the little hairs on the side of your ear! Are you familiar with this little niche, which makes such a pretty shadow?

your mad GABRIEL

Very best wishes and affectionate greetings to my future brother, sister and niece.

22   GABRIEL FAURÉ to MARIANNE VIARDOT

Cauterets
Thursday morning 5 [actually 6] September

Having wet his dark snout in the cup of sulphuric pleasures and his body in the marble bath whence rises a pleasant fragrance of rotten eggs, Toto shakes his ears, shines his horsehair, stretches out a paw to his pen, and finishes off a succession of morning jobs with the most pleasant of them all. He would love, *der unglücklich Kettenhund, sein dick Kopf schwarz legen* [the hapless watchdog, to place his fat, dark head] upon the hand of the fair mistress of his fate, whose poor quality *barkings* hold him at a distance! . . .

Again, there is nothing since yesterday evening – except that *I've* had my little nightmare too, and so you've no longer sole rights over bad dreams. The one I've had I blame on my reading a chapter from *Germania*, over which I fell asleep yesterday evening. Thus I dreamt that the low-lying hollow of Cauterets and the steep mountain confining it, changed into a gigantic nocturnal vase (with all due respect) made out of porcelain; at the bottom of it, sick and able-bodied people were swarming pell-mell, attempting unsuccessfully to climb up the smooth, slippery sides; sliding, falling down, and unceasingly renewing their fruitless onslaughts. By means of a prodigious, inexplicable liveliness, *I* had succeeded in hoisting myself up as far as the edges – the only thing I had to do to be saved was to step over them – where an invisible hand hurled me down into the vase, where in the act of falling, I crushed Field-Marshal MacMahon[39] who was passing through. I was dragged before a Tribunal who, instead of sentencing me, congratulated and decorated me! I came running up to give you this piece of news (it's here that the dream takes a turn for the worse), when I heard from the postman in Luc weeping bitterly that you had just married the Archbishop of Paris! Fortunately I woke up at the very moment when I was about to pass an organ pipe from the Madeleine through my body!

After these ineptitudes, it only remains for me to give myself indigestion while having my lunch, and to be very ill so that I can atone for so many of these absurdities! I shall tell you this evening if I have been successful. Farewell then, I hope you have a more Allemanic time than we are having – also a delicious and truly health-giving bath.

Your escapee from a lunatic asylum
TOTO

Can you credit that I have only just heard today's serious worrying news – the death of M. Thiers? I very much fear that this event will have unfortunate consequences as far as the republic is concerned! Let us try to stay alive in order to see! I do hope that I'm wrong.

23   GABRIEL FAURÉ to MARIANNE VIARDOT

Cauterets
Friday morning 7 Sept[ember]

Weep O torrents, weep thou rocks, weep O fountain,
Thou spring of Mauhourat, weep,
The choirmaster at the Madeleine
Is about to delight you by displaying his nose!   [original text p. 208]

I could not leave this place without placing my hands upon the muse of the inspired poet! May Cauterets find in this lyrical morning rapture such happiness that I'm experiencing at the thought of clearing off in a few minutes!

This, therefore, is the last note I shall be sending you once I have soaked up the final glass of water. I am writing it on a small sheet of paper with one of M. Martigny's illustrations which he did one evening while we were gossiping in my enormous bedroom. I found this loose sheet while putting my knick-knacks away, and I have picked it up so that I can send it to you this morning, covered with my scrawly writing.

I shall write to you this evening from Tarbes, when I shall be even happier than I am at present since every moment from now on will bring me closer to you. It is really important for me to tell you that the supreme happiness I have experienced here is due to your sympathetic letters, and for which once more I thank you. My stay has been transformed into poetry and has been captivated by them, whilst my letters have sometimes been compromised by *verses* whose unseemly character I am unable to excuse.

Who is this plump little horsewoman?[40] Only Martigny knows – let's not ask him to divulge his little secret! While we're on this drawing, I do not, unfortunately, deserve the complimentary remarks you made on my ascent of the Raillère! This sketch is also by Martigny, and I should indeed be clever if I could draw like that. Profiles are my speciality: fat, lumpy ones. Beyond this I am incapable of anything.

The hour strikes, the hour of deliverance! Farewell, dearest Marianne; I am determined not to loathe Cauterets where I have had, through you, some very happy hours, and I send you my last kiss: somewhat *icy* as it will come to you from 1000 metres higher up than Cabourg.

Till this evening, and above all *till we meet again soon*!

GABRIEL FAURÉ

24   GABRIEL FAURÉ to MARIANNE VIARDOT

Paris
Monday evening 10 September

Dear Marianne, I have got back from Les Frênes and will quickly relate
to my *absent one* how we spent our quiet evening.

I got there by the 5.15 express and found your mother and our Uncle
in the billiard-room, where I was happy to bring them news of a *great
Russian victory*! Then we were all reunited round the dinner-table, and
almost immediately afterwards we had some music; your sister's overture
seems to me to be somewhat on the more usual scale of her works than
the one which she had composed at first. It is full of lovely details. Paul[41]
played us a new and an old composition, plus the *Folia*:[42] then I treated
the assembled company to *my voice*, a reading of some religious pieces
by a Swedish composer. I nearly forgot the recent songs of Paladilhe,[43]
one of which (among others) is remarkably pretty. All that took us up
to a quarter to ten; and I must confess that this time it was I who picked
up my hat before people began to remark on the lateness of the hour! I
hope that nobody noticed. Everybody asked me if I knew when you
were coming back! '*Non so*', I replied, '*ma spero lo sapere tomorrow*',
[I do not know, but I hope to know (tomorrow)].[44] I told Uncle that I
was going to write to you this evening, and he loaded me up with
baggage – lovely things for you, all *overweight*! I haven't told you that
I brought back from Tarbes the little piece of work which my niece did
for you. It consists of a little handkerchief sachet in shrimp-coloured (!!!)
satin, covered with English lace. You may possibly find it *very ugly* but
you realize that she is very willing and has the best of intentions.

I promised you a *portrait* of the *maid*, so here it is. Small, thin, oldish!
A southern accent and French enough to make the hair on M. de
Carillon's wig stand on end. Thus both eye and ear of my poor Marianne
could well be frequently disconcerted. If you can excuse these trivial
details, the rest of the information is excellent. I am relying on what my
sister has said and what she herself has told me concerning the very heavy
and very varied work she does in the house she is in at present. Naturally
I have left her absolutely in the dark on the matter. You will see her
when you get back, and can decide. What have I done, or said or seen
that can possibly be of interest to you? My binder has brought me the
eight volumes of Uncle's complete works which for affection's sake as
much as for good taste I want us to have. You agree with me, don't
you? Over the last four years I have not bought a book without wishing
that you might be able to read it one day. I do hope that you are happy
with what I have chosen! I shall also ask Uncle to come up to my house
one day so that he can see two or three engravings and tell me if they
would not be unworthy of being hung in our humblest corridors. One
of them is a reproduction of Raphael's St Cecilia which had been given
to me by M. Villot and which is, it seems, a very fine print. I also have
a water-colour etching of Regnault,[45] some Fantin[46] lithographs on the

Nibelungen and *Tannhaüser*, two large photographs of *papas* Mozart and Beethoven, etc, etc . . . .

This is turning out to be a letter resembling an inventory after decease! Thank God, I am alive, really alive, and am quite ready to *take offence* if you do not recognize me!

To tell you about the furious music which the locomotives make for me when I write to you is impossible. They really ought to put them to bed at the same time as children! It's quite intolerable!

This evening I prowled around the house, I looked at your shuttered window, I had a trip round the cottage! Not the slightest sound from the closed windows! But what sadness these September evenings if you do not come back soon to enliven them! When in your house I do my utmost not to let myself see how much the family seems *reduced*; I am as cheerful as possible so that I don't get *scolded*! Farewell, dearest Marianne, until tomorrow. I shall sleep well because from it I hope for a *happy awakening*, in the form of a *solemn promise* that you will *return promptly*, and I wish you the *goodnight* you will merit if you accomplish this good deed.

Your
GABRIEL FAURÉ

This evening, the omnibus and railway train on my return home from Bougival had soporific qualities against which I struggled painfully, so do excuse this insipid letter!

25 GABRIEL FAURÉ to MARIANNE VIARDOT

Paris
11 September, Tuesday

If you could see me, dear Marianne, you would see someone *very cheerful*, and *very happy*! One thousand thanks for having taken the decision to return on Thursday, since I hope very much that there is no fear of there being any connection between 'probably on Thursday' and 'in a day or two' over which I felt I had every justification to quibble when I was at Cauterets! To be absolutely honest, Toto has to confess that when his pen made an effort to write 'stay', his heart followed the movement sorrowfully. Just think: I am in the twenty-fifth day of a most abstemious Lent! So I can rejoice in your homecoming since you will be returning in excellent health and since my stock of patience is almost completely *exhausted* there will be no need on my part to renew it! . . .

So return home; the weather will no longer be *damp* and *dull*, for the sun has come back, and you will find as many *donkeys* as you wish – even *sea bathing* at the *Pont Royal Frigate*! And all of us will attempt the impossible so that you won't miss Cabourg-on-Sea too much – I was starting to call it *Cabourg-on-glue*! I shall not hesitate to have my apologies at the ready for this respectable borough if you have truly recovered your health and *rosy cheeks*, as your sister and Georges claim.

I have been so bored since I got back that I've started to miss Cauterets
because of it! At least down there I was not prone to give *humiliating*
answers, whereas here I am questioned every minute of the day on
matters which no longer ought to be matters of an unknown quantity
from my point of view! In short I hope that when you return light will
be cast and that I shall be able to take up a more *dignified* posture. I have
had enough of hearing myself make foolish complaints as that great fool
d'Eichtal[47] did yesterday; and I feel convinced that you will understand
my position and will reproach me less for it than anyone else. My organist
[Dubois] has left in my hands the responsibility for burying concierges
and other social inferiors of the parish, whereupon it follows that I have
a great deal of business in church. This will only last for a fortnight after
which I shall have just my usual jobs to attend to.

I've just been past the Rue de Douai to tell your mother what you
had written to me. I found her very worried over the condition of Mme
Léonard's mother, who is almost on her deathbed. Possibly Mme Viardot
will remain in Paris this evening if she feels it to be necessary. I'll give
you further information when I get back to Bougival. No. 50 Rue de
Douai has assumed the airs of a victor with its fresh, bright distemper
which is quite in keeping with my state of mind. It no longer has that
often dark look of the Sphinx which caused me such distress! Away with
unpleasant memories! And may my happiness last for the two days that
remain before I see once more my *beloved* Marianne!

I tried to see Saint-Saëns just now but met only his mother. As for the
young 'China fowl' he is not being faithful to cousin Flora, he's encasing
himself in the sand at Boulogne. You're aware perhaps that the business,
or rather the *quarrel*, over Délage has been sorted out and there can no
longer be any misgivings on Saint-Saëns's part concerning the friendly
relationship and affection of your mother towards him. This was really
worrying me, and I am very relieved that explanations have been made
on both sides.

Who is the recalcitrant ass who lets himself throw you out on the
streets like that? Could it be my poetic approbations which have annoyed
him? Tell him I withdraw them on condition that he behaves better.

Till this evening with my last scribble, meanwhile thanks from my
cheeks, *swollen with happiness* and pride under the sweet pressure of
your lips! Farewell, dearest cherished Marianne! How good it is to think
of Thursday and how I shall be counting the hours!

Ever yours

GABRIEL FAURÉ

I shall set off at half past three with Mlle Charlotte.

26 GABRIEL FAURÉ to MARIANNE VIARDOT

Paris
Wednesday [12 September]

Dear Marianne, An absolutely ridiculous reason deprived me yesterday evening of the pleasure of writing to you: a complete dearth of *lighting*! I went to bed by the light of the railway station gas burners and had no less sleep because of it – as far as the locomotives permitted, anyway.

Like the day before, yesterday evening was quite dead, and in spite (or because) of the presence of fat mummy Albini and Mme de Kossakowska[48] we didn't have any music. Paul and Mlle Mouki played billiards, the men leaned over the pages of their newspapers, and the ladies looked like the side of an omnibus that was full up!

Thanks to the darkness and Mme Kossakowska's prudent lethargy I missed the ten o'clock Tarbé train, and had to wait for the next one in the kennel at *Patapouffialalère*! When I add that during the day I went to see the *touchy* Lévy household, that I have just heard neither better nor worse news of Mme Léonard, that every minute I have things to do at the Church for the sake of my unfortunate organist who turns this millstone throughout the year, then I shall have told you everything.

I am forced to stay there for the time being. This evening, by the glimmering light of a *completely new* candle, I shall write to you about the day's happenings. I almost forgot to give you a piece of news which will certainly give you great pleasure: Mme Kossakowska's engagement with the Théatre de Lyon for 2000 francs per month starting from October. She is delighted, as we all are along with her. Farewell, till this evening, and much love meanwhile,

GABRIEL FAURÉ

If *by chance* it *really* is Friday when you are to return, please don't fail to let me know the time your train gets in. If you like, in a few days we can have an outing to Montmorency, the classic place for burros: nothing could be simpler, and you will see at the same time some quite pretty countryside which you do not know, I think. Think about it!

Re-farewell!

Among the many friends who must have been happy at Fauré's good fortune
was Romain Bussine. The following letter from him was probably typical of
many Fauré would have received during that summer. Bussine's letter, headed
simply 'Saturday', is probably the one referred to by Fauré in a letter to
Marie Clerc dated 'Monday evening' and from its content is more accurately
dated by Nectoux as 17 September 1877. On this evidence, letter 27 can be
dated 8 or 15 September. The music example in the first paragraph is that of
the main theme of Beethoven's G Major Piano Concerto op.58, as played by
the orchestra after the opening piano solo.

27   ROMAIN BUSSINE to GABRIEL FAURÉ

168 R[ue] d'Etretat
[Le] Havre
Saturday [1877]

My amiable and elected friend, Here I am, where I have been since
Saturday evening. There is no need for me to tell you how splendidly
Madame la Fée and her spouse received me. There is no need for me to
say any more than the fact that we talked only of you, of your good
fortune. As for me, I have had to listen to the moans and groans of Mlle
Lefèvre, who was stirring things up for you – and yesterday evening she
did not play at all well the concerto of M.

which she had played last year under your guidance... The absence of
that guidance can be felt in her piano playing, something I find serious...
Finally I told her you were so happy that it was unnecessary to think of
other things – she and her whole family chorussed, through their
disappointment, that they are really glad to know that you are happy...
that really is nice, for her future seems to me peculiarly at risk. The
Roses... too are among those who [word omitted] and who congratulate
you, all of them uttering lovely affectionate little sighs, Jeanne especially,
who has seen Mademoiselle Marianne at Camille's house, whose eyes and
womanly heart see things so clearly, has been able to take delight in your
delectable fiancée, and is entirely happy about your marriage...

In short, my good friend, here, as in Paris, I have found nothing but
kind thoughts for you, and I pass them on to you with the discrimination
which you know I possess; and this discrimination is coming to me so
easily that I believe I could enrage you even more with the greatest
pleasure had I seen more people here.

The reason I am writing to you now is because I must present my
apologies to you, for having broken my word to you last Wednesday;
it wasn't a good idea to arrange a meeting, I forgot that I had our public
examination at Auteuil, and only remembered about it the minute I left
for the train... I am going to write to Mme Viardot, to whom I have
been very remiss in not having paid my respects before I left, the more

so as her cordiality in the Conservatoire competitions could not have been more kind – and I was most touched by it. But: Wednesday, examination; Thursday, prize-giving; Friday, preparations for departure; Saturday, speech-day at the school – departure for [Le] Havre. I can assure you that it has been impossible for me to go to Bougival... added to this has been the necessity of going on a short trip so as to be able to kiss my sister... So do forgive me, intercede with Mme Viardot on my behalf so that she will forgive me too – do remember me to your irresistible young lady, your fiancée of the Muses; I have told you all my thoughts, and will always speak in that way. You will not show my letters, for it has been brought to my attention that you do show them, you old rascal; as far as this one is concerned I can rest easy, it is not legible – you are the only one willing to show me a little affection, and the only one able to get anything out of it for yourself...

In everything which has been said about you and about our wonderful little sister (as Camille so appropriately puts it), there is general expectation that you will come to an arrangement whereby you can spend some days at Sainte-Adresse next year. Meanwhile in order that the faint echoes of things from long ago do not fade in the memory and thus will gratify our hearts still more, we intend if possible to sing the *Cantique de Racine*[49] next Sunday. This will be the very moment when you will be reunited once again at Bougival. Think therefore of us, since *we* shall be thinking of you. As a final point, I shall tell you, old charmer that you are, that the love which the Clerc[s] have for you is something altogether wonderful when they speak of you both together. For you can no longer be separated – when they think of her they think of you; when they love you, they adore her for all the happiness she will give you – for all that she is giving you at the moment... In short, these good souls are really excited: I have seen nothing as moving or even, I think I could say, unanimous, as far back as I can think or imagine... I will not quibble with you on this, you know, but you do deserve it, that's what I think – as for me, I am very happy to be able to conjugate sufficiently to come to a full close with the words:

My fine Gabriel, dear elected one of the earth. I love you,[50] with great affection,

ROMAIN BUSSINE

Unfortunately for Fauré, this idyllic period of happiness was to be all too brief. Early in November, only three months after the engagement was announced, it was broken by Marianne Viardot herself. The reasons are still not really clear, though many commentators have offered speculations. In his youth and well into old age, Fauré was always considered attractive to the opposite sex. At the time, Pauline Viardot considered that her daughter had become somewhat afraid of her fiancé, and certainly some of the Cauterets letters seem almost distracted and quite unlike most of Fauré's epistolary effusions. And much later Fauré himself said, with a possible touch of irony, that

> Perhaps the rupture was not such a bad thing for me; that charming Viardot family might well have succeeded in deflecting me from my path.[51]

Nevertheless when the engagement was terminated Fauré was heartbroken; the letters he had written to Marianne were returned to him and he kept them to the end of his life. Subsequently Marianne married the composer Victor Duvernoy (1842–1907). Famous in his day for his operas and choral pieces, he also wrote innumerable piano works, and later was a professor of pianoforte at the Conservatoire.

By way of distraction Fauré travelled to Weimar with Saint-Saëns where his friend introduced him to Liszt, who had been instrumental in arranging for Saint-Saëns's opera *Samson et Dalila* to be performed for the first time in Weimar on 2 December. This performance both Saint-Saëns and Fauré attended. No doubt Fauré hoped to recover his poise and self-esteem. Liszt's reception of him was all that could be desired, and Fauré's fondness for foreign travel persisted to the end of his life.

Inevitably his own work also proved to be some solace, and this next letter shows him attempting to gain admittance as a composer to the Conservatoire Concerts Society. Evidently not wanting to astonish the committee with one of his more recent works, he submitted to them his *Cantique de Jean Racine*.

28 GABRIEL FAURÉ to the SOCIÉTÉ DES CONCERTS DU CONSERVATOIRE

Paris
18 February 1878

Gentlemen, I beg leave to address you and to submit for your judgement a four-part chorus with orchestral accompaniment, which I have written to a religious poem by Racine. I should not have dared take such a step had I not been greatly encouraged by a few members of the Société des Concerts, who have had the opportunity of hearing the chorus performed privately; and I hope, Gentlemen, that you will be willing to take this circumstance into account so as to excuse my temerity.

I remain, Gentlemen,
Yours very truly
GABRIEL FAURÉ
Choirmaster at the Madeleine
13 Rue Mosnier
Members of the Committee of the Conservatoire Concerts Society.

In 1879 Fauré signed a contract with his first major publisher Hamelle, who bought all the rights in Fauré's works published by Choudens. The previous year Fauré had travelled to Cologne with André Messager for the express purpose of attending performances of *Das Rheingold* and *Die Walküre*, both of which made a deep impression on the two Frenchmen. In September 1879 the two composers went to Munich to hear the complete *Ring* tetralogy; and in 1880 Fauré and his senior organist Théodore Dubois went to Munich to attend productions of *Die Meistersinger von Nürnberg* and *Tannhäuser*. Although the Wagner fever was soon to reach its height in Paris, affecting composers as diverse in their aims as d'Indy, Chabrier and Debussy, it may well be that the youthful initiation into Wagner's music at the Ecole Niedermeyer by Saint-Saëns had the effect of lessening its impact on Fauré at this time. Certainly his musical idiom was hardly, if ever, influenced by Wagner, and this cannot be said for the great majority of his French contemporaries.

In April 1881 Fauré arranged his Ballade, op. 19 for piano and small orchestra; the version for solo piano had been written in 1879. In this new format Fauré took the solo part himself at its first performance on 23 April 1881 at a concert of the Société Nationale. The ease and charm of the scoring belies the oft-heard slur on Fauré's capabilities in this direction.

Fauré's first visit to England in May 1882 was again with André Messager and again to hear Wagner: the first English production of *Der Ring des Nibelungen* at Her Majesty's Theatre in London. In July Fauré and Saint-Saëns travelled to Zürich to meet Liszt again, who was presented with a copy of the Ballade in its solo version. The story is well-known that, after playing several pages, Liszt said that it was too difficult for him to continue, and asked Fauré to complete the performance. It was on this occasion that Fauré, having hazarded a suggestion that the piece might be too long, received the characteristically Lisztian reply:

Too long, young man, that does not make sense: one writes as one thinks.

Towards the end of 1882 Fauré received the last extant letter from his father. Toussaint-Honoré and his wife, in rather uncertain health, had now retired to Toulouse. Toussaint-Honoré refers obliquely to the death, on 25 November 1882, of Camille Clerc.

29★ TOUSSAINT-HONORÉ FAURÉ to GABRIEL FAURÉ

Toulouse
Tuesday 5 December 1882

Here I am, my dearest Gabriel; I must have a couple of words so I can give you our thanks for the lovely present which you have just sent to your mother, and which was chosen so nicely by kind Mme Reveillac. Over here we are glad that the bad attack of bronchitis has responded to the skilled and devoted care of our Dr Clément Maury, to whom we ask you to tender our most sincere thanks.

Your indisposition has been all the more unfortunate, in that it has not let you leave your flat at a time when gratitude and affection were needed for a family which has suffered such cruel blows, and which was calling for your 'services', your comfort. Poor Mme Clerc! How we have identified ourselves with the cruel loss she has experienced, and which has struck her children so grievously! Your mother, who is feeling over-tired, advises you to take particular care of yourself in order to recover your health and then keep it so in the best way possible.

I am watching over you myself, my dear Gabriel, for it is a long time since I took up my pen; and all of us here ask you to accept our most loving affection.

Your father
FAURÉ

P.S. Our best wishes to our mutual friends.

Little seems to be known about the early months of 1883, the year of Fauré's marriage at the age of 37. Marie Fremiet was the daughter of the sculptor Emmanuel Fremiet (1824–1910). He was noted particularly for his sculptures of animals; his masterpiece was probably the equestrian statue of Joan of Arc in the Place des Pyramides in Paris. Eventually Marie came almost to resent the success of both her father and her husband, since she herself possessed artistic talent which brought her little fame. Not unnaturally, she also resented the fact that Fauré chose always to spend his holidays alone in order to compose. Her disillusionment with so many aspects of her life grew stronger the more she became aware of Fauré's infidelities. That she never accompanied Fauré on his numerous travels was, none the less, fortunate for posterity, since he wrote a large number of letters to her which reveal a considerable talent as a letter-writer. And certainly the early years of their marriage were happy, as is shown by the affectionate letters beween them in the 1880s and 1890s, though this period of 20 years is not as fruitful in this respect as the 25 years which followed. The next communication comes from the composer Henri Duparc (1848–1933) and his wife – in reality two letters in one envelope from husband and wife – and from the context can be dated anterior to 27 March 1883, the date of Fauré's wedding, which that year fell on the Tuesday of Easter week.

30 & 31★   EMMA and HENRI DUPARC to GABRIEL FAURÉ

Chalet Ste. Claire
Near La Garde Jarès
Toulon
[1883, before 27 March]

Dear M. Fauré, We have already heard (from my brother-in-law Arthur) the news about your marriage; but the proof positive of which you have been kind enough to inform us, delights us as much as one of those fine songs which at times escapes from your languorous nonchalance (a polite way of describing your laziness). I do thank you for your acute understanding of the part we shall play in an event which for you will be, I've no doubt of it, the starting point of a long era of happiness, well-deserved happiness as the outcome of a host of lovable qualities which we shall do our best to keep in our minds for evermore – despite the dreadful nadir you have had to suffer because of your migraine.

But you do not tell us either on what day or whereabouts, in the eyes of God, your union will be blessed. I should really love to know, for I am determined on our being represented at this ceremony if only in the mind; and if you would allow it, I should be happy to offer your charming fiancée some flowers from our sun-kissed climes. They will speak of us to her, and will tell her better than I could hope to of our sincere wish to become her friends.

Jean's first thought on learning of your marriage was for the dangers of which *friendship* is well aware. 'Mummy', he said to me, 'M. Fauré will still be our friend, I expect!' So young, and already the son of his father!

Farewell, dear M. Fauré, we send you our very best wishes for your happiness; and we ask you to retain for us at the conjugal hearth a happy memory of old times, carnations, migraines, pancakes, finales and in a word, of all those funny little encumbrances of bachelorhood which, we very much hope, will again give us such happy times.

All my very good wishes
E DUPARC

[Continuation by Henri Duparc]*
You have hit the nail on the head, my old 'water's edge',[52] and this piece of good news is indeed not my business. Therefore, I do ask you to be good enough to give Mlle Fremiet my sincere good wishes. As for you, I'm not going to bother: they would be too banal. Besides, if I wanted, despite my detachment, to try to impress upon you the feelings of joy I have on seeing you so happy, it would be pure lyricism – and I feel sure you would be sufficiently sceptical to laugh at them.

So now you really have nothing more that you want: as for me, I won't speak too much about it, though I do hope very much indeed – despite all the happiness you deserve, happiness of the deepest blue – that you will not become a friend-quitter. I can see you from here, airing your gentle unconcern in the gondola of marriage, not remembering those poor devils whose affection for you has sometimes sweetened the rigours of celibacy, and serving up your clever migraines to them – done to a turn. Allow me to hope that your fiancée will once and for all get rid of this state of mind – as convenient as it is non-morbid. And, so as to allow me to count on this happy cure, do not fail – I do beg you – to offer a few words to Mlle Fremiet about the true and devoted friends you will be giving to Mme Fauré. Do I need to add that amongst that great number of friends we can lay claim to a little place, and even (why not say it?) a great one?

You have made a mistake in attributing the carnation to me; but nothing is lost: I have passed on to their rightful owner your touching reproaches over this 'poor woman' who loves my music so much. I assure you that this flatters me very much, and I should be very sorry to make fun of her except in the most innocent way. However I am inclined to think that she loves my music because Mme de Lassus loves it; and that M. de Lassus loves it because he loves my cousin, who loves me very much. However that's how you get on in this world!

Chausson[53] wrote to me the other day to tell me that Hamelle had in effect made up his mind to swallow the pill without insisting that I put the tiniest hint of sugar on it.[54] I do think that M. de Lassus – although he is not saying so to me – must be there for something, and possibly for a great deal; but something tells me that no-one has had a greater hand in this than you, and they are not going to convince me otherwise. So once again, I do thank you with all my heart; and I am giving myself something to look forward to by having printed in flashing letters at the top of a certain small *Lamento* the dearest name of my master and benefactor. But don't let's go too fast: I haven't received the slightest hint from Hamelle, and as long as he has not given me confirmation of the news himself, I shall be on my guard.

Farewell, you delightful chap. To think that I shall find in you a man who is staid, wedded, respectable, proprietor of a charming home!... I just cannot get used to the idea. Don't forget to give me your new address as soon as you know what it is, so that I can have your letters sent back there by my concierge. And above all, if you really want my opinion, do not compose any songs in the blissful state in which you find yourself: you would certainly lose that light-hearted feeling whose secret we possess, and this would be a great pity for the art of elegiac sentiments.

Farewell. – With Mlle Fremiet's permission (which she will not refuse) I embrace you fervently, and only hope you are as happy as I am. What more can I say?

H D

The following letter, undated but probably from the early months of 1883, must have given Fauré great pleasure, coming as it did from a much older composer whose music he admired greatly.

32 CÉSAR FRANCK to GABRIEL FAURÉ

Friday evening

My dear Fauré, I am very happy at your good fortune. I know that your 'future' is a woman of accomplishment and that her family is charming.

So please accept my congratulations, and believe in my true affection for you as a person and in my very high regard for your gifts.

Your devoted friend
CÉSAR FRANCK

The next letter was perhaps a reply to a party or lunch invitation on the morning after the wedding. Since, as already indicated, the wedding day was a Tuesday this would seem to be the likeliest explanation; Massenet's inability to attend is couched in affectionate terms, but his business sense evidently overrode all other considerations. However, he was not a close friend of Fauré despite their mutual associations with the Société Nationale.

33   JULES MASSENET to GABRIEL FAURÉ

Nantes
26 March [18]83

My dear friend, I very much regret that I shall be far away from Paris on Wednesday morning – *Hérodiade*[55] is on that very evening in Nantes.

But I want you to know that I am very attached to you, and that my most affectionate good wishes go out to you. Please convey my respects and feelings of admiration to the illustrious father of your wife, and believe me,

Your devoted friend
J MASSENET

Nine months after the marriage on 29 December 1883 Marie gave birth to a son. He was christened Emmanuel after his maternal grandfather, and was to become a distinguished biologist. In addition to being professor of biology at the Collège de France, he also inherited sculptural gifts from his grandfather. The final short letter from this first period of Fauré's life is an ungrammatical, poorly-written note from Saint-Saëns's mother, acknowledging the news of Emmanuel's birth.

34   MME SAINT-SAËNS, *MÈRE* to GABRIEL FAURÉ

[30 December 1883]

Thank you, my very dear friend, for the happy news you have given me, I am very happy that everything is over, and that my two friends are as well as we could hope for. I say my two, because the little one is also my friend, you would want that very much, I hope.

See you soon, every good wish to you, your old friend,

C[LÉMENCE] SAINT-SAËNS, *mère*

In my happiness I am forgetting to ask you to kiss them for me.

Notes

1 P. Fauré-Fremiet, *Gabriel Fauré*, 2nd edition, Albin Michel, 1957, p. 33.
2 Gabriel Fauré, *La Revue Musicale*, 1 February 1922, pp. 97–8.
3 Saint Saëns's transcription of the opening movement of Bach's Cantata No. 28, dedicated to Fauré.
4 Saint-Saëns's mother and great-aunt, whom Fauré frequently referred to as 'les dames'.
5 Fauré's own greeting in English: a reference to Saint-Saëns's visit to England at the time.
6 Jules Lasserre, a cellist friend.
7 Holy Communion administered to the dying.
8 Pierre-Marie Pietri, Police Prefect from 1852–8, and Jean-Alexandre Le Pays de Bourjolly who died at Tarbes in 1865.
9 Alfred Niedermeyer, son of Louis, who took over the directorship of the school on his father's death in 1861.
10 A spa town near Gavarnie which was to assume great importance in the correspondence between Fauré and his first fiancée, Marianne Viardot (see letters 16–26).
11 P. Fauré-Fremier, *Lettres intimes*, Grasset, 1951, p. 23.
12 Antoine de Choudens (1825–88).
13 Adam Laussel, fellow pupil of Fauré at the Ecole Niedermeyer, was in Saint-Saëns's piano class.
14 Jules de Brayer, organist.
15 Probably the *Trois rapsodies sur des cantiques bretons*, op. 7 for organ, dedicated to Fauré.
16 The Vatican Council.
17 This interpolation appears in the margin of the original letter.
18 Adolphe Thiers (1797–1877), statesman, journalist, historian and both founder and first President of the Third Republic in France.
19 *Après un rêve* and *Sérénade toscane*.
20 The young farmgirl Bernadette Soubirous had had her visions of the Virgin Mary in 1858.
21 Restaurant situated at 14 Rue de la Madeleine, 8th *arrondissement*.
22 Small town between Toulouse and Bayonne.
23 Hubert Léonard (1819–90), Belgian violinist and friend of the Clerc household, who tried over the Sonata with the composer as it was being written. He also taught Paul Viardot.
24 The First Piano Quartet was apparently completed by the end of 1876, but Fauré was dissatisfied at least with the finale; he rewrote it entirely, and the quartet saw the light of day only in 1883.
25 See page 30.
26 Fauré-Fremiet, *Gabriel Fauré*, p. 57.
27 Fauré is referring to an excursion he made into the mountains on a previous day, during which he was caught in a heavy shower.
28 A village near St Germain-en-Laye, where the Viardot family had a country house called Les Frênes (Ash Trees).
29 Although it seems unlikely, Fauré may have had a harpsichord at his disposal. In a letter to Marianne of 1 September he was to write: 'I should have given a great deal to be able to play the *basso continuo* in your 'joke' concert.... .
30 Ivan Turgenev (1818–93). The word *parrain* by which Turgenev was known by the entire Viardot family is literally 'godfather', but the normal English equivalent would be 'uncle'. The Russo-Turkish wars had been numerous since the end of the seventeenth century, a result of Russia's ambition to secure control of the Black Sea and an outlet to the Mediterranean. In 1877–8 the treaties of San Stefano and Berlin secured for Russia Kars and the port of Batumi.
31 A resort some 12 miles from Luc.
32 Georges Chamerot, Marianne's brother-in-law.
33 *See* letter 20.

34 The Place Vintimille (Ventimiglia Square) was to be the young couple's first home.

35 Marianne's elder sister Louise (1841–1918), who was a composer of operas and songs, and a teacher of singing successively in St Petersburg, Frankfurt am Main and Berlin.

36 The Romance for violin and piano, Op. 28, which indeed dates from 1877, was published in 1883.

37 *See* Pl. 4.

38 The 'Great Spirit' of the North American Indians.

39 Marie Edme Patrice MacMahon (1808–93), after a distinguished military career, was to become the second President of the Third Republic in succession to Adolphe Thiers. His autocratic and monarchist sympathies led to crises in 1877 when he forced the resignation of the Prime Minister, Jules Simon, and dissolved the Chamber. He resigned in 1879.

40 A reference to the sketch on this page drawn by Fauré's friend, Martigny.

41 Paul Viardot (1857–1941), Marianne's brother, was a fine violinist, and later achieved fame as a conductor; Fauré had dedicated his A Major Violin Sonata, op. 13 to him.

42 The seventeenth-century melody, used by Corelli and other composers as a basis for variations.

43 Emile Paladilhe (1844–1926), a composer of operas, songs and a few instrumental works; he succeeded Ernest Guiraud, one of Debussy's teachers, as a member of the Institut in 1892.

44 The last word of this sentence was omitted, Fauré evidently having forgotten the Italian word for 'tomorow' (*domani*). The French *demain* was added by another hand.

45 Henri Regnault (1810–78), French physicist who improved various methods of measuring heat, and a scientist who set new standards of precision in experimental physics.

46 Ignace Fantin-Latour (1836–1904), French artist famous for his flower studies and portraits.

47 Eugène d'Eichtal (1804–86), French philosopher and man of letters. He was a nephew by marriage of Marie Clerc. (*See* note 48.)

48 One of the numerous Slavonic visitors to the home of Marie Clerc's sister, Adèle Bohomolec. Two of her daughters married Eugène d'Eichtal.

49 The choral work with which Fauré had won first prize in composition in his final year at the Ecole Niedermeyer 12 years earlier.

50 The use of the verb *conjuguer* two sentences previously points forward to this 'you', since Bussine here employs the familiar *tu*, having throughout the letter so far used the formal *vous*.

51 Fauré-Fremiet, *Gabriel Fauré,* p. 59.

52 Mon vieux 'bord de l'eau' – a reference to one of Fauré's early songs *Au bord de l'eau*, to a poem by Armand Sully-Prudhomme.

53 Ernest Chausson (1855–99), like Duparc a former pupil of César Franck.

54 Hamelle was Duparc's publisher as well as Fauré's. The 'pill' here was Duparc's great song *Lamento*, the manuscript of which had evidently just reached Hamelle. The song is dedicated to Fauré, an act somewhat grandiloquently explained towards the end of this present paragraph.

55 Massenet's fourth opera first produced in 1881 in Brussels. The Nantes performance marked its first production in France. He was also hard at work on what is generally regarded as his masterpiece, *Manon*, which was completed on 15 July 1883.

2

Marriage and maturity
1884–1900

Little is known of the early months of the marriage and even less about the succeeding year 1884 when Fauré composed the fourth and fifth Nocturnes and second *Valse Caprice* for piano, the set of four songs, op. 39 and the Symphony in D Minor, op. 40. The latter was premiered under Edouard Colonne in March 1885, and Vincent d'Indy (1851–1931) also conducted a performance of it at a French Festival in Antwerp in August of the same year. However, Fauré was dissatisfied with the work; it was never published and was eventually destroyed.

The year 1885 marked the start of a period of some anxiety for Fauré: his name had by this time become recognized as that of one of the leading French composers, but publication of his music did not bring in sufficient money to support himself and his family. He was obliged to spend many hours teaching and in consequence travelling, while his wife's health caused him considerable anxiety during the 1880s. Fauré himself began to suffer a recurrence of his former illness. The greatest blow was the death of his father at Toulouse on 25 July 1885. Fauré hurried to Toulouse, although he was in the process of arranging his wife's health cure at Néris-les-Bains, near Montluçon. Soon afterwards he went to Antwerp to attend d'Indy's performance of his Symphony in D Minor.

35 CAMILLE SAINT-SAËNS to MADAME GABRIEL FAURÉ

[Paris]
30 July 1885

Dear Madame, When I got Gabriel's letter I went to Avenue Niel so as to try and find you; I learnt that your husband had returned from Toulouse and gone back to the country. Now he is in Antwerp where I shall finally be able to rejoin him the day after tomorrow. He must have been very distressed at losing the best of fathers; this is the first real sorrow to strike him in his life, a life so untroubled for him up to now. Fortunately in you he has the greatest consolation.

I have forgotten Mme Fauré's address in Toulouse, I will write to her from Antwerp.

Yours in sincerity and friendship,
C. SAINT-SAËNS.

36*   GABRIEL FAURÉ to MARIE FAURÉ

Antwerp
31 July 1885

My very dear Marie, Your sympathetic letter has deeply moved me! I
am not surprised that your heart and soul are filled with such sensitive,
tender and noble things! I am not surprised that you have never said
them to me. These things are meant to be written, not said; and you did
the right thing in putting them in writing. You couldn't enhance the
place you hold in my heart, since you possess it absolutely, but you are
everything I could wish for. You therefore make me smile when you
talk of the sensitivity of my finer feelings and emotions. Aren't you at
the very least my equal, if not my superior? Thank you from the bottom
of my heart for your confidences, and I beg you to consider what my
life would be like if I did not have you. So you really must do your
utmost to reassure me that you're taking scrupulous and continual care
of your health! When you try to ignore the advice and thoughts I try to
give you on this, you don't just distress me, you cause me *dreadful pain*!
I beg you, think of this for all time: you and I, we are *as one* for ever!

Things here, so annoying when I wrote to you yesterday, were still
more so in the evening. There is, not to put too fine a point on it, such
disorganization in the way these concerts are arranged, such ineptitude,
and so casual an attitude all round, that I am half surprised anything in
fact takes place at all. No rehearsal this morning. There isn't a single
rehearsal room available in the entire city. You get a thousand muddled
requests and not a single person to stem the flow. There is a German
faction, tenacious and crafty, which wants to make the French Festival
collapse – at the moment they're certainly succeeding.

Yesterday I heard a concert of works by Liszt, Tchaikovsky, César
Cui and Berlioz, played in an open-air bandstand by the Exhibition
Concert Orchestra with the audience moving around. Since the *concert
room* has been taken over by a floral exhibition, these are the conditions
under which they're offering to perform my symphony! I'm absolutely
against it!

Saint-Saëns arrives tomorrow morning: I don't know whether he will
succeed in controlling these belligerents we're saddled with! Such is the
situation that if the concert does not take place on Tuesday at the very
latest, I have warned these gentlemen that I have neither the time nor
the money to wait, and that I shall leave.

By dint of going to see officials, sub-officials, and sub-sub-officials, in
the end we got hold of a theatre room for tomorrow in which to rehearse.
That's something!

Such annoyances when I would far rather be near you and our darling
boy! However, I cannot regret a trip made worthwhile by my sweetheart's
letter this morning. I love you – lots of love and kisses to both of you.
Till tomorrow. Everything fine and affectionate you can find to say on
my behalf, say to our dear friends and your parents – *as for mine, alas*!

The next letter can be dated only approximately, Marie Fauré's cure at Néris being the only guide.

37★   GABRIEL FAURÉ to EMMANUEL CHABRIER

Hotel de la Promenade
Néris-les-Bains (Allier)
[End of August, beginning of September, 1885]

My dear friend, I am not cross with you and never have been: I had even intended to write to you and forestall your explanations, by telling you how I had been saddened by a certain event. Here is my excuse: I have scarcely been anywhere for the last month. At the moment I am at Néris where my wife is having treatment which, I hope, will restore her health – it's something she really did not have at all last winter. If this area were not to do her any good it really would be abominable to have come here; it's truly the most tiresome hole on earth!

Some time ago I was in Brussels, and I went to salute the façade of the *Monnaie* in honour of *Gwendoline*.[1] You can rest assured that provided nothing really serious prevents me I shall not fail to form part of the *train* of friends when the great day arrives.

People have been saying *enormously* complimentary things to me about those parts of your opera with which I am not familiar. So don't get Het Up and hot and bothered! Everything will go off very well, and all of us will be delighted about it.

Do please remember both my wife and me to your wife, and I clasp your hand with great affection, your old friend

GABRIEL FAURÉ

Fauré completed his G Minor Piano Quartet, op. 45 in 1886, the year that he met Tchaikovsky for the first time. The two composers became good friends, and Fauré inscribed his signature and an affectionate message to Tchaikovsky on a score of his new quartet. This is also the work referred to in letter 38, when Fauré wrote to Saint-Saëns to congratulate him on the first French performance of his third Symphony on 9 January 1887. The work was performed again a week later, a performance Fauré attended. Saint-Saëns's acerbic comments about the Société Nationale in his reply (letter 39) were due to his disagreements with the society over their decision to perform modern non-French works, which seemed to him to be contrary to the purpose of its original foundation.

38*   GABRIEL FAURÉ to CAMILLE SAINT-SAËNS

[Paris]
Friday [21 January 1887]

My dear composer of a splendid symphony! Dare I ask you to come tomorrow evening to the *S[ocié]té Nationale* to hear my new quartet?

You will never know what a treat it was for me last Sunday! And I had the score, something which ensured that I did not miss a single note of this symphony, which will live much longer than us two: even when putting our ages together!

All affectionate good wishes to you, and also to your mother.

GABRIEL FAURÉ

39*   CAMILLE SAINT-SAËNS to GABRIEL FAURÉ

[Paris]
Sunday [23 January 1887]

My fat cat, I've just found your letter which, for some reason or other, had escaped my attention (it hadn't been opened!). I did not go to the Société Nationale 1) because I no longer go there, 2) because I was obliged to spend the evening working. However I certainly thought about your *Quartet*, and had I not been tied to some unavoidable work I should have asked to hear the rehearsal.

I've got you a fanatic these last few days, a man with the intention of buying all your music – he's just written to me that you've put Chopin completely in the shade.

I am still busy with your wretched individual in another way – I'll tell you about this later.

And I'm grinding away at your pieces again; this time I'm getting somewhere. The more I look at them the more I love them. Especially the Nocturne in B Major[2] which I find absolutely entrancing. I shall ask you for a lesson sometime.

My best wishes to your wife
Yours affectionately,
C. SAINT-SAËNS

Fauré wrote the next letter from Le Vésinet, a few miles north-west of Paris, where he had been holidaying since the middle of August 1887. The recipient was Hugues Imbert (1842–1905), the French music critic and literary scholar. He was the author of many books and articles on topics such as contemporary French composers and Wagner. He was also perhaps the first to champion Brahms's music in France. Imbert was preparing some articles on Fauré for the *Indépendance musicale et dramatique* which he had founded. Fauré's letter was not dated and that given was added to the envelope by another hand.

Marguerite Baugnies was one of Fauré's most devoted friends: she presided over a prestigious Parisian salon. Her friend Georges Noufflard was a musicologist.

Edouard Colonne (1838–1910), an influential and experienced conductor, founded the concert series which bore his name; famous for the breadth of his repertory he was perhaps most famous for his championing of Berlioz's music.

Hans von Bülow (1830–94), pianist and conductor, married Liszt's daughter Cosima, who deserted him in 1869 to live with Wagner, whom she subsequently married.

40   GABRIEL FAURÉ to HUGUES IMBERT

[Le Vésinet]
[19 September 1887]

Dear *Monsieur*, I have received all the *Indépendance* numbers as well as the very interesting book on Schumann, and I am most grateful to you for your kind interest.

Will I soon have the pleasure of seeing you? I shall be busy on *Thursday up to 4 o'clock* and on *Saturday from 4 o'clock*. Outside these two days you will always find me ready to put myself at your disposal.

I had thought (and I quickly saw that it was impossible) that you might make use of a letter from *Cui*, written to M. Noufflard about my songs, and of which a copy was sent to Mme Baugnies, who gave it to me. In this letter Cui puts my songs in definitely too flattering a light. He says they are the best French songs to the detriment of those by Gounod which he regards as affected, those by Saint-Saëns which he regards as cold, and those by Massenet which he regards as effeminate. These assessments, doubtless intended for his correspondent, could hardly be printed without severely compromising the man who expressed them. And, if I think about it, it is a matter of considerable vanity on my part to get you to look at them.

But you would easily find in three numbers of the *Ménestrel* from last year (1886), at the time of Rubinstein's last great concerts, a series of letters by Cui dealing with the programmes which the illustrious pianist had reserved for the Parisians, and analysing them and commenting on them. This set of letters ended with the following observation, outside the actual text:

> *I regret not having seen in these programmes any mention of the names of Bramhs* [sic], *Saint-Saëns, G. Fauré and C. Franck.*

That sort of comment really touched me; and this, I think, could perhaps be extracted without offending anybody. Besides, it's *printed*!

My name appeared as well towards the end of a letter, reproduced in all the newspapers, from Hans von Bülow to Colonne. It said more or less: 'Enough of this pseudo music: let us have the Saint-Saëns, the Massenets, Francks, Lalos, d'Indys, Faurés, and... and... ' Possibly I have forgotten, possibly I have added, some names which were not mentioned; but that was, more or less, the *general picture*.

And since I myself belong to those people we are dealing with, don't you think it is better not to talk at all about the artistic preferences of a musician who is still young compared with his French contemporaries? To many people that would smack of impertinence; to others, envy and jealousy. Actually, those musicians who interest me most are our comrades d'Indy, Chabrier, Chausson, Duparc etc... in fact those who have come on the scene when it is more difficult than ever to be an original musician. As for the older composers: apart from Saint-Saëns for whom I have my passionate, wholesale friendship and deep gratitude, I cannot bring myself to take much interest in all these people like Massenet, Salvayre[3] etc... the only exception being *Reyer*[4] and certain lighter pieces by *Delibes*, those which have grace and charm.

But whether all this should be said, I'm not sure, the more so as I could be mistaken. Some musicians have genuine merit, but in such complete contast to my own thoughts and feelings that I find it impossible to understand them.

Do forgive this lengthy verbiage in which there is, alas, far too much of your very devoted

GABRIEL FAURÉ

Can you give us a part of your Sunday at Le Vésinet, next Sunday? A part or the whole day, if this does not frighten you?

Fauré had completed the first version with small orchestra of the *Requiem*, op.48 by the end of 1887. On New Year's Eve of that year his mother died. Fauré then hastily added some extra movements early in 1888 in time for the first performance on 16 January, when it accompanied the burial service of one of the Madeleine's parishioners. The work went through two other versions before reaching its final form with full orchestra in 1900. A very different work was the incidental music to Alexandre Dumas *père*'s play *Caligula*, whose first performance was conducted by Fauré in November 1888. Earlier in the year Marguerite Baugnies had organized a lottery so that Fauré and Messager could pay their first visit to Bayreuth, where they heard *Die Meistersinger* and *Parsifal*. They also met Daniela Thode, the eldest daughter of Cosima Wagner and Hans von Bülow.

41★ CAMILLE SAINT-SAËNS to GABRIEL FAURÉ

[Paris]
[18 December 1888]

My dear Gabriel, I too lost my mother this morning at 9 o'clock. Not much point in saying more, is there? Not much point either in coming to see me, I am only receiving my relations because I cannot do otherwise – unless you would like to see her for the last time.

C.ST S.

Letters 37 and 42 are the only two extant letters from Fauré to Chabrier, but both show the close friendship between two French composers whose musical styles were markedly different from each other. Nectoux dates letter 42 'around 3 June 1889' because of its allusion to the success of Chabrier's *Gwendoline* at Karlsruhe on 30 May under the baton of Felix Mottl.

42* GABRIEL FAURÉ to EMMANUEL CHABRIER

[Paris]

What a fine success, my dear friend, and how absolutely delighted we were to get the news of it here! But how annoying as well not to be able to be down there!

From my point of view it was absolutely impossible to leave Paris, and difficulties of a material kind were bound up with dreary health matters. My wife is ill in bed.

Come back soon so that we can have a good time and kiss you on both cheeks. As from yesterday Messager is a father. *He* will certainly go to hear you at the end of the week. Once again, one thousand of the most affectionate congratulations from my wife and me to your wife and you, and many many friendly greetings.

GABRIEL FAURÉ

It was in 1891 that Fauré met the poet Paul Verlaine (1844–96) who was to prove to be the source for some of Fauré's most successful songs. However, Verlaine's poetry was already well known to him. Count Robert de Montesquiou (1855–1921), a poet and society figure in Paris, was the kind of man whose ambition was to gather around him persons of genius. His enthusiasm for Verlaine was transmitted to Fauré whom he first met in 1886. Fauré set to music Verlaine's *Clair de lune* and *Spleen* in 1887 and 1888 respectively, and began work on the *Cinq mélodies de Venise* op. 58, to words by Verlaine, in Venice in the summer of 1891. The Princess de Scey-Montbéliard, later to be the Princess Edmond de Polignac (1865–1943), arranged this holiday for Fauré at her expense, and she was to be one of Fauré's most generous admirers. Born in New York, she was originally a Miss Singer, of the sewing-machine family; she married the Prince Edmond de Polignac in 1893. She hosted one of the most elegant and influential salons in Paris, and exercised a benevolent influence on a large number of composers of many nationalities. It was she who brought Fauré and Verlaine together, and her suggestion that the two men collaborate on a theatrical project, *L'Hôpital Wat[t]eau*, the subject of letter 43. Verlaine was constantly ill however, and already suffering from the alcoholism which was to kill him in 1896. Fauré managed to convince the Princess of the futility of attempting to work further with Verlaine, whereupon she suggested an opera on the subject of Buddha in which Fauré would collaborate with Maurice Bouchor. The latter suggested as librettist his friend, the poet Albert Samain (1858–1900) (*see* letter 47). The vague dating of 'early 1892' for this letter corresponds with Fauré's interest in this project throughout that year.

Thus, the final decade of the century marked the start of Fauré's increasing fame, and his genius was further recognized by his appointment in 1892 as inspector of music in the provincial conservatories, in which he succeeded the composer Ernest Guiraud (1837–92), the teacher of Debussy and Dukas. Fauré was able to give up his private teaching, but had to spend a considerable amount of time travelling. Fortunately these travels resulted in numerous letters to his wife and friends.

43   PAUL VERLAINE to GABRIEL FAURÉ

Paris
Wednesday 21 January 1891

Monsieur, My friend Charles Morice and M. Robert de Bonnières tell me that I must ask you all about the appropriate details – the size, nature of the subject, approximate time, type of verse (mixed with prose or not?), how much time there is – concerning the literary work for which you were willing to consider me. Just at present I am receiving treatment for a rheumatic disorder which, so it seems, should soon leave me in peace. My present address is then, alas!

> Hôpital Saint-Antoine,
> 5 Bichat Ward,
> Rue du Faub[ourg] St Antoine,

where I can receive people *every day* from 1 till 3, they prefer Thursdays and Sundays, but I enjoy special immunity; and if there is any difficulty with the concierge, show your card to the attendant and you can come in on such days and at such times as you wish. But Thursdays and Sundays are the regular days. (Ask for bed no. 5 in the Bichat Ward.)

Just in case you may not be able to come, be good enough to write to me, giving me all the details listed above.

Please accept, Monsieur, my best wishes
P. VERLAINE

The next letter can be dated only approximately, though it is evidently from this period.

44   PAUL VERLAINE to GABRIEL FAURÉ

[Paris]
Friday morning [Spring 1891]

My dear Fauré, Thank you for your well-timed intervention: Hamelle has been very kind. I can be seen every day from 1 till 6. Come, that is, before 3. Above all come soon +

Extraordinarily busy. I'm writing for newspapers... which perhaps(?) will never pay. Lord, what a job!

Yours ever, and shall I see you soon?
P. VERLAINE

+ and often!

H[ôpital] Broussais, Lasègne Ward, bed 30, 96 Rue Didot[5]

45 PAUL VERLAINE to GABRIEL FAURÉ

[Paris]
6 April [18]91

My dear M. Fauré, Madame de S[cey-Montbéliard] ... has promised me
an advance of 300 francs for the 15th of this month. She evidently doesn't
suspect the embarrassing state I am in. I shall be most grateful if you
could open her eyes to this. And I send you my best friend, an artist too,
who will be willing to undertake this all too painful commission.

Moreover I have started on *our* work.

Your apologetic
PAUL VERLAINE
18 Rue Descartes

46 PAUL VERLAINE to GABRIEL FAURÉ

[Paris]
Thursday 26 November 1891

Dear Monsieur, Did you receive a letter written some time ago in which
I asked you to meet me so we could agree on the business with Madame
de Montbéliard? Quite naturally your silence has paralyzed me and I
have done nothing, given the unknown and uncertain state into which
I should have been flung had I taken up my pen on this account.

However one scruple haunts me (I am *very scrupulous*, as well as
having a fair amount of pride) to the effect that Madame de Montbéliard
has advanced me a hundred francs. And since I am scarcely able to let
her have them back, what might in her eyes be the equivalent of this
sum in verse? I am quite prepared to dedicate something to her with
your music which would double its value – if my words were acceptable
to you.

Regarding the most important business, is it still on the cards? If my
presence is still needed, well here I am – but not without having seen
you and conferred together.

Alas, re-rheumatism and other complications. Result:

H[ôpital] Broussais, Lasègne Ward, bed 24, 96 Rue Didot, Paris

So do come to see me here – I can be seen every day – or write to me.
But come all the same, won't you?

And every good wish to you,
P. VERLAINE

47 ALBERT SAMAIN to GABRIEL FAURÉ

Monday [early 1892]

Dear M. Fauré, Herewith I send a revised, corrected (not too much) and somewhat expanded something which, so it seemed to me, might be called the first *tableau*. It's up to you to see whether the proportions I have given here and there to the 'voices' will allow for some curtailment when music is added at those points. That is my overriding fear. I have tried to vary the funereal impression of the opening by using the voices of both young men and young women; the mother's wailings in the same kind of mood allow for a different nuance, from sombre tragedy to desolate melancholy. There are some hints for the décor which did fascinate me somewhat.

After a moment, when the star shines alone – shadows disperse – and you see night – a night in Asia, dark blue, all dotted with points of light. In this night, where tomorrow's vague lineaments appear in a confused mass, a shepherd's silhouette takes shape, as if it were in the distance.

This single note, reverberating in the gloom, would be good, so it seems to me. If the *two* quatrains are not enough, I might be able to extend them.

Then after this incantation – more sonorous in that great silence – the stage is filled with light, rose-coloured and white, where the young women of the Gardens of Loumbini will appear.

It's up to you to tell me what you think, or better still what you feel about all that.

For the ending I have done an 'ensemble'; to my mind all the voices – from top to bottom – ought to sing it.

In addition, I have done a pencil sketch of a strophe which precedes the birth of Buddha – perhaps at this point, music alone would convey better the sensation of approaching ecstasy, or it might replace the above strophe.

I shake your hand most cordially,
ALBERT SAMAIN

Samain's venture, which might have been more worthy of Fauré's genius than the somewhat Satiesque *L'Hôpital Wateau* of Verlaine, came to nothing. Fauré knew his own limitations better than anyone. In his song writing he was able to select those poems which shared a natural affinity with his musical style; operatic subjects by their nature were for the most part beyond his scope. It is no coincidence that Fauré's two large-scale works for the stage,

Prométhée and *Pénélope*, were products of the interest in Hellenic antiquity so characteristic of early twentieth-century culture in France.

48   PAUL VERLAINE to GABRIEL FAURÉ

16 August [18]92

My dear M. Fauré, Reinach[6] tells me that because of some poetry[7] set to music by you, a music publisher owes us some money. If such were the case how grateful I should be to you, and when you have succeeded in prising from this industrialist that code of honour, the double prebend, see that what is due to me gets to me, *absolutely as soon as possible!*

Either by money order, or in banknotes if the sum calls for it; as soon as possible, I repeat: pressing needs, remaining debts, etc.

(And many many thanks for your collaboration in my benefit subscription.)

Alas! Ill once again, and my address, provisional I hope,

Hôpital Broussais, Lasègne Ward, bed 30
96 Rue Didot

All good wishes,
P. VERLAINE

Are you coming to see me? Every day from 1 till 3. I would have something very confidential to tell you about the subscription, as a matter of fact.[5]

Despite the abortive *L'Hôpital Wateau*, Fauré's interest in Verlaine's poetry remained undiminished. He began his finest Verlaine masterpiece, *La Bonne Chanson*, op.61 in 1892, completing the first eight songs of the cycle easily and quickly. (The ninth and last song was not completed till 1894.) In a letter written towards the end of his life to his pupil Roger-Ducasse he was to remark:

> *I have never written anything as spontaneously as* La bonne chanson. *I can and must add that I was helped by a spontaneous understanding at least the equal of mine from the one who has remained its most moving interpreter.*

This was Mme Emma Bardac, the wife of a rich financier whom Fauré first met probably in 1892: it was generally believed that she was his mistress. The radiance and voluptuousness of *La Bonne Chanson* tells its own tale. Emma eventually divorced her husband to live with Debussy and became his second wife in 1908. Under these circumstances is it any wonder that Fauré and Debussy were not much more than cool acquaintances? Fauré admired Debussy's aims and liked much of his earlier music, but Debussy in his few comments on Fauré's music was almost always slily malicious about it, even though there must have been much in it to attract him. Ironically, *La Bonne Chanson* was one of the few works by Fauré which elicited Debussy's express admiration.

The next letter refers to the initial attempt Fauré made to obtain a composition class at the Conservatoire, a vacancy occasioned by the death of

Ernest Guiraud. This attempt provoked the celebrated remark by the aged
Ambroise Thomas (1811–1896): 'Fauré, never, if he is nominated, I resign.'
Fauré's rival Théodor Dubois, already his senior at the Madeleine, was elected
in his stead, and Fauré had to be content with an appointment as music
inspector of the provincial conservatories. From letter 49 it is easy to see that
Fauré had his own reasons for not wanting additional teaching responsibilities.

49★ GABRIEL FAURÉ to CAMILLE SAINT-SAËNS

no date [end 1892]

My dear Camille, I am not a *donna* but I am, alas *mobile*.[8] That is to
say, I have thought it over and do not consider myself in sufficiently
robust health to increase the workload I have already, with a job as
important, as laden with responsibilities, as a composition class. I have
taken a good look at myself too, and apart from these basic truths, I have
not found a *method* for myself. I have already had some young people
through my hands, and I can remember that my teaching has varied
according to the ability of each one of them: a system which is not
possible when there are numerous people in the class, where one needs
to let fall from one's lips only such words as are not open to dispute!

So there then are the strong scruples I feel when I really should have
liked to take your advice, but I am sure you will appreciate them and
that when I come to see you one of these mornings, you will not have
too SEVERE an expression in reserve for me!

All my affectionate good wishes,
I'll see you soon, won't I?
GABRIEL FAURÉ

The following letter refers to Saint-Saëns's projected concert visit to Chicago,
a visit which in the event did not take place.

50★ GABRIEL FAURÉ to CAMILLE SAINT-SAËNS

[5 June 1893]

My dear Camille, The Second Waltz, the Third and Fourth Barcarolles,
and Second Impromptu, the Fourth Nocturne: those are the pieces I
should be delighted about if you were willing to play them. I don't have
any strong feelings either way, but it was you who wanted them. If I'm
expecting too much of you here, you can choose what you would like.
As for thanking you, I could never do enough of it, neither at the present
time, nor in the past, nor in the future, for I am quietly confident of
being able to rely on you!

All my affectionate good wishes, and I hope you experience as little
fatigue as possible, many dollars, and above all superlative good health!

Your wretched pupil
GABRIEL FAURÉ

Letter 51 refers to Fauré's first attempt to gain a seat in the Institut, with all the wheeling and dealing which inevitably accompanied such manoeuvres. Unlike Massenet or Saint-Saëns, Fauré had no opera to his name, while his predilection for songs and piano music had gained him a reputation as a mere salon composer. Neither situation was conducive to success in an election where genius was not the only attribute to take into account. Requiny, otherwise a shadowy figure, was evidently a man of some influence, as Fauré saw it.

51   HENRY REQUINY to GABRIEL FAURÉ

Marly
2 November 1893

Dear friend, My sister has told me about your letter. I can well believe that you must put yourself forward! You are, as they say in Rome in the conclave, among the *papabile*.[9] I cannot see that there are circumstances any more favourable for trying to nudge you in. It sometimes happens that an election is all arranged beforehand: either by some indication clearly resulting from previous elections, or a candidate may be a particular favourite either because of a mass of outstanding credentials or because of a group of sympathetic activists. Now, out of those last lucky academics, it seems to me an insult that Joncières[10] is an everlasting candidate, destined to reap the doffing of hats and never to hear the *dignus intrare*.[11] Dubois has a certain advantage, his position as professor of composition at the Conservatoire; the camaraderies of Rome[12] would be worth a considerable number of votes. One can certainly be sure of that. No link with either of these two factions. Among those who are applying as candidates for the first time, I see only you and Godard[13] having candidatures which could be regarded as of paramount importance. If poor old Gounod were alive and the vacant chair was someone else's, you could have counted on his active support.[14] How many times had he not spoken to me about you, with a genuine admiration for your genius, and a real affection for your very self? In his absence, you have the sponsorship of Saint-Saëns, which is considerable, and who will be in a position to say, with all the authority of his critical appraisal, what your work is all about and what your work is worth.

For a long time I thought that Paladilhe would be very sympathetic towards you. One of the last times he saw Gounod they spent the evening with him playing you, and Gounod singing you. It was Paladilhe who told me this, he was really profoundly impressed by what happened to him that evening. I fear that his long-standing and close friendship with Dubois will pledge him *to* him in the final vote, but in the section classification he will have the chance of demonstrating his feelings for you. I shall see him. As for the other friends I have in the Académie des Beaux Arts, I have much less influence over them. However I shall make every effort to act upon Gustave Moreau,[15] and Paul Dubois,[16] Falguière,[17] M. Blanchard,[18] and Détaille.[19] Last time Détaille voted for Joncières. He will have to drop him. Get him on your side right away. Foolishly he had been persuaded to lend his support to Joncières, whom he knew at Offenbach's house!!

We are still at Marly, Villa Niélesville, 10 Rue des Vaulx. If you can, do come and dine with us on Saturday – that is to say, the day after tomorrow, or Sunday if you prefer, at 7.30. Come earlier if you can. The tram brings you as far as the horse trough, and from the horse trough to the house there is a park for 6–8 minutes. We can chat better and more usefully than by letter. Your father-in-law must be able to do a great deal, unless the close family relationship he brings to your candidature is a stumbling block for him, which sometimes happens. Try to come, we shall be very happy to see you and very glad if we were able to do something which might be useful or agreeable on your behalf.

Very cordially yours
HENRY REQUINY.

52*   GABRIEL FAURÉ to CAMILLE SAINT-SAËNS

[Paris]
[3 November 1893]

My dear Camille, Mme Guyon[20] has spoken to me about Paul Dubois, and she is urging me to ask you to complete the work which, so she says, she has certainly begun. With a couple of words from you we should get Paul Dubois.

Mr Gérôme[21] has also expressed himself in my favour, as has also the painter Jules Breton.[22]

If I could get up to half a dozen, that would be respectable!

Till Sunday at St Séverin, and many thanks,

GABRIEL FAURÉ

Despite these overtures, Fauré's application was unsuccessful. The Institut committee postponed its decision until May of the following year when Théodore Dubois was elected. This was neither the first nor the only time that the careers of the two musicians at the Madeleine were to interact.

The year 1894 was relatively uneventful for Fauré, save for a trip to Geneva and a second visit to London. In England interest in Fauré's music was slight but gradually increasing, and in 1896 Fauré managed to set up a contract with the London publishers Metzler & Co.

1895 was also fairly uneventful, except that the post of music critic to *Le Figaro*, for which Fauré had applied, was given to the composer Alfred Bruneau (1857–1934), much to Fauré's disappointment. The following year was, however, one of the most momentous in Fauré's life. Having visited London in 1882 and 1894, he paid his third visit there in April 1896 and was once again in London in December of the same year. From this time onwards, far more letters are extant from Fauré to his wife than previously.

At the same time as his April visit to London, Fauré was again attempting to gain admittance to the Institut, with all the attendant tensions and worries felt by both Fauré and his family.

53   JULES MASSENET to GABRIEL FAURÉ

Paris
21 April [18]96

Dear friend, I am absolutely sympathetic to your letter, to your calling – so I should like to see you – but when? how? – you are so busy at present – that it seems to me not only very difficult to arrange a time for you and for me – but it is [also] very injudicious for me to appropriate one moment of your time – I shall come to your house – I shall try to meet you –

I am well disposed to you,
In friendship and admiration
MASSENET

Fauré left Paris for London at the end of April, resulting in the usual correspondence between him and his wife. Marie Fauré would have been an interesting study for a psychiatrist. Overshadowed by the fame of her father and husband and left behind whenever Fauré was compelled to travel, she quickly became a woman embittered. The numerous flattering attentions bestowed on Fauré by other women, which he evidently did little to discourage, win her our sympathy. She was easily upset by domestic trivialities, as letters 54–8 show, so on weightier matters the scenes which must have taken place between her and her husband are not difficult to imagine. After the first few years of marriage, there must have been very little of the original love that had undoubtedly been present at the start. Fauré remained fond of Marie right to the end, but it is easy to see that her bitterness and irritability may have provided Fauré with the ideal excuse for his infidelities.

Marie Fauré dated letter 54 merely 'Tuesday'. Another hand, possibly that of Philippe Fauré, added in pencil '28 April 1896, addressed to London, Old Queen Street 22, Westminster'. This was to be Fauré's London *pied à terre*, the home of Frank Schuster, one of his most devoted English admirers, and in the words of Robert Orledge,

> the wealthy son of a Frankfurt Jewish banking family who chose to devote his life to the advancement of the arts rather than business.[23]

54★   MARIE FAURÉ to GABRIEL FAURÉ

[Paris]
Tuesday [28 April 1896]

My dearest Gabriel, We are well, we have had your telegram from Dover, we are thinking of you and are talking of papa (you) every minute. Yesterday I slept the whole afternoon, today I'm feeling better but I have Marcelle's white collar to do; Philippe claims he wants to climb the ladder today – don't worry, he's still not standing up straight.[24]

Meg has written to me, she tells me that she has seen Falguière who will be voting for you; and she is offering me for little Emmanuel a *complete* set of clothes for his first communion – I'm accepting with enthusiasm! So there you are.

It is dark, we have storm clouds and the temperature is registering 22 degrees outside. Tomorrow, I shall write more for you; forgive me for today, the little ones kiss you – oh! and me of course!!

MARIE FAURÉ

You can burn my letters if you want, but do not leave them lying about.

55★ MARIE FAURÉ to GABRIEL FAURÉ

Thursday 30 May '96 [actually April]

My dearest Gabriel, Yesterday was somewhat difficult: I felt it was necessary to warn the *Abbé* Vautroys that *possibly* I would be forced to ask that I be allowed a certain degree of latitude for Emmanuel; and that I was no longer able to rely on the promises of the priest – that I needed another summons from him – or I would take appropriate measures myself. Actually he is charming, our *Abbé*; he will come with us on Sunday at 3 o'clock to a first retreat meeting, at which I intend to be present since I shall not be taking Emmanuel to the morning retreats; and the *Abbé* wants to come with us so he can set us up comfortably and with some semblance of authority.

I've had your letter, full of such important and wonderful things. Our life at the moment is in absolute mind-boggling confusion!

And now the important matters: 'Philippe is continuing to improve, Emmanuel is fine' and I am better. The end of your letter gives me strength for everything! I am going to increase twofold my health (and my sweetness!). All the same it is annoying to be dependent on someone else at this time; one word of disapproval from you is sufficient to get me into a panic, but since you rate me so highly I am going to be gentle with the priests.

Everything you say regarding the Institut will be said again to papa – and afterwards, for the Lord's sake, I do beg you not to get het up about it, whatever happens. We will send a cable to you – to where I am sending my letters. I've heard nothing about Saint-Saëns. At home today we shall soon have mummy, Emma and the two little communicants. I shall leave Philippe in the bedroom and in bed; don't worry about him, we'll deal gently with him, only one person at a time will go in.

I am as happy as I possibly can be over everything you tell me about London, I revere these people who understand you so well – how happy I should be if I were there! Here I cradle and protect the *future sailor* [Emmanuel] – he has a priest's determination for that; he seems to have an immutable will of his own: the painting of Mlle Bérenger's parents, overwhelmed with grief by one of their sons who, in spite of them also wanted to be a sailor and died as a result, does not affect him at all.

You will never guess what he wants to ask his Aunt Emma for his first communion present (an illustrated, special nautical dictionary).

Oh! the monster! Do not worry about anything here, I am happy to know that you are happy over there! Do not make into a tragedy all the things I am telling you about over here, you know me: you know I easily get excited and do not know how to conceal things – I have to tell you everything.

I kiss you, I adore you, thank you for your letter, I must have forgotten to tell you about things which I shall doubtless recall soon. But do not worry if you are without letters for a day, I have a lot to do – and Philomène is coughing and spitting in a disgusting manner. Tomorrow I shall take her to [Dr] Gruby by using my bag of tricks. He'll see the point of it.

MARIE FAURÉ

56* MARIE FAURÉ to GABRIEL FAURÉ

Thursday 30 May [actually April]

Oh Gabriel! How happy I am during this worrying period of elections to the Institut to sense that you are the centre of all those festivities in which you are the moving spirit; but how I am suffering at being alone, sacrificed as prey to these two priests; how troublesome it is (and what an opportunity!) to have to resist whatever they want, which with cat-like stealth they are attempting to slide in like a lever. But I shall succeed: truth is mightier than trick. Our dear *Abbé* is maintaining his domestic arrangements; on Sunday he will be coming to fetch us in his carriage so that we can all arrive at the church together; haven't they got such kind thoughts! They don't give you the option of being an independent arbiter; but I shall be the strongest: I shall leave in a docile manner with him, and on the stairway I shall hand him a letter (of which I shall send you a copy), saying to him: that not having time to chat before going into church, I am asking him to read this letter (in church) and in consequence, to use his influence with the priest – for this letter is the expression of an immutable resolution.

I have just been hearing about the first communion at Passy, and with us it will be just the same in that microscopic church: no hassocks, every seat you can think of must stay put, (long) sermons, and hungry children who go into church at 7.30 and don't come out till 9.45. During lunch Marcelle was so pale and agitated that *papa himself* saw to it that she was put in the drawing-room on her own, and she goes to school every day! And she is worn out when she gets among a crowd!

In the programme of retreats, communion, confirmation, etc. I have made a marvellous discovery: it is the renewal (in best clothes) of the first communion on Sunday *7 June*; the *Abbé* of Passy (he had lunch at Emma's house) has had the same idea for Emmanuel as I have: he says that each year delicate children should take their first communion at this renewal, where the mass lasts half-an-hour instead of two hours, and when it is not jammed up with parents and as a result no crowds. After this I can take decisive action and without vouchsafing any more arguments: I think you will approve of my action. From now until Sunday, each morning, I shall reread quietly my draft letter, toning it down and removing every unnecessary word.

Now make sure you don't come back until you want to, Emmanuel will be taking communion on 7 June. To have another engagement would not be right. So there!

Just consider the weather, and should the sea be too rough on Wednesday, oh well! Send the Péreire dinner packing and a telegram instead; at least promise me this if you love your little ones!

Do not worry at all about my aggressive disposition. Women are tolerably monkey-like, I shall profit by their example; a taciturn and lovable obstinacy, to say yes, to sit down smiling, and then to leave on tiptoe; I shall be a model of gentleness, referring to my letter at every attempt to have a discussion. When necessary I should put Emmanuel to bed with the shutters closed and a dry compress on his head. (This is a joke.)

Your letter I received this morning is doing me good, I feel so alone in this struggle! However I think it is better if I am alone. Thank you for all the loving words you say to me, you give me the courage to complete my task without faltering, I am speaking the truth: with the upbringing of children, the first communion is only incidental.

Perhaps there will come a day when I shall be acquainted with the duet! Perhaps there will come a morning when I shall go to see St Michael in the drawing room! All for love of the little ones! But it is not without tears. You tell us to kiss ourselves and one another on your behalf; therefore we are feeding ourselves on kisses, hideous things! It's certainly the least we can do while they are there under his protection.

I must finish my letter, I am getting sad. My thoughts are with you unceasingly; see you soon, we kiss you tenderly,

MARIE FAURÉ

57* MARIE FAURÉ to GABRIEL FAURÉ

[Paris]
2 May

I am sad, my poor Gabriel, not to be at your side this evening, and I would like to be sure that you are going to sleep well and not suffer any nervousness; papa is feeling indignant[25] and we have to soothe him – today there is not one of his colleagues who does not fill him with dismay.

I should like to have your news; I hope that all those great bonds of affection which surround you and all the success you are enjoying will prevent your blowing up this thorny problem out of all proportion.

Listen to some good news. This evening our darling Philippe stood upright *without any support*, and then with a little frightened face he said quite softly 'But it's happened all of a sudden'. Emmanuel is more gentle and more agreeable than usual; I think he is concerned to see the difficulties I am having in my struggle with the priests.

He is very docile in everything he is asked to do, like his prayers.

Forgive me if tomorrow I do not have time to write to you; the day will be complicated because of the first retreat to which I *must* go if I am to show willing, and then during the course of the morning I have yet again to look at, tone down and recopy my two letters.

Today I went to buy a completely new sailor-suit and a warm jersey for Emmanuel and a jersey for Philippe too; Mummy paid me everything on my return, *100* francs, less 10 sous! Emmanuel is going to put them on. I've also bought a little book by Bossuet (*Meditations on the Eucharist*) which seems to me simply his meditations on the gospels.

Ah! I'll see you soon, everything is fine; in a few hours it will be Sunday. I kiss you as hard as I can, and I love you, how I do love you.

MARIE FAURÉ

58* MARIE FAURÉ to GABRIEL FAURÉ

[Paris]
4 May

My dearest Gabriel, When papa and mamma were leaving here the day before yesterday they went by M. Bohomoletz's house, and Meg's, to tell them the result of the election: Mme Bohomoletz was just as she always is: wonderful and sensible. Meg has been extraordinary: papa says that she was in bed, they went into her bedroom and saw her: quite a small woman in the middle of an enormous bed, who when she saw them began to shout 'Oh! The swines, the swines' and then sulked and put her head in both hands, all the time repeating: 'Lenepveu? Why Lenepveu?'[26] and that lasted a quarter of an hour.

Your telegram yesterday did me a lot of good, for I was worried about you, at least that is what I thought; anyway let's not talk any more about that, think about all the happy memories you will be bringing back from London, and really do try to tell me everything (without being too modest).

My day yesterday rather wore me out, my letter was good compared with the reality! For it convinced our *Abbé, he read it here in the drawing room*, and the result of this victory has, I think, been as unexpected as any literary figure might have devised: he came towards me, saying, 'You are charming, I must kiss you!' And we kissed each other on both cheeks! He took his to the priest. I do not know the result yet, but I will not yield one inch.

In spite of everything I have had a quarter of an hour's struggle with the *Abbé*, who was having the confirmation in Aravers (which *I* was having next year!), he said too that since the renewal was like the first communion (imagine that: priests' words!) we should not be gaining anything. But he had to give way before my response: we shall have a more equable temperature in June, we shall have Emmanuel rather more inclined to go out, we shall have a mass lasting half-an-hour instead of two, and we shall have only a quarter of the communicants and helpers. He really did have to agree with all that; as for all the other points I said to him 'But, *M. l'Abbé*, I have foreseen that, there is an answer to everything in my letter – read it a second time while I put my gloves on, a single reading is not sufficient for a letter like that'. He read again for a long time, and everything ended just like I said to you.

We have been to the retreat together, and it lasted two hours. Emmanuel behaved impeccably; he was as pretty as a picture (with some trepidation), he was between his mother and his *Abbé*; despite this, a nasty verger said to him 'And what are *you* doing there! Why *are* you there?' 'By order of the priest' we replied.

Our poor *Abbé* slept a little (in the retreat) and fidgeted a great deal; as for me, you can't imagine how tired I was; and Emmanuel, nicely got up regarding his clothes and so on, came out saying to me *Oh! I am glad I am with my equals.*

Today both of us will go back to the three-and-a-half-hour retreat and our *Abbé* will not come until next week; I have shown him quite a small book by Bossuet which I have bought entitled *Meditations on the Eucharist*; it does not quite agree with the words of the curate on our retreats, but we will carry on with Bossuet. So there.

All affectionate good wishes from the depths of my heart; oh! how alone I feel in this struggle! Tomorrow I will write no more! and after tomorrow! Oh! I shall kiss you all the more!

MARIE FAURÉ

59★   EMMANUEL FAURÉ to GABRIEL FAURÉ

Tuesday 19 May 1896

My darling papa, Just think – I have managed to fit my lock to my box which I have made, and this box locks itself. I have put inside it, before giving it to mummy, some flowers and two stamps. Philippe has made a lovely boat.

On Sunday I went to mass with mummy, afterwards we went to Madame Bohomoletz's house; Adèle tells me that she will be going to Russia, and would be seeing some chickens born. I am working at fractions, it is very easy.

All affectionate good wishes,
EMMANUEL FAURÉ

60★   PHILIPPE FAURÉ to GABRIEL FAURÉ

19 May 1896

My darling papa, I am almost walking, and we are very well. But I annoy mummy a bit, and I have made a boat for mummy, and I am very happy because I am going with mummy.

Darling papa, I love you very much indeed.
PHILIPPE

On 2 June, soon after Fauré's return to Paris, he was appointed principal organist at the Madeleine in place of Théodore Dubois who had been appointed Director of the Conservatoire on the death of Ambroise Thomas. This was only a small consolation for Fauré after failing in his bid for election to the Institut. Massenet had hoped to succeed Thomas as Director of the Conservatoire, but only if he were appointed for life. This condition being refused, Massenet resigned from the Conservatoire altogether. This spate of musical chairs was to have further repercussions for Fauré in the autumn. Before this however, Fauré paid a further visit to Bayreuth where he again met Wagner's family. Letter 61 was sent by Saint-Saëns to Bayreuth, where Fauré was staying from 4 to 13 August 1896. Fauré was about to apply for one of the two Conservatoire composition classes (those of Dubois and Massenet). As usual, Saint-Saëns was ready to further Fauré's professional career by working hard behind the scenes on his friend's behalf. (Saint-Saëns's reference to Widor is slightly confusing. In 1890 Widor had succeeded Franck as Professor of Organ at the Conservatoire; on Dubois's promotion, Widor took over his composition class.)

61★   CAMILLE SAINT-SAËNS to GABRIEL FAURÉ

[Paris]
Tuesday (4 or 11 August 1896)

My dear Gabriel, With the recent nomination of Dubois, it is quite obvious that we wouldn't want to be unpleasant to him and that his recommendation will stand. Now you've got all you need. If I were you I should let Widor follow Massenet, and I'd take the organ class. It's done no harm either to him or to César Franck.

If I were in Paris I would try to see the Minister, I'll drop a line to Roujon[27] – it's all I can do. I will leave matters in the air so as to give you every opportunity to double back in the way I've indicated, which would be the astute thing to do.

[CAMILLE SAINT-SAËNS]

62★   GABRIEL FAURÉ to MARIE FAURÉ

Bayreuth
10 am 4 August 1896

I'm writing to you immediately, and will run and take these lines to the post office in the next village, but I haven't the faintest idea as to when and on what day they will reach you.

I've had an excellent trip, without sleeping *for a single minute*... I remained all night in a fine, massive armchair in the smoking-room, watching night disperse and day dawn, something I really love!... What a room, and what a view! It is so enormous that the little ones could have had their beds there too! Before my very eyes there is an enormous park, and a veritable forest of fir trees with their troughs and crests; it's quite marvellous...

63★   GABRIEL FAURÉ to MARIE FAURÉ

Bayreuth
Wednesday morning 5 August 1896

I'm having to write to you very early (it's nine o'clock), as I must go to Bayreuth and return before lunch. We are a good three-quarters of an hour from the town!... I suspect that this short distance from Bayreuth plays a rotten trick on us by delaying the delivery of letters by one day! The one I wrote yesterday is very likely still a long way from you. I'm very well: sleeping well and eating well! Cheerful for a minute, then just in fits and starts, and above all in such a way that people can see that my enjoyment is due to them! Besides, the performances are very good: I'm ashamed to admit it, but every time I hear one of these works I realize I didn't know them at all well. I believe one's whole life wouldn't be enough for them!

However, Fauré did not admire Wagner's music dramas without some reservations. In a letter to Marie dated 6 August he believed that, '*The Ring* is stuffed with a philosophy and a quantity of symbols which are only manifestations of our misery and nothingness – no help at all.' In Bayreuth Fauré managed to find some relief in private performances of his own music.

64★   GABRIEL FAURÉ to MARIE FAURÉ

Bayreuth
7 August 1896

Yesterday, music here with Risler,[28] the pianist, and Miss Palisser, a singer from London who sang some of my songs. With Risler we did *Shylock* for four hands and the Allegro Symphonique.[29] Tomorrow we will be playing a quartet and the sonata. But all this will be in front of just a few people, and there won't be any show about it.

65★ GABRIEL FAURÉ to MARIE FAURÉ

Bayreuth
Saturday 8 August 1896

Today they're coming from Bayreuth to play one of my quartets (the second), and the sonata. Risler will play the piano, Fridrich, a fairly good violinist from Paris and two other orchestral players from Bayreuth will play the other parts.

The fourth cycle which I am going to hear again will begin tomorrow and finish on Wednesday. So I shall leave on Thursday morning, I hope. I am full to the brim of this *Ring*, it's haunting me night and day! I do not believe that these works are straight-forward archetypes and that it is possible to imitate them. But some benefits and things we can learn none the less come from them in a general sort of way. Such things seep into you just like water seeps through sand.

66★ GABRIEL FAURÉ to MARIE FAURÉ

Bayreuth
Sunday 9 August 1896

You write *much* better than I do, and you find so many charming things to say! Your letter this morning was exquisite!

Yesterday we had music here: the *two* quartets were played very well. In the evening it was Mme Wagner's weekly reception. A *pot-pourri* of people, some good, others as ridiculous as you can imagine. For the buffet supper, there was everything, even *legs of cold mutton!* Everything there is at one and the same time German, affected, pedantic and naïve. You have to see it, but not too often. Mme Wagner's daughters are pleasant, unaffected. The mother is less likeable, despite all her airs and graces!

And today we shall once more be immersing ourselves in epic sonority! I am fairly tired the whole time, and yet we're not doing much. The weather is almost invariably muggy and humid; I believe the climate is equally muggy. Despite the wonderful landscapes, I prefer our Parisian atmosphere and our Parisian people, in spite of our faults! How tasteless people are here for everything plastic, well-ordered or comfortable! Always pretentious barbarity. They're remarkable only for their brains and their obedience!

So I prefer Paris, and when in Paris I prefer everything to Paris! Man alive! oh wretch! oh little crumb, as you so beautifully express it! But between such little crumbs as we truly are, you and the little ones, let us love each other most dearly: it is the one really beautiful thing, along with books, statues, pictures and the music of those rare human beings!

I think really that Tuesday, the day you will get this melancholy letter (even so it has been a marvellous stay, where everything is charming, everyone wonderful, and where I'm hearing such marvellous things! Aren't I being difficult!), I think that Tuesday will be the last day to write to me. I will get your letter on Thursday before I go.

67* GABRIEL FAURÉ to CAMILLE SAINT-SAËNS

[Paris]
[24 August 1896]

My dear Camille, I am very sorry that you are not here at present and I hope you will be back and enclosed by Paris before too long.

I have been to see Deschappelles[30] today, and this is what I've managed to glean: The Conseil supérieur (to which people had assured me I would be admitted – and to which I will definitely *not* be) will meet around 20 September and will make a decision as to whether there are grounds for maintaining three composition classes or reducing the number to two; creating from this (for those two classes) two posts of assistant professor who will be instructed to teach Counterpoint and Fugue.

If this arrangement is adopted, it is Widor who will be appointed: besides, he has already announced his appointment to different people with as much eagerness as the fact that he has contrived to forget that he *had promised me* not to come forward against me.

But this matters little: all of us are more or less forgetful or fickle.

As for his organ class it will be reserved for Guilmant[31]. Besides, I would not offer myself for the organ class in any case. Never will I undertake to learn to improvise fugues to students who do not even know harmony.

On the other hand my expenses are too heavy for me to be able to give up my time in exchange for a salary of 1500 francs.

So the situation is such that I should be very grateful if you could try to be present at the meetings of the Commission and to act in my best interests there: that is to say, to complain about the amalgamation of three classes into two, which [would then] reduce my chances of succeeding Massenet. If the opposite happens, it's the Institut which will be put back indefinitely, for Widor will have a title in addition, and a very considerable title. My only hope would be to succeed you in forty years, and I swear to you that I like you much more than the Institut!

We would be fairly well here if it were not for my little Philippe who is again rather unwell. There seems no end to it!

Herewith very many warmest greetings, and my affectionate good wishes,

GABRIEL FAURÉ

I shall be leaving for Dinard on Sunday until 15 September.

The next letter can be dated with reasonable accuracy from the context.

68   GABRIEL FAURÉ to THÉODORE DUBOIS

154 Boulevard Malesherbes
[end of August 1896]

My dear friend, I hadn't wanted to talk 'Conservatoire' to you during the Competition period since you are so engrossed in it; then I left for Bayreuth and, on my return, it was you who was no longer in Paris. So I am obliged to pursue you into your country retreat in order to ask you the most indiscreet of questions:

Would you be good enough to take an *interest* in my application for one of the vacant composition classes? I realize you could reply that this is no business of yours, that a committee will be called upon to appoint candidates of the Minister's choice. But *that* would be the reply of the Conservatoire director, and I hope I might be in a position to expect a reply which would be more amicably frank. In everyone's opinion the committee in question is only destined to play to the gallery and to conceal what it really wants. At least that's what people are saying. On the other hand I have learnt from M. Trélat (who has *begged* me to say nothing about this, and in the same way I implore you to do likewise) that Widor has been nominated. Widor himself has mentioned this to various people, adding (which might raise my rather forlorn hopes) that he was taking your class and Massenet's which would be amalgamated; and there would be a tutor for Fugue whom *moreover* he had *chosen* so as to replace him in the organ class, then its traditions could be respected there! So I cannot even be a candidate for the organ class! And what about the committee? What will be left for it to do?

There remains, my dear friend, a real favour you can do for me. If you are aware of any prejudice against me which would lead to my isolation from the official world of music, as your colleagues in the music section suggested to me at the time of the last election to the Institut (I speak of the hierarchy), if you have just a sneaking suspicion, tell me in all sincerity. I shall bother nobody any more, nor myself; and in my corner I shall continue to perpetrate my work which is probably detestable and certainly inferior!

I hope that you are resting, as you really must in the wake of the competitions, and I hope that Madame Dubois is completely well again and has recovered the complete use of her hand.

Do please give her my regards and believe in my most devoted sentiments.

GABRIEL FAURÉ

The organ repairs have begun.

69 GABRIEL FAURÉ to THÉODORE DUBOIS

Paris
5 September

My dear friend, Your response has brought the most kindly testimony of your affectionate interest in me, and I thank you from the depths of my heart.

I didn't pass on a personal impression in speaking to you about the committee: I said to you what others have said, certainly hinted, since we do not yet know of whom it will consist.

As for our colleague's indiscreet remarks, I present them to you as organized and consistent, it seems to me, with his hearty self-satisfaction. Anyway, regarding what concerns me, I do thank you for having reassured me on what I feared was a prejudiced faction in the Conservatoire.

Certainly I can confirm that I am doing my best (as well as I can do), but I am unable to declare that I am hoping to satisfy everybody. Still, the shortcomings with which I am reproached are precisely those I detest the most, and music moves me all the more when the methods used are clear, correct, precise and even concise.

It is clear proof that frequently one is not the best judge of oneself! But what, above all, I am determined to convince you of is that your letter has made me perk up, and while the information you were willing to give me (and which I shall keep secret) does not raise my hopes, at least it expresses acquiescence and a devoted feeling of friendship for which I am deeply grateful.

I shall be away up to 23 or 24 September. But when I get back, if you yourself are in Paris, I shall be entirely at your disposal if you need to speak to me.

Please give my regards to Madame Dubois, together with my most sincere and devoted sentiments and once again my thanks,

GABRIEL FAURÉ

In September Fauré paid a visit to Saint-Lunaire, near Rennes, staying in the villa of his English friends Frederick and Adela Maddison. According to Robert Orledge[32] Fauré had met them in London in 1894 and they became devoted admirers of his music. Maddison was a lawyer and a director of the

publishers Metzler and Co., which led to Fauré making arrangements with
them to publish many of his works in England. Adela Maddison was herself a
composer, and was almost certainly another of Fauré's mistresses. She left her
husband in 1898 to live in Paris and thus to be nearer Fauré. Fauré dedicated
his Seventh Nocturne, op. 74 to her, a work which dates from August 1898.

70★   GABRIEL FAURÉ to MARIE FAURÉ

Saint-Lunaire
Re-Wednesday! 23 September 1896

I'm adding a sentence to my first letter, written in great haste, to tell you
that our preoccupation in business matters is not going to upset me. I
remember what the Prince de Polignac told me recently about the
extremely keen interest of Mme de Rothschild in us two. I do not believe
that the charming way she proves it to us could vanish at a stroke. On
the other hand, the Maddisons firmly believe that I shall succeed, perhaps
even this year and certainly in a year's time, in being able to give a
concert in London for my benefit – and to repeat it every year in a
country where they are used to well-known people, where everything
always gets better as it goes along, slowly but surely. They say that these
concerts ought to bring in *at least* three thousand francs each time. It's a
pity they are not able to give them in their own home because they do
not have permission to give public concerts, they can only have an invited
audience. But for that we'd have done it already. I want to avoid
worrying grandfather in this respect – and it is really for that and the
ceremonial side of the business which would please him in spite of
everything, that I'm desirous of access to the conservatorial shop! It's
certainly not for the gratification of becoming the *Dear Colleague* of a
good many mediocre people which makes me want this.

71★   GABRIEL FAURÉ to MARIE FAURÉ

Saint-Lunaire
27 September 1896

The sunshine is poking fun at me because I have to leave. The sea is
calm, beautiful and sparkling! What an abominable practical joker! I shall
leave this afternoon then, and will be in Rennes tomorrow.

Is the arrival of the Tsar[33] keeping Emmanuel and Philippe occupied?
What a boring time we have in store, and how much better it would be
to be a *wine-merchant* at the moment! *They* at least will get some
consolation from this hubbub!...

Despite Fauré's pessimism, he did in fact take over Massenet's class on 10
October, with Guilmant taking Widor's former organ class. At last he had
arrived! Once again he visited London to take part in the first English all-
Fauré concert on 10 December, a visit resulting in letter 72. He stayed with
Frederick Oliver Robinson, Earl de Grey.

72★   MARIE FAURÉ to GABRIEL FAURÉ

[Paris]
9 December [18]96

Thank you for all your telegrams, my dearest Gabriel; I am sending you a letter from Fernand which I thought was more for Emmanuel than you, and in reading it I see the opposite is true.

Forgive me for only giving you a health report today; I am in a flap at my inability to succeed in sorting out myself and the little ones (as to clothes); I should like to have done with it, and I am dreadfully weary.

I am thinking of you, of your rehearsals and of the good which this affectionate and appreciative atmosphere must do you; and in spite of my loneliness I thank all of them, and especially the Maddisons.

We are well and send you all our tender love, and I promise to write to you better (if I am capable of doing so); for I do feel somewhat that my body is made of wood. But I am well – till tomorrow, I love you dearly.

MARIE FAURÉ

Fauré's appointment as a composition professor at the Conservatoire did not absolve him from the need to continue his time-consuming labours as inspector of the provincial conservatories. These two short notes to Marie underline the dislike Fauré entertained for this job.

73★   GABRIEL FAURÉ to MARIE FAURÉ

Dijon
25 March 1897

This is the most boring [inspection] of all! All the same I suppose it will come to an end; but it is long-drawn out, meticulous, loaded with stupid details!... Between two clarinets and a double bass I am quickly writing a few lines to you, not knowing if I'll have time for it later. Tomorrow, Friday, write to me at Rheims, Hôtel du Nord. I am absolutely tired out by this ceaseless work, with no interruptions *except* time for lunch and dinner and *nothing more*: I've a pain in my stomach from it! Forgive this minor point. Many kisses once more.

74★   GABRIEL FAURÉ to MARIE FAURÉ

Dijon
26 March 1897

I've been able to go on an outing for one hour by carriage today, and it has done me good. This evening, *an important concert* in the Conservatoire! I shall leave tomorrow at six, will be in Langres at nine, will set off again at three, and will be in Rheims at half-past seven...

Letter 75 is famous, and is the only extant letter from Marcel Proust to Fauré. Undated, one can only surmise that it represents Proust's initial reaction to Fauré's *Le parfum impérissable* which was composed and published in 1897.

75   MARCEL PROUST to GABRIEL FAURÉ

[1897?]

Monsieur, I not only love, admire and venerate your music, I have been, still am in love with it. Long before you knew me you used to thank me with a smile in concerts or gatherings when my uproarious enthusiasm made your disdainful indifference to success take a bow five times over! The other evening I became intoxicated for the first time with *Le parfum impérissable*, and this is a dangerous intoxication for since then I have returned to it every day. At least it is an unclouded intoxication, for I have said things to Reynaldo[34] about this *Parfum* which even from a musical point of view seemed correct; and heaven knows, he is critical of pronouncements on music by literati. So there you are, Monsieur, a hundred times less well than I *could* tell you, for I know your work enough to be able to write a volume of 300 pages and more; but through diffidence I would never have said more than a hundred to you. Only as you have had the extraordinary idea of thinking that I was angry with you, I feel I must offer you these initial outpourings. Thus, I am grateful to you; and I ask you to be so good as to receive my gratitude along with my respectful feelings.

MARCEL PROUST

Fauré went to London again in December 1897. From there he wrote the following affectionate letter to the composer Guy Ropartz (1864–1955). A former pupil of Massenet and Dubois, in 1897 he was Director of the conservatory at Nancy. In 1919 he was appointed Director of the Strasbourg conservatory, and in both institutions his work was extremely influential. His published compositions run to almost 200: the psalm mentioned in Fauré's letter was his setting of Psalm 136 for soloists, chorus and orchestra. Charles Malherbe (1853–1911) was a musicologist, minor composer, and from 1899 archivist-librarian of the Opéra.

76   GABRIEL FAURÉ to GUY ROPARTZ

London
20 December [1897]

My dear friend, I have received the fine psalm which you sent me, on which you have inscribed my name in so friendly and flattering a manner. Thank you very much indeed, but at the same time I thank you with all my heart when I tell you most sincerely how much your work has pleased me and in which I have taken a deep interest. It is *very fine*!

As far as the competition is concerned I shall write to Schmidt[35] [*sic*] immediately to urge him to despatch his work with an apology for the delay, and to Malherbe. (But the latter replied that it was in order.)

Another thing. Could I ask you to ask the chapels for someone other than me to deputize at *the organ*. I have had replacements in my stead at the Madeleine since 1 August (5 months), I shall again be away on 20 January for your concert and then for inspections, then again for holidays here! This adds up to too much leave, not to speak of other necessary absences. Will you please do me the favour of calling on one of your colleagues, as well as mentioning the reasons I am giving you.

I am thinking of returning to Paris for Christmas and you will find [me] there.

Do please tender my regards to Madame Guy Ropartz, and again my very deepest gratitude with one thousand affectionate wishes and as many excuses.

GABRIEL FAURÉ

Fauré paid three visits to England in 1898, in March–April, June–July and October. For his first visit he was again the guest of Frank Schuster. The principal reason for this journey was the first (and only) performance of *La Bonne Chanson* in Fauré's own arrangement for tenor, string quintet and piano, a version since lost. Evidently Fauré enjoyed these visits to London, where his music was beginning to be well-known in the drawing-rooms of the wealthy. He visited the Maddisons again, renewed his friendship with the portrait painter John Sargent,[36] and generally was in the thick of a social and musical whirl. That this was the case in both London and Paris from the 1890s onwards is a possible reason even today for Fauré's undeserved reputation as a salon composer. The fact was that even as late as the end of the nineteenth century a composer writing in the smaller forms found that his music, especially when it was disturbingly unconventional, was appreciated most of all in these small and élite social gatherings.

77* GABRIEL FAURÉ TO MARIE FAURÉ

Calais
25 March 1898

I have taken refuge in a small hotel in the town, for the terminus of the Harbour Station was chock-full of travellers who arrived last night, and were none too keen on being bounced up and down on the water. Exposed to wind and rain I have been to see what the sea was like on the side of the jetty (but *far* away from the jetty!) and I saw it was so rough that I thought I might get through a fair amount [of work] while waiting for it to calm down. But how boring, how annoying to be marooned in this wretched little town! What is there to do until tomorrow? For I do not have to leave tonight... So if the weather is *average* I shall leave tomorrow. If it is as second-rate as today, *I shall wait* again! But today is the third windy day, and generally it changes on the fourth.

I am in a small bedroom of a very small, very peaceful hotel. I shall have dinner and go to bed *immediately*. Impossible to go out: it hasn't stopped raining. I've got a good fire, and I shall dream in front of it while trying to think up English themes... Till tomorrow, dearest Marie; today I am a bit like La Fontaine's pigeon, trailing its wing and dragging its feet, as the fable says... !

78★   GABRIEL FAURÉ to MARIE FAURÉ

Calais
26 March 1898

Yesterday, after everything I said, the boat which I despised, despised itself and did not leave. Just now I have been to see if another one was leaving, but they are not letting me make the attempt. Still, the Lord knows that I am kicking my heels here and am bored under this onslaught of wind and rain. I don't know what I'm about, I come back, I go out, I take carriages to go and see... nothing! I go to make enquiries about the sea and ships! It's boring, and I can only leave tomorrow at one o'clock. The weather's changing, and since midday (it's now five o'clock) the wind has been abating hour by hour. Good Lord, what a stupid adventure! Oh for a bridge, a tunnel, a balloon, anything at all to get rid of these absurd crossings! I am very well, but I am so bored I could *scream*. There is a theatre here, Thursdays and Sundays. I might even have gone, out of desperation.

79★   GABRIEL FAURÉ to MARIE FAURÉ

London
28 March 1898

I finally arrived in London at seven o'clock, and at half-past eight I was at the table, in Schuster's house, sitting down to a sumptuous dinner, after which we had a great deal of music. I have lost only one rehearsal, which we shall make up for later.

80★   GABRIEL FAURÉ to MARIE FAURÉ

London
29 March 1898

First of all, I've had a rehearsal of the *Naissance de Vénus*[37] with a sufficiently large chorus much better than I'd hoped, and satisfactory soloists. We'll try *La Bonne Chanson*. The first run-through will probably be very prickly. But we shall rehearse again on Thursday to make up for the rehearsal lost on Sunday. I fear there will be mistakes in the copy in spite of the care taken by the poor little copyist. Bagès[38] is there, in very good form, in very good voice. As for me I am neither in good form nor in good *fingers*. Once again, if only I could have done some work during those two days of exile in Calais! Oh God, what a memory!

Have you chosen the fan you want to finish for Mme Rothschild? I cannot tell you how much I love the way you work on painting; you love it, and every one you produce gives me so much pleasure!

It's terrifying how many invitations I've had here. I hardly know what to do unless I hand myself round in little packets. People are always as kind to me and as ready to help as they possibly can be.

81★ GABRIEL FAURÉ to MARIE FAURÉ

London
31 March 1898

I didn't have a minute yesterday: *La Naissance de Vénus* was sung here, at Mme Maddison's house, really very well – and in truth I was quite moved by the efforts they made and by the results. Yesterday evening we were at Lady Charles Beresford's. Bagès had a great success. Today I've got rehearsals again.

82★ GABRIEL FAURÉ to MARIE FAURÉ

London
1 April 1898

A really thick fog after a whole day's sunshine yesterday. I am writing to you with the light on! The day before yesterday – in the evening – there was, at Schuster's house there, a supper party which got me to bed dreadfully late, and yesterday caused a lot of general scurrying about. In the evening we again rehearsed *La Bonne Chanson*. My impressions of it after the first rehearsal were fairly favourable. Yesterday evening I thought it was hateful and *useless*! We shall see this evening. At Mme Maddison's house *La Naissance de Vénus* made a very, very favourable impression on Wednesday. She is delighted with the way it turned out, and it wasn't at all an easy result to get...

Here, everybody seems steadily more and more pleased with me, and it only remains for me to be pleased with everybody. But the days are over in a flash, it's terrible!

83★ GABRIEL FAURÉ to MARIE FAURÉ

London
Saturday, 2 April 1898

I went to bed last night at four o'clock. After the Schuster party, several musical people stayed behind, and we recommenced singing and playing until that absurd hour! Just like the Maddison matinée, the Schuster soirée could not have been more successful. Everything went to a 'T', the Franck quintet and *La Bonne Chanson*. Bagès sang admirably, and the success has been extraordinary. Mme Marchesi[39] had a great success too with *Le [sic] Cimetière* and *En Prière*. However for my own part, I continue to find that this accompaniment to *La Bonne Chanson* is superfluous, and I prefer the simple piano accompaniment. But I've had a great success: Schuster, Sargent and Mme Maddison were *weeping* with emotion.

This evening, Schuster is again having a gentlemen's dinner, and Bagès has sworn that he will sing all my songs afterwards. It's terrifying. Tomorrow I am lunching in town, and then there's a matinée at a conductor's house. On Monday evening there's a dinner and my *two* quartets at Sargent's. I wanted to leave on Wednesday, but Schuster has begged me to stay until *Thursday* so that a sculptor here can outline a bust for him. I shall be posing on Monday morning. It was difficult to say no.

My dear sweet Marie, where can I find the money for my tours of inspection which I must start on the 18th... ? I shall not be bringing back much out of the 500 francs I have earned: I handed over 80 francs to the organist who was deputizing for me, and I still owe him about 100 francs. Oh God! How I wish I could put a price on the enthusiasm people show me here! How expensive life can be!

After this pleasant trip, Fauré recommenced his provincial tours in France and, as letter 84 indicates, had the incidental music for Maeterlinck's *Pelléas et Mélisande* very much on his mind. He had been commissioned to write this for the first performance of the play in England, which took place on 21 June 1898 at the Prince of Wales' Theatre in London. The score was orchestrated by Fauré's pupil Charles Koechlin (1867–1950), who accompanied Fauré to London on this occasion. Fauré took three of the original pieces, *Prélude, Fileuse* and *La mort de Mélisande*, and formed a suite from them. He orchestrated this himself, though Koechlin's version served as a starting point. The final version, which adds the well-known *Sicilienne* originally written for cello and piano, dates from 1909.

84* GABRIEL FAURÉ to MARIE FAURÉ

Aix-en-Provence
April [?] 1898

I finished my operations yesterday in Montpellier at midday, after examining the choir and listening to High Mass in the cathedral. Then I left on the slowest train at one o'clock, arriving at Aix after thirty stops at eight o'clock in the evening. It's been very warm here in the Midi ever since I arrived. The trees are all in leaf and bloom, and smell so good! I shall be beginning my inspection straight away; it should be over by three o'clock tomorrow afternoon, so that I can go to bed at Digne... Really I am very well, I don't mind doing all this, but I shall be really glad to see the end of this labour. I hope to finish on Friday evening, arriving in Paris on Saturday... I know nothing about anything any more. I only know that I will have to grind away hard for *Mélisande* when I get back. I hardly have a month and a half to write all that music. True, some of it is already in my thick head!

85★ GABRIEL FAURÉ to CAMILLE SAINT-SAËNS

[Paris]
[14 July 1898][40]

My dear Camille, I have been prey to a sculptor: he undertook to do a bust for me, and made me pose every morning those last few days of that latest trip to London – where it was impossible to come to see you, unfortunately, since you were only free in the mornings. On my return I found the magnificent Preludes and Fugues[41] for organ which I shall never be able to play properly, and to my great joy I saw my name at the top of one of them: I do thank you very much for this nice, delightful surprise! My regrets at still not having written the organ piece which *you ordered* are all the deeper as a result!

I haven't written an organ piece, it's true, but I have written the competition flute piece, 'andante cantabile' and 'allegro folichono', and I can't remember anything at all that has given me so much trouble![42]

Isn't it actually today that *Henry VIII* receives its première? How I should have loved to stay just for that! – See you here soon, I hope, and 30,000 tender wishes now from your very affectionate and 1,000 times grateful

GABRIEL FAURÉ

Fauré visited England for the third time in 1898 when he appeared at the Leeds Festival in October, conducting *La Naissance de Vénus*. His activities during 1899 are less well documented. In letter 87 we come across the name of Fernand Castelbon de Beauxhostes, a rich patron of the arts at Béziers in Languedoc. He took a great interest in the large amphitheatre there, the construction of which had started in 1896 for the purpose of staging large-scale performances of opera and drama in the open air. He had commissioned Saint-Saëns's opera *Déjanire* which was staged there in 1898, an opera which Fauré conducted in Béziers when it was revived in August 1899. Fauré was given a similar commission, the lyric drama *Prométhée* op. 82, which was to receive its first performance in August 1900. Fauré was well aware of the responsibilities such a performance entailed, and of the immense prestige and fame that it would probably bring.

86★ GABRIEL FAURÉ to MARIE FAURÉ

Montpellier
Tuesday morning, 23 May 1899

Here I am at Montpellier where I've been since late yesterday evening. The journey was vile, due to the heat, the dust and the general herding together of the passengers. The first class [coaches] were filled with third-class citizens! Whitsun holidays are the same everywhere, and there are people from Bougival everywhere in France: at Arles, where I stopped for two hours, I *nearly* saw a very savage, very genuine bullfight in the old Roman arena, along with these southern people who shriek so loudly. But I did not allow myself the temptation, in spite of the presence of

Mistral,[43] who was in charge of the festival along with Mlle de Chévigné, daughter of a lady I know well, the very Mlle de Chévigné who had been elected the previous day for a year as 'Queen of the Félibres!'[44] How extraordinarily crazy all these Provençal folk are.

The next letter cannot be dated with any degree of accuracy, though Fauré must have written it some time before August 1899.

87   GABRIEL FAURÉ to HUGUES IMBERT

[1899, before August]
154 Boulevard Malesherbes [Paris]

Dear friend and... victim! I am here again to use and abuse your kindness! Here's what it's all about. It appears that Saint-Saëns wants me to conduct for him the rehearsals and subsequent performances of *Déjanire* at Béziers – this year he only wants to be present at them as a spectator! And for this occasion the festival organizer, M. Castelbon de Beauxhostes, is begging me for a small page of biography which would go with my photograph. Only the programme booklet.

Since you know me better than I know myself and possess such an expert sleight-of-hand, would you be good enough to undertake this short monograph? Then I can tell you how much I should be in your debt: and M. Castelbon also.

Do please forgive me, and you may be sure once again of our very devoted and affectionate sentiments.

Your grateful,
GABRIEL FAURÉ

You will be willing, won't you, to put your name to the twenty lines in question?

Fauré had known Eugène Ysaÿe for some years, and the violinist was Fauré's greatest admirer and supporter in Belgium. February 1900 saw Fauré briefly in Brussels, going to concerts, playing at concerts, and meeting his old friend once again.

88   GABRIEL FAURÉ to MARIE FAURÉ

Brussels
4 February 1900

All morning I've been running about the streets and squares of this amusing city, trying to think about *Prométhée*; but without success. My overriding concerns are with the things I have to do here, and do in the best way possible.

Ysaÿe's return has been announced here for tomorrow. A whole group of his friends seems quite anxious to look after me: too much in fact, for everything tires and bores me at present. If I am unable to think of the musical side of *Prométhée*, I think a great deal about the heavy responsibility I've taken on there – with too little time! Well, I shall have to succeed there, even so.

Yesterday I did a little playing with a lady who's giving a party in my honour tomorrow, for which Mlle Eustis and a violinist from Paris are coming. This lady looks like a dried fish !...

89★   GABRIEL FAURÉ to MARIE FAURÉ

Brussels
5 February 1900

I saw Ysaÿe at his orchestral rehearsal this morning. When I came in, he tumbled down from his stand, took me in his big arms, and kissed me with evident emotion. And then he introduced me to his orchestra like this: 'I present to you one of the greatest musicians of the time..' Over there: ovation and general racket. In short it was very kind and very cordial.

Dinner yesterday evening was very smart. There were the King's first Chamberlain and the Burgomaster of Brussels. I accompanied Mlle Eustis in heaps of songs during the soirée which followed. The Conservatoire concert earlier in the day was very fine. Afterwards in a tavern, their customary meeting-place, I found almost all the present-day musicians here, including Messager on his way through Brussels.

Tonight there's a soirée at the home of the smoked-fish Lady. Tomorrow evening, the Concert du Cercle; and Wednesday morning at 8 o'clock, my departure...

Soon Fauré had to confer with his associates at Béziers. He had at his disposal enormous forces. They included about 200 singers, some 400 instrumentalists in three groups (including military bands from regiments at Béziers and Montpellier), and other singers, players and soloists from Paris and Brussels. There were to be nearly 800 performers in all, including 20 harpists. The orchestration was to be undertaken by Charles Eustace, conductor of the Montpellier regiment. Fauré paid a preliminary visit to the Midi in March to meet Castelbon and Eustace; for the first performance in August he was in Béziers some time before and wrote letters almost daily to Marie. His account of the activities in Béziers is extraordinarily vivid, and there can be little doubt that the production of *Prométhée* was a major event in Fauré's career.

90★   GABRIEL FAURÉ to MARIE FAURÉ

Montpellier
Tuesday 20 March 1900

Having got there yesterday at three o'clock, I was seized immediately by Castelbon and my musical director. Yesterday evening I heard in the Barracks concert-room the two fragments of *Prométhée* I've prepared, and the same thing this morning in the open air. I think that this is as much as I can do in a genre which is not one I like best! But there are many things I have still to do! Really, I'm dreaming of them constantly every night. I confer with Eustace over the music I've brought him so that he can orchestrate it. Tomorrow I shall be leaving for Perpignan, with a two hour stop at Béziers. I can't tell you how much I'm longing to get back. Everything is hustle and bustle. I've had interviews with journalists here. So that's it !... My hosts are bewildered by my bold harmonies in *Prométhée*; to me they seem just like platitudes, something to do with the latitude!

91*   GABRIEL FAURÉ to MARIE FAURÉ

Perpignan
21 March 1900

I left Montpellier this morning at 10, with Castelbon: I had lunch with him at Béziers at one o'clock. I set off again at 3.30, arriving in Perpignan at 6 pm. After dinner I made a half-hearted attempt to go out, a voyage of discovery across the dirtiest little town I've ever seen (after Digne and Foix). I hope the cold light of day will hold some pleasant surprises for me!

My short stay in Montpellier will have been useful. Unfortunately every meal in Eustace's house was like a banquet! It was terrible. We talked usefully about *Prométhée*; on the other hand I felt that I had got really stuck. It was almost the start of an execution. And then I got the feeling that in this part of the world it is an event which is long-awaited and even talked about with some excitement. Long before the performance I have become a celebrity. I've seen it in Béziers too. Castelbon had invited to this lunch some of those people who had helped and been with us (Saint-Saëns and me) at the time of *Déjanire*: and so they knew me and treated me with some sort of respect. But today these unfortunate people were rooted to the spot, they didn't dare speak. At a stroke I have become Saint-Saëns himself! These little observations are always amusing!

Tomorrow morning at eight o'clock I shall start extracting teeth at the Conservatoire. I shall be free, I think, on Friday at 6 pm, and as I must go through Béziers to go to Rodez, I shall doubtless sleep there ... If you have time, would you send me at Rodez the libretto by Hérold and Lorrain for *Prométhée*?[45] I'll have them to keep myself occupied on the return journey.

92*   GABRIEL FAURÉ to CAMILLE SAINT-SAËNS

[Paris]
[20 June 1900]

My dear Camille, I am very sorry not to have the whole of *Prométhée* and not to be able to submit it for your inspection. It's gone for a walk to the engraver's, or to the copyist, or to Montpellier, at Eustace's house!

Here is the motif to be used as Prelude to the work, and which often recurs:

I would love to see you! But time is short, and I am obliged to remain *screwed* to my table!

Many, many affectionate good wishes!
GABRIEL FAURÉ

93★ GABRIEL FAURÉ to MARIE FAURÉ

Béziers
6 August 1900

I've had a tiring journey, oppressively hot, and when I arrived at half-past one in the morning I was met at the station by Castelbon. He kept me up until three o'clock, explaining a thousand things to me. I finally got to bed, but today I have a *real* migraine with all the usual miseries.

I heard the ladies' choir rehearsed this morning. There are a lot of them, and they're reliable. I think it will be alright. This evening I shall have the men's choir. I am told they are excellent, that they learn very well. Their part is not long, but it is very difficult.

In a feeble sort of way I had implored Jambon,[46] before he began his modelling, to have the scenery as low down as possible (and all of us concerned recommended this), and he has raised it by two metres. It's a disaster! I have *ordered* them to lower it by one and a half metres. If he's not happy about it, it's too bad. It seems, essentially, that it's all I shall be able to get, but at least I shall *get* it. All these fellows have eyes only for their own ideas, plans and impressions; they throw out the rest. There will be difficulties, but I'm also discovering a great deal of good will and enthusiasm . . .

94★ GABRIEL FAURÉ to MARIE FAURÉ

Béziers
7 August 1900

The two main conductors here, the civilian and the regimental, still show no inclination of getting themselves heard. Both of them invent silly reasons. They have no intention of displaying themselves in a state of disarray, when they're well and truly wrong! My presence would be more useful to them now rather than later. But I cannot insist, since they are doing this to please me. The men's choir is good at learning things by heart. But they have terrible accents, and sing jerkily and harshly. There'll be some work to do there. But we'll succeed.

I've slept fairly well, in spite of the very oppressive heat of a storm which has been threatening since Monday and hasn't broken.

If all three of you were able to be here it would be really lovely and even funny, thanks to the somewhat comic side things always take here: you just can't get angry ... !

95★ GABRIEL FAURÉ to MARIE FAURÉ

Béziers
10 August 1900

I didn't write to you yesterday. I was tired out, irritated, in the doldrums, and in addition the post from Paris did not bring your letter. The mail is dreadfully slow ... As for work, it has reached a low point. Everything I have done seems ugly, and outrageously imitative of Wagner. So I am in a fog, and bored to death! I have paid a pleasant visit to the colonel who lends us his musicians. That poor old infantry, accustomed to playing polkas, marches or fantasias on *Robert le Diable*[47] is having a dreadful time dealing with the exigencies of its task. And circumstances have made its task the weightiest and most difficult. They have to accompany the main characters and this is the most complicated part, as far as details go, of the whole of the music in *Prométhée*. I went to hear them this morning at eight o'clock in the barracks. They don't make a bad shot at it, but there aren't enough of them!

I shall never be too weary to say that everybody is showing exceptional keenness and goodwill. I think it's only me here who is bored!

At three o'clock we shall be going to the sea, which I haven't yet seen, and will return for dinner. The weather is still very close and tiring. Everyone tells me this is unusual for Béziers. Saint-Saëns wrote a letter here this morning – it was furious, mad – nobody could understand any of it. He hadn't even taken the trouble to sign it! In the end I gathered that he was angry because there was a printing error in his *words*! That affects him much more than mistakes in his music. Ever the violin of Ingres ...

96★ GABRIEL FAURÉ to MARIE FAURÉ

Béziers
11 August 1900

When you receive this letter it will be eight days since I left: it seems very much longer to me. Yesterday I went to the sea (since our choristers had asked for an evening off) ... Down there, at the mouth of a small river, there are fishermen's huts, with thatched roofs, separated by enormous clumps of maize, giving the illusion of landscapes from central Africa, near a Lake Chad or Oubangui!

Today I'm living in hopes of getting close to seven or eight hundred men and women on the move. Looking at a new large poster gave me this idea. By tomorrow this conceited behaviour will be tiresome and the worse for wear! ...

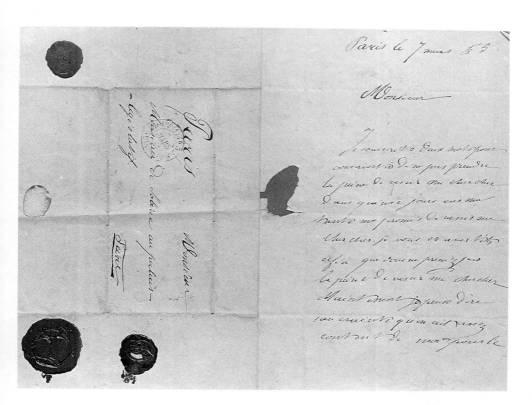

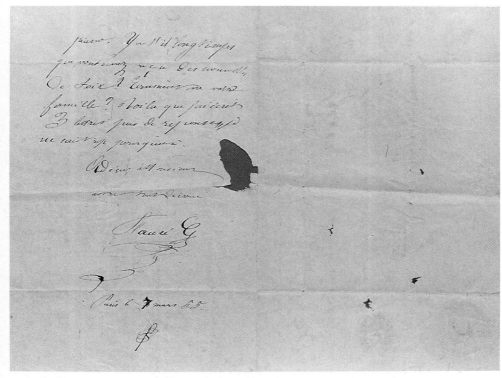

1 Gabriel Fauré to Dufaur de Saubiac, 7 March 1855 (Letter 1)

2 Camille Saint-Saëns to Gabriel Fauré, *c.* 1874? (Letter 13, first page)

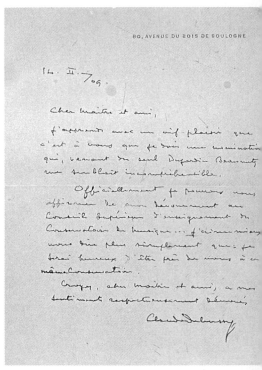

3 Claude Debussy to Gabriel Fauré, 14 February 1909 (Letter 160)

4 Gabriel Fauré to Marianne Viardot, 4 September 1877 (Letter 21, first page)

Maurice Ravel to Gabriel Fauré, 21 April 1910 (Letter 166)

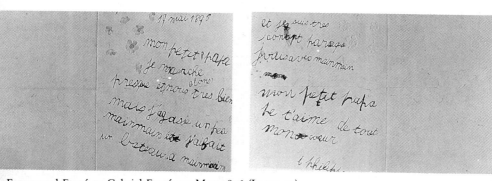

Emmanuel Fauré to Gabriel Fauré, 19 May 1896 (Letter 59)

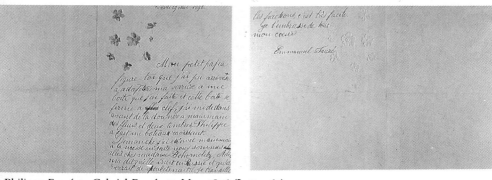

Philippe Fauré to Gabriel Fauré, 19 May 1896 (Letter 60)

8 Queen Elisabeth of the Belgians to Gabriel Fauré, June 1923 (Letter 297)

Bruxelles 24 Juin 1923

Cher Maître,

J'ai entendu votre beau Trio qui m'a causé une profonde émotion. Cette œuvre est si grande et pleine de charme poétique et j'ai été envelopée par cet inexprimable délice qui se dégage de vos compositions.

Combien j'ai regretté que vous ne soyiez à côté de moi à ce moment.

Les artistes qui ont si bien interprété votre Trio m'ont rejoué « ma sonate » dont la dédicace du grand et cher Maître m'est si précieuse.

Croyez moi

Votre affectionnée

Elisabeth

Portrait of Fauré by John S. Sargent RA, *c.* 1896

2 Fauré composing *Pénélope* at the Grand Hotel Metropole et Monopole, Lugano, 1911

3 OPPOSITE ABOVE Fauré's piano at his final home, 32 Rue des Vignes

4 OPPOSITE Marie Fauré's telescope, 32 Rue des Vignes: she and Saint-Saëns shared a passion for astronomy

5 Fauré, with the inevitable cigarette, c. 1914

You sent me a letter from one of Schuster's friends, asking for information on how to get to see *Prométhée*. But except for Schuster and Bardac, there are still no definite requests for accommodation and seats. Six months ago all my friends were to have come *en bloc*. The Polignacs will probably come, but it isn't absolutely certain. And really, bearing in mind the distance, I dare not insist on it; especially when I'm not sure about what is going to happen, and whether all of this is worth being so very hot, sleeping badly and eating badly for two whole days! Today however, I do experience, *like a breeze*, the feeling that things won't be so bad. But I did tell you I was conceited...

97★ GABRIEL FAURÉ to MARIE FAURÉ

Béziers
13 August 1900

The weather has been marvellous since Friday. Brilliant sunshine, unbelievable sky and a soft sea breeze. It's the kind of weather I had last year and appreciated so much. May the Lord see to it that we get similar weather for the two days when we have the performances.

Today we have a great deal to do. Besides, old Eustace is coming from Montpellier to spend a few hours here in order to bring to my attention those dubious sections to do with his orchestration. In turn I shall be going to Montpellier to hear his music on Friday or Saturday, sometime between morning and evening.

I hear that two or three young musicians from Paris, Büsser[48] (a friend of the Gounods and Halphens), Koechlin and a third person, will be coming to hear *Prométhée*, and this pleases me very much. Alas! It doesn't seem so long ago that I was a young musician myself! How quickly time flies! It's terrifying...

So far we have dined every evening in the courtyard of the house, an interior one like those in the old houses of the Midi, or in Spain. But new arrivals, more numerous every day, mean that we have to go back to the dining-room, and they don't make the meals any shorter, unfortunately!

Here you hear nothing of the Exhibition,[49] politics, China, or anything. Good old crystallized folk in that sweet life of indolence which fine vineyards provide for them!

98★ GABRIEL FAURÉ to MARIE FAURÉ

Béziers
16 August 1900

I'm sending you a letter from Fernand[50] which I've just received. I shall be very happy to go and look them up just for one or two days, in other words to go and stay with them on 31 August (or on the 30th if I can flee from here on the 29th which I doubt for many local reasons) and on

1 September. What I should really like, if you didn't think it *too* unreasonable, would be to borrow five hundred francs from Hamelle on *Prométhée* (it's true there was already a similar advance three months ago!) and send one hundred francs to Juliette[51] so that she can come here with her father, an avuncular proposal which might not offend them. I would be so happy, in the absence of you and the children, grandfather and grandmother, to have at least Fernand and his daughter with Margot.[52] If you agree, as I do, that they might enjoy this, and this would make me very happy too, send me a reply by telegram. I would write to Fernand that it's me and you who would like Juliette and him, if not his whole family, to be able to hear *Prométhée*. I do not have enormous outlays here. I have bought only a rather pretty doll for Mlle Castelbon...

Just think, I'm beginning to know the meaning of fame: in the smart bootmakers' shops here they're selling boots in a dark Havana colour surmounted by the following sign:

Latest creation, the elegant Gabriel Faurés!

You'll be thinking I'm doing cartwheels! There are *Prométhée* shoes too!

The ballet, or rather the plastic postures, is making me furious. The choreographer, who is from the Opéra, is determined to have his own way, and *I* am determined to have mine, Hérold says nothing, and Lorrain is not there. To throw a sop to this balletic mountebank we're putting on the *Pavane*[53] for him — it will be danced and sung at the concert on Monday 27th.

Here we are going through the frantic, somewhat bewildering period. This afternoon we are going to try on stage the music which has to accompany the main characters. This is the dangerous part of the business, and I am longing to know whether or not we have miscalculated.

Mme Maddison has asked me to find five rooms for the Polignacs and herself, and for two guests she doesn't know. Having found nothing suitable in a single house, the kind gentleman who put up Polignac has offered his house all of a sudden, where they will be all together and very comfortable — for nothing. Schuster has asked for three rooms, which I *have* got, but I cannot be responsible for the bugs! The people here tell you quite candidly in their *dialect*: Eh! Monsieur, the Midi without bugs — that's not possible!.. They're used to them from their cradles.

I am certainly under pressure today; there are five rehearsals in different places! Saint-Saëns should be arriving this evening.

I have just heard that three Rome prizewinners will definitely be here: Rabaud,[54] Max d'Ollone[55] and Büsser. I am very happy at the interest taken by these young people.

Letter 99 refers to Emmanuel Fremiet's promotion to Grand Officier in the Institut, an event which gave Fauré genuine pleasure. His father-in-law had followed Fauré's career with affectionate interest and, like Saint-Saëns, had done much to promote it.

99★   GABRIEL FAURÉ to MARIE FAURÉ

Béziers
17 August 1900

I have just learnt, with great joy as you can imagine, of grandfather's elevation to the rank of Grand Officier. I am relying on you and the children to convey to him my most loving congratulations, and to grandmother as well. I am sure that each time he receives an honour he must remember his early years and think of his mother, whose ambitious hopes for him had never dreamt of reaching such heights, whatever aspirations of fame she may have had for her son! As for me I am really happy for you too, since you will find in it some sort of compensation for all the toil and troubles in your life of sacrifice.

Yesterday's experiment was very unsatisfactory regarding the music for the scene changing: (1) because this wretched little infantry music is insufficient; (2) because they had been given (by Jambon) a totally unsuitable place to stand. We had to have this little scene so that people could agree that I was right when I protested beforehand about these arrangements... In short I'm starting to think that the real battles and the really tiring business have yet to begin.

The *strings* will not be here till Tuesday, and the harps Wednesday evening. All that is too late, *far* too late. So, since there is a God for drunkards, we must hope there will be one for musicians.

We had a tremendous storm last night. I slept little and as a result am feeling tired.

100   GABRIEL FAURÉ to MARIE FAURÉ

Béziers
21 August 1900

I am needed by so many people at the moment that I'm going slightly crazy, and as more artists for *Prométhée* arrive, lunches and dinners get longer! This morning I've already had a choir and ballet rehearsal; at 2.30, any minute, we rehearse with the soloists at the college; at 3.30 the ballet again, at 5.00 in the arena, at 8.30 the choirs at the college. Ouch!... One of the new arrivals, Jean Lorrain, is making our heads spin by wanting everything changed. We're squashing him!

Everything is settling down more or less, and I hope we won't have any big hitches or cataracts from heaven.

101* GABRIEL FAURÉ to MARIE FAURÉ

Béziers
26 August 1900

The close, threatening weather of these last few days, which on two occasions suspended our rehearsals, has just knocked us to bits, almost as we were about to begin with the circus chock full of people. A veritable whirlwind, with a thunderbolt striking the arena. A two hour deluge! We have finally just left the arena, and I cabled you immediately.

What rotten luck to get this storm! The scenery is ripped; we shall have to work on it all night and all tomorrow morning. It's really upsetting.

Winnie,[56] Mme Maddison, Bardac, Schuster and Georges Macquay [*sic*] and another Englishman arrived last night. I have scarcely seen them for a moment this morning, and I do not yet know the full effects of the storm. *I* had taken refuge in the artists' box in the theatre. I shall go back to change my clothes, but I was hardly wet.

I was not able to write this morning: we have had separate rehearsals again!

102* GABRIEL FAURÉ to MARIE FAURÉ

Béziers
27 August 1900

I did everything I could over the arrangements for my friends' stay here before they arrived. They all know one another and live to some extent in groups, and I see them when I can – that is to say, at fairly rare intervals. They are all invited to Castelbon's house this evening, after the performance and before the concert at nine o'clock.

This morning the weather is magnificent, no less! I was not going to tell you about my fears, but the whole week the weather has been threatening us and had even spoilt our first big rehearsal on Friday. In fact we shall be performing this evening after *one* dress rehearsal.

The storm was frightening. The thunderbolt fell on the arena, on the very spot (by coincidence) where Prometheus was to steal the fire! The scenery was dreadful at six o'clock. They worked on it all night. Jambon had fortunately brought with him one of his splendid lieutenants.

How seven thousand (and more) people were more or less able to take shelter during those two terrifying hours I shall never be able to understand. People had talked of irreparable damage, of sodden harps. Fortunately it's not as bad as that. But you can imagine the sadness of the evening. So, we are hoping for a glorious retribution today. Saint-Saëns was soaked to the skin, fortunately he is not ill.

I am going to have the *Pavane* rehearsed for the concert. I am constantly busy, and have to deal with everything. The organization is so poor! People are saying that Larroumet has been unable to stay today because he couldn't get a bed last night. You cannot imagine to what extent I've had to see to everything on behalf of other people.

Yesterday I had several telegrams from friends in Paris wishing me success. Oh well, that will be for this evening, I hope.

103★ GABRIEL FAURÉ to MARIE FAURÉ

Béziers
28 August

Everything has gone marvellously, I got an ovation; I had to appear on the stage between two of the players! At least the weather was very fine, with clear skies, but too much wind. Today, we've got the second performance.

Fernand, his daughter, Margot, along with friends and relations of ours, arrived yesterday at four o'clock. I saw them yesterday evening, and they were present at the concert in the theatre. I shall be lunching with them, and it's from their hotel that I am writing to you. Last night I had to go to the station to wait for Pierre Lalo;[57] at three in the morning he hadn't arrived. I received in his stead Prince Henry of Orléans, the one who has been to Tibet. I am dead with fatigue, but happy at what's been happening. But how awful that you weren't there!

Saint-Saëns said to me, after a moment's silence and reflection: 'With your *Prométhée* you have astounded us all, your colleagues and myself included, and I don't feel the slightest resentment, rather the reverse.' No point in adding that he is exaggerating enormously. But his satisfaction with my work has given me great pleasure, as you can well imagine!

The performance was as fine as it possibly could be, but the wind engulfed the loud sounds a bit. Today once again, alas, the wind is fairly strong. Last year's fine and calm weather is avoiding me.

We shall talk a great deal about all this, and I shall try not to forget anything. The artists (in the drama) have been *marvellous* to me, very taken with my success alongside theirs and as much as theirs. I will write at greater length to you tomorrow. I got up late.

104★ GABRIEL FAURÉ to MARIE FAURÉ

Béziers
30 August 1900

So everything is now over and has gone well. The concert on Monday evening was amusing. The *Pavane* was sung and danced, but it would be unwise for me to say that it was understood by the very provincial audience that evening. With Saint-Saëns I played his variations for two pianos.[58] Yesterday, a banquet; in the evening, illuminations in honour of *Prométheé* on all the municipal monuments and promenades, with a concert in the open air. Today, farewells!

I am finally satisfied with my work, which was done so *rapidly*. What a pity that I have other things to do apart from composition!
I have lost my glasses; I have lost my walking-stick, and have been given

another one by someone here who likes my music; and I have found mine again, and also found my glasses again! I have spent a great deal of money: I've no idea how much, keeping the choristers in drink from time to time, carriages, and the alpaca costume! But I have got 500 francs from Hamelle, received yesterday.

I shall spend the whole of tomorrow in Foix, and on Saturday at two o'clock I shall arrive in Bagnères-de-Bigorre. I am tired today, and am worried to excess by everybody. They're having me sign my scores and give autographs. Forgive me for being so brief.

After a short visit to his relations in the south-west, Fauré returned to Paris and to his teaching responsibilities at the Conservatoire. His constant concern over his pupils and friends is well illustrated by letter 105 to the young composer Paul Ladmirault (1877–1944), who had evidently written to Fauré asking for his advice. The friendly opening was a prelude to a more serious matter which had obviously been worrying Fauré for some time.

105   GABRIEL FAURÉ to PAUL LADMIRAULT

Paris
20 September [1900][59]

My dear friend, It is a very rare occurrence for me to be consulted over the appointment of a professor, but you may be assured that in the event of any such possibility I would think first of you. Why don't you go and see Schmidt [*sic*] who will certainly be leaving behind some pupils in Paris: in the same way he is giving up the organ of the Dominican church on Rue du Faubourg St-Honoré. I will write to him to appraise him of your visit. You are among the most interesting [of my pupils] and I should be very sorry to see you in the grip of unfortunate financial problems. Have you been working hard? I should like to see you in class frequently, and to see you undertake a composition of some substance. And while we're on the subject I want to give you some advice: I would prefer you not to disappear like a little scurrying rat as soon as you have shown your work to me! This smacks a little of superciliousness, or at the very least, a lack of interest in the work of your comrades for which I have to reproach you: so come to the class often; and show that you are in a little less of a hurry to get away from it! And above all, produce lots of work, and you will give me a great deal of pleasure.

During these last few days I have been rereading a chorus which you had very kindly dedicated to me, musically charming, but containing some desultory mistakes which a literate person such as you ought to avoid if anybody can! I will speak to you about it with the music in front of me.

Now, very quickly, go and see Schmidt, 49 Boulevard Péreire, and you will find he is expecting you.

With very best wishes
GABRIEL FAURÉ

Fauré visited Brussels again in October to attend Ysaÿe's performance of his *Requiem*. He also heard Puccini's *La Bohème* and Saint-Saëns's *Samson et Dalila* there, both operas eliciting comments from him of the sort one would expect.

106   GABRIEL FAURÉ to MARIE FAURÉ

Brussels

27 October 1900

After lunch on Thursday I acquainted Ysaÿe with several things in my most recent music, and, as always, he gave me a good deal of encouragement.[60] At four o'clock we had a rehearsal – excellent, very well prepared, with a keen response to all my wishes without my having to express them. Ysaÿe understands my music as if he had composed it. At seven o'clock we put on evening dress just where we had been rehearsing, and after having dined at some speed in a restaurant, we were present at the première of a dreadful Italian work called *La Bohème*. I know the directors, I know the composer Puccini whom I had met twice at the Saint-Marceaux's[61] house, I wasn't able to escape. After this première we had supper with all those concerned, and we went to bed at two o'clock. Yesterday, Friday, another rehearsal at nine o'clock, absolutely excellent. After lunch, music again at Ysaÿe's house with a pianist from Berlin, engaged for the same concert as the *Requiem*, in which he will play a Beethoven concerto;[62] I acquainted him with several of my piano pieces. At six o'clock we went back to rejoin Saint-Saëns and Durand[63] at the Grand Hotel to have dinner with them and the directors of the Theatre. But Saint-Saëns was unwell, and appeared only to have a cup of tea.

The performance (the fiftieth one of *Samson*) was very successful, and gave me a great deal of pleasure. Saint-Saëns is leaving again this morning, due to the Institut, so I've scarcely seen him. And today at two o'clock a public dress rehearsal, that is to say, the first test of what tomorrow's concert will be like... Everyone is charming to me here, and very friendly. There is a fine musical atmosphere, serious but not pedantic.

Notes

1 Chabrier's opera *Gwendoline* was to receive its première at the Théatre de la Monnaie in Brussels on 10 April 1886.

2 The second of the three Nocturnes, op.33, which were published in 1883. The B Major was to remain one of Saint-Saëns's favourite works of Fauré.

3 Gaston Salvayre (1847–1916), most famous in his day as an operatic composer and music critic.

4 Ernest Reyer (1823–1909), composer of operas and choral works.

5 Postscript written down the edge of the left hand side of the page.

6 Théodore Reinach (1860–1928), French historian, musicologist and archaeologist, and an authority on the music of ancient Greece.

7 Verlaine is referring to the *Cinq Mélodies de Venise*.

8 A reference to the Duke of Mantua's aria in Act 4 of Verdi's *Rigoletto*.

9 'People who have a chance of becoming Pope.'
10 Victorin de Joncières (1839–1903), critic and minor composer, best known for his operas. His real name was Félix Ludger Rossignol.
11 'Worthy to enter.'
12 A reference to the *Prix de Rome*, the composition competition at the Conservatoire.
13 Benjamin Godard (1849–95), a composer best known for his salon music for piano.
14 Gounod had died two weeks earlier on 18 October; it was his seat in the Institut which was being contested.
15 Gustave Moreau (1826–98), painter.
16 Paul Dubois (1829–1905), sculptor and painter.
17 Jean Alexandre Joseph Falguière (1831–1900), sculptor and painter.
18 Auguste Thomas Marie Blanchard (1819–98), engraver.
19 Edouard Détaille (1848–1912), painter.
20 Thérèse Guyon, to whom Fauré had dedicated *Le pays des rêves* from his songs, op.39.
21 Jean-Léon Gérôme (1824–1904), painter and sculptor.
22 Jules Breton (1827–1906).
23 Robert Orledge, *Gabriel Fauré*, Eulenburg, 1979, p.17.
24 Fauré's younger son Philippe, born in 1889, suffered from poor health as a child and at the time of this letter was apparently unable to walk unaided, even though he was six years old.
25 About the result of the Institut election. (*See* letter 58.)
26 Charles Lenepveu (1840–1910), a not very successful composer, had taught at the Conservatoire from 1880, and thus his election to the Institut can be seen as a political rather than a signal honour.
27 Henry Roujon (1853–1914), writer and administrator, was Director of the *Beaux Arts* from 1891 to 1903. His works include *Dames d'autrefois* (1910), as well as numerous literary and critical articles.
28 Edouard Risler (1873–1929), French pianist of German birth. He studied at the Conservatoire, and gave many recitals throughout Europe. Chabrier's *Bourrée Fantasque* (1891) was dedicated to him.
29 A movement from the early unpublished first symphony in F, op.20, later transcribed for piano duet by Léon Boëllmann as op.68, a version published in 1895.
30 Theatre chief clerk to the Minister of Education and Fine Arts, relating to the Conservatoire.
31 Alexandre Guilmant (1837–1911), French organist and composer. He was organist at the Trinité in Paris from 1871 to 1901, and with d'Indy and Charles Bordes founded the Schola Cantorum in 1894.
32 Op.cit., p.16.
33 Tsar Nicholas II landed at Cherbourg on 6 October. His visit to France was intended to seal the new Franco-Russian alliance, which was greatly welcomed by the French people.
34 Reynaldo Hahn (1875–1947), French composer and conductor, a pupil of Dubois and Massenet, and a great friend of Saint-Saëns, Proust and Sarah Bernhardt. He was best known for his songs and numerous stage works, in which the influence of both Massenet and Saint-Saëns is noticeable.
35 Florent Schmitt (1870–1958), French composer of large-scale works, was one of Fauré's earliest pupils at the Conservatoire. He was competing for the Prix de Rome, although he was not successful until 1900.
36 John Singer Sargent (1856–1925), born in Florence of American parents, achieved his greatest successes as a high society portrait painter, particularly in London. His achievements were recognized in France too, as his numerous distinctions show.
37 Fauré's 'Mythological Scene', for soloists, chorus and orchestra, composed in 1882.
38 Maurice Bagès, who was to première the new version of *La Bonne Chanson*.
39 Blanche Marchesi (1863–1940), French soprano who had made her début in London on 19 June 1896, and was to make her operatic début in Prague in 1900, singing

Brünnhilde in *Die Walküre*.

40 Date established by Fauré's reference to the first performance of Saint-Saëns's *Henry VIII* at Covent Garden, which Saint-Saëns attended.

41 Saint-Saëns's Three Preludes and Fugues for organ, op.109, composed and published in 1898, of which the first was dedicated to Fauré.

42 *Fantaisie* for flute and piano, op.79. Its two sections were eventually given tempo markings of Andantino and Allegro.

43 Frédéric Mistral (1830–1914), French writer and authority on the language and literature of Languedoc.

44 Of the Félibrige – a literary society founded in 1854 whose main purpose was to preserve the Provençal language.

45 Jean Lorrain (1855–1906), French writer of short stories, poems and articles for journals. He collaborated with Ferdinand Hérold in preparing the libretto of *Prométhée*.

46 Marcel Jambon (1841–1908) was known for his work at the Universal Exhibition in Paris in 1889, and his décors for a number of Wagner's music dramas were famous.

47 Opera by Meyerbeer (1791–1864), produced in Paris in 1831.

48 Henri Büsser (1872–1973) [*sic!*], French composer, pupil of Franck, Widor and Guiraud at the Conservatoire.

49 The Universal Exhibition which was then taking place in Paris.

50 Fauré's elder brother, who still lived in his native *département* of Ariège.

51 Fernand's daughter.

52 Daughter of Casimir Fontes, the husband of Fauré's elder sister Rose.

53 *Pavane*, op.50 for orchestra and chorus *ad libitum*, composed 1886–7.

54 Henri Rabaud (1873–1949), French composer and conductor who had been a pupil of Massenet. He succeeded Fauré as director of the Paris Conservatoire in 1920.

55 Max d'Ollone (1875–1959), French conductor, critic and composer, a pupil of Lenepveu and Massenet. He was best known for his operas.

56 The Princess de Polignac.

57 Pierre Lalo (1866–1943), son of the composer Edouard Lalo (1823–92), French critic who worked first of all for the *Journal des Débats* and then for *Le Temps*. He was famous for his diatribes against 'Debussyism'.

58 Variations on a theme of Beethoven, op. 35, composed in 1874.

59 Fauré did not indicate the year, but it is confirmed by the fact that Florent Schmitt won the Prix de Rome in 1900 and was leaving Paris as a result.

60 Fauré was perhaps referring not only to *Prométhée* but also to the Piano Quintet in D Minor op.89, on which he had been working for nearly ten years and which was to be dedicated to Ysaÿe.

61 Marguerite Baugnies had married the sculptor René de Saint-Marceaux in 1892.

62 The composer and pianist Feruccio Busoni (1866–1924) who played on this occasion Beethoven's G Major Concerto.

63 Jacques Durand (1865–1928) the publisher of Saint-Saëns and Debussy; Fauré was to engage him as his third publisher in 1913, after a seven year association with the firm of Heugel.

3

From *Prométhée* to *Pénélope*
1901–13

For Fauré, increasing fame yielded increasing commitments and responsibilities. He renewed his links with the Ecole Niedermeyer by his appointment as a professor of composition there in 1901. When in Paris his life appeared to be comparatively uneventful, although his love-hate relationship with the capital ensured that he made as many trips as possible to get away from it. Fauré eagerly took up an invitation to return to Béziers in August for a revival of *Prométhée*, to be accompanied by the ballet *Bacchus mystifié*, a collaboration between Max d'Ollone and the mayor of Béziers, Dr Sicard. The composer Jean Roger-Ducasse (1873–1954) was one of Fauré's favourite pupils, whose critical judgement he increasingly came to trust where his own compositions were concerned.

107 GABRIEL FAURÉ to MARIE FAURÉ

Béziers
16 August 1901

It is cool, the wind is actually rather disagreeable. I can't see the unfailingly clear blue sky we had two years ago, the sky of *Déjanire*; rather it's a cloudy, sullen sky, like last year's uncertain weather. Well, let's hope for the best! Last week, the important week, was all set for trouble: Sicard's ballet doubles the orchestra's work, and it never occurred to Castelbon to double the rehearsal-time. This present week should already have been assigned to it. Then too, *Prométhée* is almost new for the performers after a year's break; and among the string players especially the performers are not the same as before. I foresee a certain amount of trouble there! ... Saint-Saëns hasn't arrived yet, but he is expected every day; Hérold has come to us, twice over: he has a youthful spouse with him. We already knew her: he had brought her last year disguised as a cyclist ... And so we're led to believe it's a cunning extra-Béziers reunion! But the Parisians continue to disdain us – I'm speaking of the official Parisians, the Leygues, the Roujons, or those Parisians you see everywhere where *great Art* is present! We are not worthy of their attention!

108 GABRIEL FAURÉ to MARIE FAURÉ

Béziers
28 August 1901

All's well that ends well. All I feel now is a considerable fatigue and great excitement, and they will soon go away. I am unable to release Castelbon immediately, the more so as Saint-Saëns is still here. But I shall leave on Friday evening for Bagnères, stopping for a few hours at Toulouse. Yesterday's performance was rather less successful than Sunday's because of the rather strong wind and the untimely arrival of the War Minister [General Louis André]. Having got into the arena in the middle of an act he was the cause of a noisy demonstration from the entire rabble, and we were compelled to break off. He had to go for his train in the middle of the last act and so he disturbed us again. Saint-Saëns told me that he (the Minister) had been *bowled over* and *very* impressed. It's annoying that this was apparently possible without having to arrive at the beginning or leave at the end!

Ducasse has been our companion until this morning. He seemed very content and very happy to be brought into perfect and very friendly relations with Saint-Saëns, who has been delightful the whole time. Ducasse is travelling through the Pyrenees for a few days and will see me again in Bagnères. Tomorrow, all of us, Saint-Saëns, Castelbon and his daughter, and the schoolteacher, are spending the day at Lamalou.[1] On Monday we shall be by the sea. I confess to having been in a boat – but with the young Miss Castelbon, that is to say under the aegis of a fine fisherman incapable of anything imprudent. All this time Ducasse has been like a seal in the water! And I have found *two cousins here*.

This evening, concert in *the open air*, one has to say it come what may. And the moral is really that Castelbon has truly great *ability*, and will again do great things here.

109 GABRIEL FAURÉ to MARIE FAURÉ

Béziers
30 August 1901

A very early word. Back from Lamalou late yesterday evening I wasn't able to write. Saint-Saëns was in incredibly good form. He is *completely* under Ducasse's spell, he finds him remarkable in every respect.

The receipts here have been mediocre, 73,000 francs as opposed to 111,000 last year. There are many reasons I could mention – one is clerical! – and the threatening weather in particular has kept many people at home. I wanted to stop at Toulouse and go to my parents' grave at Gailhac. But I am tired, and this journey was very complicated – train times, through coaches, etc. I'll make straight for Bagnères.

110*   GABRIEL FAURÉ to MARIE FAURÉ

Bagnères-de-Bigorre
31 August 1901

Yesterday I actually had a quiet day in the train. I left Béziers at ten
o'clock, and arrived at Bagnères at half-past six. Fernand is putting me
up, he'd made sure of a room in advance. Perhaps I shall be able to work
in two or three days. For the time being I must relax. Just think, I was
so all-in last week that I dropped everything I picked up! Thus I have
broken a fine dessert plate at the Castelbons, then the small drinking-
glass in my bag, then one of the flasks in my dressing-case. What a lot
of breakages!

Saint-Saëns has been marvellous, affectionate and charming the whole
time – and with a child-like merriment. Yesterday I had an hour to kill
in Tarbes, so I took a carriage and reviewed all the little nooks and
crannies in the town where we all were in 1877. I hadn't been back there
since. Many many times in the course of the day I thought of you and
the youngsters and your parents – and I really would have loved to have
you there so much, just as I would have here! Do I have to say it? Of
course I do. I was aware of it with Saint-Saëns. I told him casually the
day before yesterday at Lamalou: I am unaware of the affectionate things
I never tell him because I know he is *absolutely convinced* of my affection
for him; and as a result all this put him in a good mood in that it
strengthened those feelings which he might have been uncertain about.
How we can all get worried and touchy, myself more than anyone!

.   .   .

Casimir Fontes, Fauré's brother-in-law, was now very deaf and his affliction
spurred on Fauré to seek advice over his own hearing problems. Letter 111
contains the first hint, as far as is known, that Fauré was suffering from some
aural discomfort which led ultimately to the serious deafness which was to
cloud the last 20 years of his life.

111   GABRIEL FAURÉ to MARIE FAURÉ

Bagnères-de-Bigorre
1 September 1901

Poor Fontes is dreadfully deaf, and has become so almost overnight. He
is very upset. You have to *shout loudly* in his ear to communicate with
him. This puts the *wind* up me! I shall run along to my ear specialist as
soon as I get back and shall consult him on a regular basis once more. I
fully realize the misery of this affliction which, for me, would be the
worst of all evils!

Fauré again travelled to Béziers in 1902. He was to assist Saint-Saëns with the production of the latter's *Parysatis*, commissioned for Béziers as *Déjanire* had been three years before.

112   GABRIEL FAURÉ to MARIE FAURÉ

Béziers
17 August 1902

The weather has remained gloomy all day, then about six o'clock, when they were starting to rehearse the last act of *Parysatis*, the rain began to come down in earnest. In spite of the optimism of Castelbon, who assured us that the sun will be shining at midday, it seems impossible to me that the performance can take place. It's sad, and I wonder how the day will turn out for all those people who have come so far! Saint-Saëns is very calm. He will make use of the afternoon by having his own kind of rehearsal of the two small comedies which they're having to perform tomorrow.

More than once yesterday I had the annoying experience of hearing various people say to me about *Parysatis*: 'It's not as good as *Prométhée*'. Obviously that sort of remark is hardly pleasant for me on account of Saint-Saëns, and besides I am convinced that on the contrary the great mass of the public will have quite a different opinion.

113   GABRIEL FAURÉ to MARIE FAURÉ

Béziers
18 August 1902

Yesterday Saint-Saëns had a great ovation. The weather, so awful in the morning, brightened up towards one o'clock, and became resplendent at five. As the performance went on, so the sky became more and more beautiful. The work has been very successful. But it is obvious that it has its detractors and has not pleased everybody. Someone said to me: '*Prométhée* effused an Olympian impression, while *Parysatis* effuses an Olympic impression'. Certainly there's sometimes a circus feel about it all. Yesterday morning in addition to worries over the weather, we learnt about eight o'clock that the main singer had had a miscarriage during the night. Fortunately another young performer (who must have been delighted with the turn of events!) knew the part and could replace her. But you can imagine the uproar the next morning. In fact everything ended in a great apotheosis. Saint-Saëns and Mme Dieulafoy and her little jacket and breeches kissed each other on the stage amidst general rejoicing.

In spite of the morning's bad weather, the daytime has been wickedly hot, and today is going to be stifling. But what a wonderful evening yesterday with that moon!

Saint-Saëns has just conferred with me over Neptune's troops. Both of us were literally in our shirts in the middle of my room. The sight of this conversation as seen in my wardrobe mirror was most amusing. I am going to have my lunch at the seaside, by invitation of the publisher Durand. Saint-Saëns is staying behind in order to rehearse his comedies which they will be playing this evening. Tomorrow will be a very busy day; there will be inaugurations, ministerial banquets, etc., etc. ...

From 1903 onwards Fauré had even less time for composition, since in March he was appointed music critic of *Le Figaro*. Inevitably this was more than merely a matter of writing articles, since the operas and concerts themselves had to be attended, and in the case of unfamiliar works, studied in detail. Fauré took his duties far too seriously to neglect the smallest aspect of them, and his organ playing at the Madeleine, his composition classes at the Conservatoire, and his tours of inspection in the provinces all continued relentlessly. Like César Franck before him, much of his music could be written only during holiday periods. In 1903 Fauré spent much of the summer mostly at Aix-les-Bains in the Haute Savoie, then at Lausanne.

114   GABRIEL FAURÉ to MARIE FAURÉ

Aix-les-Bains
1 August 1903

They're playing my music for *Pelléas et Mélisande* with orchestra at the Cercle on Wednesday. They've just rehearsed, and it will be fine. They will also play *Clair de Lune*, *En prière* and the *Pavane*. Mme Gandrey, wife of the Administrator of the Opéra-Comique in Paris and the Cercle here, has got me to come; she will be singing that day as well as the next, Thursday, in the chamber music concert, in which I shall be playing my Sonata and, perhaps, the first Quartet. Unhappily, the *Pelléas* rehearsal has been very painful and sad from the point of view of my *ears*! However I have not neglected my treatment, even to the extent of lying down yesterday evening...

115*   GABRIEL FAURÉ to MARIE FAURÉ

Aix-les-Bains
3 August 1903

Like you and as much as you, I am sorry that I have composed nothing for almost a year now. I think this period of holidays and rest will get me going again. In any case I have always sought quality rather than quantity, and I feel certain that the vague ideas which came to me this winter were not worth my dealing with. You also know that since December *Le Figaro*, even before it fell to my lot, occupied and preoccupied me beyond all reason. This will be even more the case now. I continue to look after myself carefully. I am starting to get an extraordinary appetite, something which has not happened for some time.

Le Figaro dealt with the dignity of the Conservatoire prize-giving in a rather disrespectful way. However it did give a part of the Minister's address. It says there that Lefebvre has been appointed *officier* because he is a highly-respected composer (!) and I have because I am a good teacher. On top of this *Le Figaro* calls me its 'beloved collaborator!' *That* is some comfort after the Minister!

116 GABRIEL FAURÉ to MARIE FAURÉ

Lausanne
12 August 1903

I am stunned by this curse which has struck me in the very place which I most need to protect. It is disrespectful, or at the very least inconsiderate, to think of Beethoven. Nevertheless the latter half of his life was *nothing but a long period of despair*! Now there are areas of music, sonorities, where I can hear *nothing, nothing*! Of my own, as well as others. This morning I put some manuscript paper on my table; I wanted to try to work. Now I feel only a dreadful mantle of misery and discouragement on my shoulders...

117* GABRIEL FAURÉ to MARIE FAURÉ

Lausanne
16 August 1903

I am working a little because I really want to – without too much fatigue, and above all to get certain things fixed in my mind. I can assure you that I am not over-exerting myself in any way.

At the very beginning of September there will be an important première at the Opéra-Comique; important because of the personality (!) of Sardou,[2] the librettist, and the bizarre school of music to which the composer of the music belongs, Puccini. They consist of three or four fellows who have conjured up a neo-Italian art which is easily the most miserable thing in existence; a kind of soup where every style from every country gets all mixed up. And everywhere, alas! they are welcomed with open arms.

118 GABRIEL FAURÉ to MARIE FAURÉ

Lausanne
20 August 1903

Apart from my ears, I feel very much better and look well. However every day is different and as yet this does not indicate a complete recovery... If what I have begun here goes well I should really like to make something of it! And I always make my way so *slowly*. I have never been one (possibly this increases their value) not to tinker and retinker with my work and linger over it *ad infinitum*! *Without being as yet too sure about it*, I think it is a sonata for a violin and piano buzzing around in my head – I have sketched out several vague ideas for it. In any case I hope it will be some chamber music.[3] On the other hand, in my isolation here I have rethought *Prométhée* considerably, which I was quite sick of originally, and then I acquired a taste for it again. I believe it is my feeling that any likely performance would always be heavily cut, and this is the reason I feel estranged from it. Perhaps it will be, on Colonne's part, only a lip-service, with decidedly insufficient forces, an 'approximation'.

119   GABRIEL FAURÉ to MARIE FAURÉ

Lausanne
25 August 1903

I am fairly happy with my work. There's nothing very sizeable as yet. It's just like a strong door which I would have had to open and which I *have* opened at least halfway. And I finally believe that this will be the second movement of the Quintet, whose first movement broke down a long time ago! The second will compel me to take up the first again. We all have these bees in our bonnets. There is a quartet by Schumann which bears dates like, for example, 1843–48[4]... The air here makes me go to sleep early. I have not sat up late a single evening, except once when I became exasperated by the stupidity of mankind when I went to the one small theatre which is open here in the summer season.

120*   GABRIEL FAURÉ to MARIE FAURÉ

Lausanne
27 August 1903

Thank you for what you told me about this new essay in chamber music; you are right to appreciate the genre as you do. It really is, along with symphonic music, *true* music and the most sincere expression of a genuine personality. I shall not stop working on it until it is completed.

Colonne has written to me again to ask what I could give him this year. It's very embarrassing; I should really like to talk to him about *Prométhée*. But there is always this worrying business over *approximation*; choirs insufficient in number, soloists mediocre! I will talk to him about it none the less, but *with an open mind*. From every point of view it is *his* locale which would be the most propitious... I continue to go out and about on the large and small railways, and the aim of my outings is always to arrive somewhere around half-past four in order to partake of chocolate, or even coffee with milk, according to the local custom.

After returning to Paris, the winter and spring were uneventful, and in 1904 arose the usual question of where Fauré should spend his working holiday that summer – as always, leaving Marie behind in Paris. To begin with, Fauré returned to the idyllic setting of Aix-les-Bains. Unfortunately the Haute Savoie was visited by a heat wave in August, and Fauré moved on to Zürich, where he stayed for the remainder of the summer and managed to complete the first two movements of the Quintet.

121*   GABRIEL FAURÉ to MARIE FAURÉ

Zürich

14 August 1904

Your nice telegram was sent on to me at the *Pension Sternwarte*, where I found it after I had just put my letter in the post. I am very comfortable and nicely set up. This district is built entirely of villas, hotels and pensions, and is known as the 'Zürichberg', that is to say, mount of Zürich. I occupy, in a beautifully and carefully maintained house, a very large bedroom in the corner; it is kept light by a window on the north-east and a large glazed bay-window all the way along the room on the south-east; this bay-window has access to a superb terrace, where I have a table, some chairs and a large rocking-chair where perhaps I shall doze off from time to time. The room is spick-and-span, and furnished with chests-of-drawers and wardrobes, where yesterday evening I carefully put away all my linen and other belongings. In the small German bed with its damned flat bolster I did in fact sleep very badly last night (the first). I shall exercise my wits to get round this one inconvenience.

On my terrace yesterday evening up to half-past nine (the time I claim to go to bed each evening) and this morning were both delightful because of the wonderful freshness of the air.

I mustn't forget that in the middle of the room there is a large, handsome table, on which I have placed a considerable quantity of manuscript paper – quite white – it's now a matter of turning it black.

Because of the Assumption holiday I do not know whether this letter will be delivered to you tomorrow, Monday. I should be very sorry if it were unable to bring you in time my best wishes for the holiday, both for you and for mummy. I hope you will all have dinner together.

P.S. I can read *Le Figaro* and *Le Temps* here. I am therefore familiar with the week's events and of the truly unfortunate death – and so dramatic, too – of Waldeck Rousseau.[5] He was an asset, and this is rare amongst men of state.

122   GABRIEL FAURÉ to MARIE FAURÉ

Zürich

21 August 1904

I dream of finding here, and it really ought not to be impossible, some kind-hearted scrapers in order to try over at some stage what I've been doing. There is no shortage of musicians here. Unfortunately they are German to the marrow and full of suspicion, when not openly scornful, of French music as soon as it is not gay, skipping, comic, or amiably sentimental. Moreover, as soon as you leave your own home, you are struck by the feeling of superiority which each nation tends to let through in everything and for everything. People only allow *us* to be 'smart' and good-tempered. It's not much!

I had a good day yesterday. Naturally I ask for nothing better than to try to get on as far as I can with the quintet. But it will, without doubt, seem to take an awfully long time as far as I'm concerned.

123   GABRIEL FAURÉ to MARIE FAURÉ

Zürich
26 August 1904

I paid my debt to a migraine most of yesterday. It was absolutely unremitting, right up till evening. Then, thanks, I believe, to a quasi-diet, I felt better towards nine o'clock; and as I had dozed off almost continually throughout the day, I copied out again up to half-past eleven my previous day's work. Till tomorrow, my dear Marie, I am completely wrapped up in the quintet.

124   GABRIEL FAURÉ to MARIE FAURÉ

Zürich
31 August 1904

I'm getting along fine. However I'm not sleeping all that well, although I work a little each evening so as to go to bed a little less early; moreover, the terrace offers me no more than the convenience of contemplating the myriad little points of light which the Zürich gaslights make, and the moon plays a dirty trick on me by rising at the back of the house.

Yesterday I worked from half-past one till half-past six without stopping. Then I went through the apple trees and meadows overlooking the pension until a quarter to eight, and finally I worked after dinner till half-past eleven. I heard all the solemn clocks in the city striking midnight, which I had not heard before.

Here is how matters stand: the first movement, *completely reworked*, is at its *peroration*. But it has to be stunning [*épatante*], and it is *this* I am working on ceaselessly at present. This first movement is long, by the way. The Adagio is half-way there. I hope I can get to grips with it in three or four days. Two other movements are taking shape quite clearly at the same time. But this very painstaking labour of reworking, balancing and improving the first movement has been very hard work. And now when I read it and hear it in my head, it seems to me that it has an air of spontaneity which is deceptive, *quite* deceptive!

125 GABRIEL FAURÉ to MARIE FAURÉ

Zürich

3 September 1904

I worked a great deal yesterday, and in the end fruitfully. I feel I can glimpse the ending of this devilish first movement fairly clearly – I hope it will be completed tomorrow evening or Monday at the latest. In fact for the last 48 hours I have not eased off, and I reckon I shall remain rivetted to this fiendish ending until its last note has been written down. The funny thing is that the *final bars* have been written ever since yesterday! It is the penultimate ones which still have to be decided on completely, definitively.

Yesterday's grey weather was auspicious for me. It is grey again today. It's a good sign. I went out early in the morning, and for one hour in the evening, before dinner. And this appalling battle involving perhaps 500,000 men over there – my mind is full of it, my rotten quintet would prefer it to remain empty.[6]

126★ GABRIEL FAURÉ to MARIE FAURÉ

Zürich

12 September 1904

I have worked till five o'clock, again not as fruitfully as I would have liked. It's hard, so hard! But do not worry, it will come out alright in the end.

I have been enjoying myself in one of those places where the Zürich folk take their quiet amusements. They had there a gigantic gramophone which, among other things, played a complete scene from *The Master-singers* by Wagner; the piano accompaniment could be heard with fantastic clarity. The reproduction of the voice, on the other hand, made it sound dreadfully vulgar! And it was rather ugly. But the interesting thing, bearing in mind the sort of people who were there, was the choice of pieces. In Paris, it would be the *Père, la Victoire* or the songs of Bruant, *A Montparnèsse!*[7]

Till tomorrow, I shall try to do a good day's work and get it all over and done with!

127★ GABRIEL FAURÉ to MARIE FAURÉ

Zürich

19 September 1904

This morning you sent me a beautiful letter from Ysaÿe. He asks me to have the *Pelléas* music sent to him, he's going to do it on 16 October in Brussels. And he asks me to send him the most meticulous details about it that I can. *This* is conscientious, as well as being warmly affectionate.

And here's a thought which has occurred to me and which seems quite simply sublime! Ysaÿe is engaged every year, along with his quartet, for the Société Philharmonique de Paris. Since my Quintet will be dedicated to him, I shall reserve its first performance for when Ysaÿe comes to the Société Philharmonique. And this will rid me of all other offers and will even allow me not to speak of this quintet to anybody.

128   GABRIEL FAURÉ to MARIE FAURÉ

Zürich
21 September 1904

My work progressed well yesterday. The movement which will be responsible for, I won't say a few white hairs, but the loss of some hair, is in its final stages. Will I be able to finish it before Monday or Tuesday? Perhaps, but I'm not sure. Great perorations are always difficult. In any case, I shall make every effort to that end, since the weather is not involving me in going on excursions far-afield; I did not go out yesterday afternoon till half-past five, my head spinning and my eyes exhausted. Besides I feel as well as I possibly can be. But since my work hardly goes out of my head when I am out in the highways and byways, it is not a natural consequence that in leaving my table I cease working. This time I believe I have not tried out on my piano three notes of what I have written! My equanimity is such that I can hear admirably in my head.

On one of these last few days I got hold of a really comical apparition. While I was thinking of lots of other things, things of no importance in fact, there came into my head a kind of rhythmic theme rather like some Spanish dances. And this theme trotted around and didn't engross me in the least. But the most important aspect of it was that while I was continuing to think about lots of other things, this theme was developing, was being dressed up in the funniest harmonies, was modifying itself, modulating, etc., that is to say it was working itself out all on its own. Obviously it was making use only of what my memory had stored up ever since it first came into the world, and of material which has become a part of me. But isn't it idiosyncratic that there is this two-sided aspect in the way the brain functions? This distinction between one part and another? Had *that* been written, it would have had its own structure, complete!

Fritz Steinbach (1855–1916), mentioned in letters 129 and 131 was a conductor, a composer and head of the Cologne Conservatory. He was famous for his interpretations of Brahms's orchestral music, and directed the first Brahms festival in Munich in 1909.

129*   GABRIEL FAURÉ to CAMILLE SAINT-SAËNS

[30 December 1904]

My dear Camille, On 10 January next I have to play in Cologne my sonata and my first quartet. If, by any chance, you see Fritz Steinbach – it's him who's getting me to come – do tell him that I am not an idiot and do remember me to M. and Mme Ahn whom I used to call on when *Hélène* had its première at Monte Carlo [18 February 1904].

I hope they will again play the *Timbre d'Argent*[8] at Cologne on 9 January. Every good wish, and on behalf of us all, a Happy New Year! GABRIEL FAURÉ

And I fear, alas, that I shall not be in Paris for the première of *Hélène*! [18 January 1905]

130 GABRIEL FAURÉ to MARIE FAURÉ

Cologne
10 January 1905
Dom-Hôtel
Eau de Cologne on all floors!

I was fed very well yesterday in German style and at German times; that is to say, I lunched at two o'clock and had supper at ten after going to the theatre, where they did *Norma*,[9] which I had never seen. It is filled with melodies with which our forefathers were filled with enthusiasm, and it needs a style of singing which has been totally lost.

The city is enormous, very lively and very clean. There are numerous fine old churches here, not to mention the Cathedral, 'the Dom' which is just there, ten metres from my room – it is universally famous. But what a lot of equestrian Emperors everywhere, perched high up! On the banks of the Rhine – very wide, very beautiful – I saw the statue of that unfortunate Frederick.[10] It is gigantic and he is represented by a broad, commanding gesture which seems to address itself to the whole of the universe. And when you think of his sore-throat reign, you get a pretty good idea of the funny way mankind functions.

And it's just because of this that they are so formidably powerful, these Germans, so profoundly different from us. To see them still so tough, so licked into shape, you ask yourself what they must have been like in the fourteenth century. But what power and what order, what solidarity in everything, everywhere, for everything... It's depressing!

I shall be going to rehearse again at midday. Then the concert this evening, and tomorrow morning I leave for Frankfurt.

131 GABRIEL FAURÉ to MARIE FAURÉ

Cologne
11 January 1905

The concert took place yesterday evening at seven o'clock. I played more cleanly than usual, and my partners appeared to devote their very greatest care and interest on my behalf. The public was somewhat reserved after the first movement of the sonata, and were so again just after the last movement. Then they applauded warmly and called for me. After this, a Beethoven quartet was played. (They were to have played a quartet by Saint-Saëns,[11] but they had given up that idea for fear of frightening the public with three new works.) Finally, with my quartet, the same thing happened as with the Sonata. The same reticence at the beginning, and a fairly warm response at the end. All this finished about half-past nine or a quarter to ten. I had supper at ten o'clock with M. Fritz Steinbach, whose character would take too long to go into here. But, fundamentally, such haughtiness! Then I repacked my trunk, went to bed, and am now ready for off.

132   GABRIEL FAURÉ to MARIE FAURÉ

Frankfurt
12 January 1905

Here I am in an environment more artistically inclined and immediately sympathetic. I have already had an excellent rehearsal yesterday evening, and here I can count on interpretations which are both penetrating and impeccable.

The journey from Cologne to here was most interesting. From Bonn as far as Mainz you go alongside the Rhine; and after Coblenz, in particular, the river flows between really high walls of rock and mountains crowned by sturdy old castles. It was superb. I had more than enough time to enjoy the journey.

I was met at the station here, and taken to the hotel, where I am very well set up, too well set up despite the price they put on an artist. They brought me a piano just now so that I can keep my fingers trim.

Yesterday evening at seven o'clock I was present at a fine orchestral concert given in the Opera House. The room was most beautiful and stylistically very fine. A large audience and very well-dressed (not me!), and then I had some supper and went to bed. It is very silly for the Strasbourg concert to take place only next Wednesday, when the one here takes place tomorrow [Friday]. So once again it's a long week before I return to Paris. Today, a fresh rehearsal just to suit dedicated artists.

P.S. As many Emperors as in Cologne!

Soon after this, Fauré's life was to undergo profound changes. Since 1896 when he had been appointed to a professorship of composition at the Conservatoire, a steady stream of gifted pupils had been passing through his hands. The greatest of these was Ravel who, despite increasing fame as one of France's most promising composers, had failed several times to obtain the Prix de Rome. In 1905 he was forbidden to enter the competition and the obvious prejudice against and suspicion of his music provoked a storm of protest. As a result, Théodore Dubois was compelled to resign the Conservatoire directorship, and to the surprise of everybody Fauré was nominated in his stead. Although he himself had never studied at the Conservatoire, Fauré was recognized as the man most fitted to carry out the very necessary reforms there. These included a broadening and strengthening of the curriculum and a greater willingness to accept and promote new music. One of the most far-reaching appointments ever made to any musical institution, it was due to the support of François Dujardin-Beaumetz, the Under-Secretary for Fine Arts.

133★ GABRIEL FAURÉ to MARIE FAURÉ

Zürich

14 August 1905

I worked so well yesterday that I have almost finished my seventh *Barcarolle*. I think I can send it tomorrow morning to *Le Figaro*. And I shall be delighted to have as a result a work completely ready for January as a starting-piece for Heugel.[12] If this five-page movement goes away tomorrow I shall go to Lucerne and Fluelen and will return to it on Wednesday. And then I shall really get down to the remainder of the quintet.

And tomorrow it's your birthday. I do ask Emmanuel and Philippe to kiss you warmly for me, and to kiss grandma warmly also, and to give her my best wishes.

134★ GABRIEL FAURÉ to MARIE FAURÉ

Zürich

18 August 1905

I have started on the quintet again. I have to get back into it before carrying on. I foresee, therefore, some days of marasmus[13] which you must not worry about. And really the question is this: I wonder whether it will be necessary to give it four movements, or whether three (as in the fine quintet of Franck) will not suffice. We shall see. The piano piece left yesterday evening, *by registered post*, and I have an excellent copy of it here.

135★ GABRIEL FAURÉ to MARIE FAURÉ

Zürich

15 September 1905

It's very true that I'm in quite a nervous state.[14] I am sure that once I am in the thick of things and can see through them, I shall be able to make decisions in a happier frame of mind. I have got on a lot these last few days. I certainly won't have it finished before leaving. But I shall be really busy from morning till night in Paris only from Monday 16 October. So I still have some time to make use of, and I shall be able to press on again, while conceding that I shall be unable to finish by that date. In any case, I have done more than half of the Finale.

I still intend to leave on Thursday. I am not familiar with the museum in Basle, and will take the opportunity of visiting it, since I have to stay overnight there.

Returning to the quintet I have to say that in any event I needn't talk of one further year for it to be completed. Yes, I shall indeed have enough to keep me busy in the Conservatoire. But don't forget I shan't have anything else to do. The Sunday evening concert articles were keeping me busy from the *Thursday* morning! There will be nothing of that sort from now on, except (rather infrequently) operas. No more classes or the Madeleine. That is sufficient to brighten up the sky. And, above all, no more matinées to celebrate my works right and left. *I shall no longer have the time.*

And I must get on with the organization of this mode of life because a thousand and one things are buzzing around in my head which I want to commit to manuscript paper . . .

136★   EUGÈNE YSAŸE to GABRIEL FAURÉ

Brussels
6 November 1905

My dear old friend, A very quick word to tell you of the joy we all feel with the prospect of our having you here during the winter and in being able to shed light on this cherished quintet which we have awaited with so much impatience for so many years! How proud I am of being the first to think of asking you back to see us, our friends shouted enthusiastically, and today when we received your reply in the affirmative we are giving free rein to our delight with the most hellish rhythms all round!!!

Twenty times, my dear Fauré, I wanted to write to tell you of the happiness I felt when I heard of your entry into the Conservatoire as Commander-in-chief; now I am the *last* to congratulate you, but it is less banal and no less warmly-felt; geniuses ought to do nothing but composition, but one does think of all the good they can do at the head of a great institution, one forgives that kind of unfaithfulness to the Muse, who on the other hand will benefit from your enthusiasm for the task.

I embrace Rouvier,[15] the whole of France, I kiss the ponies in the *Faubourg Poissonière*, and sing your praises in the old modes! . . .

Do you want to talk about the date and programme? Give me your thoughts on it, or have them written out for me.

Yours ever, very affectionately,
E. YSAŸE

My wife and children send their best wishes.[16]

Ysaÿe was referring to the visit Fauré was to pay to Brussels in March 1906, where on the 23rd the Piano Quintet in D Minor, op.89 was to have its first performance. Fauré remained in the Belgian capital for a week. There were to be several other concerts, including performances of the *Requiem* in Brussels on 20 March and of the two piano quartets in Ghent on 24 March.

137   GABRIEL FAURÉ to MARIE FAURÉ

Brussels
Monday 19 March 1906

The journey, very short, went very well. From half-past seven this morning right up to ten o'clock I was busy getting on with my marking [of parts for the quintet]. Then I was at the rehearsal which did not begin until half-past ten and went on till one o'clock. This took place at Ysaÿe's brother's house where I stayed for lunch. At this first rehearsal we only got through the second movement of the quintet. The other two really need a very thorough rehearsal. Unfortunately *this* (with Ysaÿe) can take place only on Thursday morning! True, we can make it last as long as it needs to. Ysaÿe returns tomorrow. But he is having his orchestra rehearse all afternoon, and on Wednesday will be in Antwerp all day.

Tomorrow I shall have a piano in my room, which will be useful for working on my finale. This evening a rehearsal of the *Requiem*, and performance tomorrow night. And tomorrow there's also a rehearsal of my two quartets for Ghent, where I am being asked to play them at the house of an artist who is in touch over matters concerning the Paris Conservatoire; this will be on Saturday. Also tomorrow, at two o'clock, a matinée in the home of Octave Maus.[17] What a pile of engagements! I'm longing for bed-time. The weather is very cold.

138★   GABRIEL FAURÉ to MARIE FAURÉ

Friday 23 March 1906
Café de l'Horloge
Brussels

I finally had this rehearsal with Ysaÿe, yesterday. But so many annoyances! Marching orders were that I would lunch at their house at half-past twelve, and would rehearse afterwards. However, the first thing Mme Ysaÿe does is to have the silly idea of inviting in other people. On the other hand Ysaÿe, who got back from Antwerp at two o'clock in the morning, did not come down till one o'clock. Then we had a leisurely lunch, Flemish style, and time went on. I was cross, and naturally had to keep smiling. At last, at half-past two we eventually got down to rehearsing the second quartet to give the guests time to leave, for I certainly did not want to work – and the Lord knows there was certainly work to do! – in front of them. Finally at half-past three we were able to slog away at the quintet, and we remained glued to it until half-past six without a break! That sort of thing will only come off in Paris, after the first lot of work has been digested, although we do have another rehearsal today, around three o'clock.

Ysaÿe finds the style of the quintet grander and more elevated than in my quartets, more obviously free from all seeking after effect: music, pure and simple. I am very glad he has had this impression: all the more so as at present, music aims for everything save music itself.

Ducasse may not perhaps approve of this piece, but it's all the same to me. I have this feeling deep down that my methods are not comprehensible to *everybody*!

For relaxation I have had a brilliant soirée with the sonata, the first quartet and some songs in a very elegant setting, but it is a place where my music is very well-known. And this evening, at the Cercle, I shall play the second quartet and the quintet, then eight songs with Mlle Féart. Along with all this, it's three degrees below zero: winter through and through.

Tomorrow I will be playing to the citizens of Ghent. The whole of the Ghent Conservatoire is all of a flutter. And on Sunday evening, around half-past eleven more than likely, I shall be in the Boulevard Malesherbes. I shall send you a telegram around midday to tell you how things went at the evening soirée. And then, further details on Sunday evening ...

P.S. Ysaÿe says that my quintet is *youthful* and has the quintessence of goodness. You will never believe it!

By now, Fauré's music was being published by Heugel, with whom he was to remain for seven years. For his working holiday in 1906 Fauré again returned to Switzerland, staying first at the picturesque little town of Vitznau on the Vierwaldstättersee, east of Lucerne. He arrived on 7 August, remaining there for three weeks, before moving on to Pallanza in Italy, with the aim of finding somewhere cheaper and off the beaten track. Fauré's chosen hotel proved to be extremely noisy, so he continued to Stresa, on the opposite shore of Lake Maggiore from Pallanza; a steamer service connected the two towns. A severe stomach upset resulted in his moving to Lausanne where he was tended by Dr Combe, who had attended Emmanuel Fremiet two years previously.

139   GABRIEL FAURÉ to MARIE FAURÉ

Pallanza
30 August 1906

Here the countryside is wonderful, with a charm which gets more fascinating as each day goes on. But the hotel is poor, noisy, a veritable barracks of commercial travellers or Italian officer-underlings. There is an orchestra which makes a row every evening in a café nearby until eleven o'clock. I go to bed at half-past nine, while my neighbours above and below come back at eleven, making so much noise that they seem to encourage the one who makes most. Half-past three in the morning. The carriage to fetch travellers from the Simplon stops in front of the hotel. It has four horses, each of which has 3000 little bells! Not cow bells. Oh! At first it's a delightful noise in the night. But after ten minutes it becomes infuriating. Finally the carriage sets off. I get back to sleep again; but at five o'clock it is back again and has not lost one bell on the way back. Noise of travellers and luggage on the stairs.

And daytime? Yesterday I wanted to work at my table. I was in very good form. But in front of the hotel, situated on the main square, which is paved, there is a carriage stop for excursions. Horses, irritated by insects and horse-flies, paw the pavement unceasingly, toss their heads and toss, in consequence, their bells. (The latter are elevated to the status of cowbells!) If they were all pawing the pavement at the *same* time and *in* time, that might be of some assistance. I could follow their rhythm. But they have no conductor. I shall go crazy. The moral is to look for somewhere else. Pallanza is just like all other places. What is very good is very expensive. Saint-Saëns had to put up at the Pallanza-Hôtel or the Eden, which are outside the town and in the shade, but they are very expensive. Otherwise, I am very well, and when I have found a hotel where it's possible to sleep, I shall be even better. And I really do want to get on with my work and put it into some sort of shape.

When I was in Vitznau, five or six times I went in a boat past the house [Triebchen] where Wagner lived from 1864–72 and where he wrote his principal masterpieces. I really cannot tell you how much that played on my emotions. This house is situated on a small headland. It is quiet and surrounded by large trees. Then there is a garden and meadow which slopes very gently down to the lake, to the very water. There are also some beautiful poplars there, and two benches where dreams miraculously become realities. You cannot look at this quiet spot set in such a beautiful landscape without being very deeply moved.

140* GABRIEL FAURÉ to MARIE FAURÉ

Stresa
3 September 1906

I do hope that grandfather's cold comes to nothing: the high temperatures will be a help if he can avoid draughts, for I see in *Le Temps* that you're getting as high as 32° in Paris! At the same time I am worried for you... It's quite probable that it is as hot here; only I do get the shade in my room all day, and it is wonderful. Everything lights up before me like a reflector. It's magical! You may think I am talking drivel, but I cannot say what I want to in sober fashion over everything in front of my eyes at the moment, this atmosphere which is a source of such comfort to me. Never, never have I experienced anything like it before.

So as not to be ungrateful, I'm working as well as I can. Yesterday I slogged away from eleven till half-past twelve first of all; then I carried on at *14.30* (that's how they say it here) till 1800 hours. From this period of labour I still only came up with odd sketches, but I feel that everything is going to be alright. It consists, in short, of this poem: *La Chanson d'Eve*, by a Belgian poet, Van Lerberghe. I have already borrowed *Crépuscule* from this poem. Now, I am trying to place it at the beginning with the intention of getting together a number of pieces which would form a cycle and a pendant to *La bonne chanson*. The differences of character between the two poems would of necessity entail different musical settings, and from this point of view the project interests me.

Post from the Conservatoire had been behind the dam during my peregrinations; now the lock-gates have been released and I am, alas! inundated this morning.

141 GABRIEL FAURÉ to MARIE FAURÉ

Stresa
11 September 1906

Nature overwhelms me today with tender care. Since I am a recluse in my room she has prepared this admirable spectacle: wonderful sunshine, very strong wind, a very green, very rough lake with superb waves and limitless white horses on them, and a panorama of incredible clarity far away into the distance. It is grandiose and wonderful. With all this you can remain all day in a comfy armchair.

That lovely letter from Philippe thus came at just the right moment to amuse me; and it is charming and the analysis is so appropriate that one might actually believe that this finale describes everything he sees there. Only I have to confess to him that I never thought of any such thing and even never thought of anything at all in this case.[18] But it is true that the C # C # D C # B sounds like a cock-crow!

Only once, in the andante of the second quartet, do I remember having translated – and it was almost involuntarily – the distant recollection of the sound of bells, which in the evening at Montgauzy (you can see how far I'm going back) we used to get from a village called Cadirac when the wind was coming from the west. Over this pealing would rise a fleeting reverie which, like all fleeting reveries, would be literally untranslatable. Surely, though, it is common for external factors to make our minds sluggish in this way when it is a question of thoughts which are so imprecise that in reality they are not thoughts at all? However they are something in which you can take pleasure. A desire for non-existent things, perhaps; and that *is* the domain of music.

Fauré's international eminence was now an acknowledged fact, as the next two letters demonstrate.

142 RICHARD STRAUSS to GABRIEL FAURÉ

Berlin IV.15
Joachimsthalerstr[asse] 17
16 October 1906

Most honoured Master! Would you be able to recommend any pupils, with all that glory provided by the Paris Conservatoire, for the positions of first flute and oboe at the Royal Opera in Berlin?

I should very much like to engage instrumentalists from the excellent French school, and I should be most happy and grateful to you, Sir, in the event of your being able to accede to this request.

With the assurance of my highest regards,
Your very devoted
DR RICHARD STRAUSS

V[ice] Kapellmeister

143   ALEXANDER GLAZUNOV to GABRIEL FAURÉ

St Petersburg
6/19 October 1906

Dear Sir, I had the honour of making your acquaintance in Paris during the 1889 Exhibition and, taking advantage of this memorable meeting, I am permitting myself to address you today, to recommend to you Mlle Sokolnitzay, a diploma student from the St Petersburg Conservatory of Music, who would like to perfect her art in Paris. Mlle Sokolnitzay completed her piano course of instruction in the classes of Mlle von zur Mühlen, and possesses the title of 'free artist' which was conferred upon her by the Council of Professors.

I have been able to appreciate personally her remarkable musical thought as well as her very genuine talent, and it is for this reason that I am allowing myself to introduce her to you, and ask you to grant her the favour of your regard.

In hoping you will be able to look favourably on my request, I thank you in advance for all that you may consent to do for Mlle Sokolnitzay; and I ask you, Sir, to receive the assurance of my most distinguished considerations.

ALEXANDER GLAZUNOV
Director of the Conservatory of Music at St Petersburg

The year 1907 marks the start of Fauré's work on his only completed opera *Pénélope*, the progress of which was unusually well-documented in letters to Marie Fauré. The composer's wife had by this time become his confidante as to the state of his work, and the letters to her became increasingly interesting in this respect. Fauré was introduced to the librettist for *Pénélope*, René Fauchois (1882–1962), by the French soprano Lucienne Bréval (1869–1935) who was to sing the title role of the opera at its première in Monte Carlo in 1913.

Letter 144, written in a very shaky hand, came from the 85 year-old

Pauline Viardot, who for a short while in 1877, had been Fauré's mother-in-law elect.

144   PAULINE VIARDOT to GABRIEL FAURÉ

February 1907

My dear Fauré, I am asking you to take note of a charming pupil whom I had some years ago; her past history, painful and interesting at the same time, merits your kindly attention, and I would be most grateful to you for everything which you might be willing to do for this most interesting person.

Thank you in advance, my dear, my dear Fauré. Please accept my best, rather elderly, wishes

PAULINE VIARDOT

For the summers of 1907 and 1908 Fauré returned to Lausanne. He chose this city in 1907 partly because of its attractiveness and partly because he thought it prudent to be close to Dr Combe in case his stomach ailment of the previous summer should recur. In the event Fauré had to consult an oculist M. Dufour, who told him that the symptoms affecting both his eyes and ears were attributable to the same disorder: sclerosis. This was to trouble Fauré more and more right up to his death. Fauré arrived in Lausanne on 22 July, and though far from Paris, important events which were his concern were communicated to him. One of these was the sudden death of Antonin Marmontel (1850–1907) who had taught at the Conservatoire since 1901. His father, Antoine (1816–98), had also taught there for 50 years, numbering Bizet, Debussy and d'Indy among his pupils.

145   GABRIEL FAURÉ to MARIE FAURÉ

Lausanne
24 July 1907
Hôtel Mont-Fleuri

A piece of very sad news has just arrived here by telegram, the sudden death of Marmontel. This ill-fated and very good friend was present at the prize-giving the day before yesterday. He seemed very well, he was cheerful, in good form and so happy at his pupils' success. I am deeply moved by his death, which deprives me of a professor, who was *irreplaceable* from the point of view of the enthusiasm he brought to his teaching, and of a real friend.

The French pianist and conductor Alfred Cortot (1877–1962) was in constant touch with Fauré from the time he was appointed to a professorship at the Conservatoire to replace Marmontel almost up to Fauré's death. Between 1902 and the outbreak of the Great War Cortot conducted the first performances in France of such works as Beethoven's *Missa Solemnis*, Brahms's German Requiem and a concert performance of Wagner's *Parsifal*. His prowess as a pianist was legendary and Fauré always regarded him as one of his great interpreters, though Cortot's enthusiasm cooled somewhat over Fauré's late piano works. Cortot's somewhat gushing attitude towards the composer is demonstrated by letter 192; his adulation towards Fauré tended towards sycophancy and Fauré was undoubtedly aware of this.

146 GABRIEL FAURÉ to MARIE FAURÉ

Lausanne
31 July 1907

Well, Cortot is making himself available to replace Marmontel. He would be a first-rate acquisition. He would enhance in the most brilliant fashion the list Chevillard,[19] Risler, Lucien Capet.[20] It would answer the Conservatoire's purpose, and would do me honour too. But there will be much, much opposition when it ought to go through of its own accord, since Cortot is infinitely superior to other possible candidates, whom I know only too well, alas!

Pénélope is not suffering from these other distractions. I am thinking a great deal and working...

147 GABRIEL FAURÉ to MARIE FAURÉ

Lausanne
4 August 1907

Since the day before yesterday the heat has been terrific. Yesterday I worked with the windows and shutters closed by the light from the corridor – north-facing – on to which I had opened my door. I was right into the composition of the prelude; but as I encountered the brick wall, one which never fails to appear, I decided not to be stubborn any longer; and I began the handmaidens' scene, those women who spin and quietly turn their spinning-wheels. As it is very hot in their house, and very hot in mine, it works out very well. While all this is going on, I'll chew over the continuation of the prelude in my head.

Alfred Cortot is quite ready to apply, which makes me very happy. Under the pretext of expressing my regrets at not having been able to see him before my departure, I have written a long letter to M. Dujardin-Beaumetz, where, in passing, I spoke to him of Cortot's application, of the candidate's high calibre, and of my earnest wish to see him come to the Conservatoire. In this way the die can be cast.

148 GABRIEL FAURÉ to MARIE FAURÉ

Lausanne
1 September 1907

My work is up and down; one day goes well, the next badly. However I feel sure that this work will not take me as long as I first feared, and that it should not be more than two years, from the time when I first began to think about it (last April), before it is *performed*.

Undoubtedly the *considerable* task of orchestration will take longest; as far as the actual *composition* is concerned, I have every hope that it will progress relatively quickly.

Fauré's optimism was somewhat misplaced, as the composition of *Pénélope* took six consecutive summers, though the total time-span involved was just under 12 months. This was not unreasonable by Fauré's standards, especially as he also produced various smaller works during the period from 1907–12, the most substantial of which was the song cycle *La Chanson d'Eve*, op.95.

149★   GABRIEL FAURÉ to MARIE FAURÉ

Lausanne
20 September 1907

Here I am with 49 written pages before me. No doubt this is not an enormous figure unless I take into account the fact that in these 49 pages there is the raw material which will provide me with what is to follow, when it decides to appear. But the librettist has given me too much text. He has not reflected on the fact that music can make poetry dreadfully long-drawn-out, and that what can be read in two minutes, when sung takes three times as long at least. Therefore I am forced to cut distichs or groups of four or eight lines here and there, and to see that the general sense is not losing anything in the way of clarity. It's not always easy! These damned suitors have endless *discussions*! . . .

My latest photographic saunter was aimed at a property called Champs-d'asile where I lived for four months after the Commune, when the Ecole Niedermeyer was set up there temporarily. I haven't seen the prints yet. But if they come out well, I shall have several copies made, then I shall be able to send them to good old Gustave Lefèvre-Niedermeyer[21] and to Messager who was a *youngster* there!

When I tell you that Sarah Bernhardt is in our midst and I'm leaving her here, I'll have given you all the news.

150   GABRIEL FAURÉ to MARIE FAURÉ

Lausanne
1 October 1907

Right: I have just given the copyist my last piece of work, and I am calling a halt there to this part of the work, an unbroken sketch. I've got to a scene which has to be shortened in a very finely-balanced way if I've got the job of doing it myself. So I'm crossing this bridge and will go beyond it: but here I shall only – just as I began it yesterday – outline a few sketches. In short, not counting the three pages of the prelude I have written but haven't numbered, I shall bring back 55 pages fully written out, and these could be printed immediately. From what I have done since yesterday, some completed pages might possibly come out, and could take their place in the succeeding scenes.

Fauré was again to pay visits to England in both the spring and autumn of 1908. These visits probably represent the high-water mark of his reputation in England, and Fauré undoubtedly enjoyed these trips, not least because of the contacts he made with the British aristocracy and Royal Family. There is nothing, however, to suggest that his pleasure in these contacts was prompted by snobbery.

The Ravel work mentioned in letter 151 was the *Rapsodie espagnole*; letters 151–4 were all written from 22 Old Queen Street, Westminster, the London home of Frank Schuster.

In 1905 both Emmanuel and Philippe Fauré had added to their surname that of their maternal grandfather, possibly at Marie Fauré's instigation.

151* GABRIEL FAURÉ to EMMANUEL FAURÉ-FREMIET

London
[17 March 1908]

My dear old Emmanuel, I was delighted by your letter, it was so funny. Your description of the Ravel has to be right: it really is in this case the result of new-fangled musical procedures (so-called). But I do find you too severe on Franck's [Symphonic] Variations, where the conception is lofty and truly expressive. It is one of his works which I like best.

But who in heaven's name was able to get you to go to the Revue du Théâtre Marigny? You must have heard some crazy, obscure things there!

A very fine musical soirée yesterday. One lady, who really seemed to know what she was talking about, paid me this very splendid compliment in French: very briefly, but it spoke volumes, 'What strikes me, among other things, in your music is its sense of form; it is so economical, like Mozart's.'

I confess I savoured this not-so-banal eulogy. It is indisputable that Ravel, and those like him, know only about lavish profusion; and so all they can manage is big effects!

I will speak to Sargent about grandpa's request, and will try and get him to arrange for me to see the President in question[22] face to face. I still don't get up till ten and again I manage to sleep in the evenings from six till half-past seven before dressing. And Schuster is still making me walk for one hour, twice a day. What healthiness!

Do kiss mummy and Philippe for me, as I kiss you very tenderly,

GABRIEL FAURÉ

I have seen some really superb portraits by Sargent with, here and there, a certain amount of carelessness over the human features – that really gets on your nerves. But all the same, they're jolly good. I shall be going to lunch at our ambassador's. Roger Ducasse forgets only one thing: my Ballade!... It's nothing!

Jeanne Raunay (1869–1942), who came to be regarded as one of the most authoritative interpreters of Fauré's songs, was in London during Fauré's visit, and assisted him on several occasions. Like the pianist Marguerite Hasselmans later, she became almost an artistic companion of the composer, and Fauré wrote many of his later songs with her very much in mind.

152*   GABRIEL FAURÉ to MARIE FAURÉ

London
19 March 1908

I was unable to write to you yesterday after the concert. It took place at half-past three in a pretty music room of Bechstein pianos (Berlin).[23] The second half of the room was filled with critics or professional musicians and singers. On the other hand, the first half was very much like a salon where everyone knew each other.

First Mme Raunay sang songs, old and new; then an excellent London pianist[24] played my *Ballade*, which I accompanied on a second piano; finally Mme Raunay ended with *La bonne chanson*. A charming and very warm reception for all these different things, very well interpreted too.

Despite expenses, which are extremely heavy here, we shall get a small profit of between 950 and 1000 francs between us. It's much more than we feared might be the case.

And then the splendid receptions take their course: very brilliant but very friendly as well. You couldn't be pampered any more than I am. The Queen and dowager Empress of Russia had had charming letters written expressing their regret at having been unable, due to a previous engagement, to come to the concert.[25]

Tomorrow evening I am invited to a house where the Prince and Princess of Wales will be too.

153   GABRIEL FAURÉ to MARIE FAURÉ

London
21 March 1908

Yesterday evening I accompanied Mme Raunay in my songs before the Prince and Princess of Wales. As for the Queen [Alexandra] she again expressed her regret through our Ambassador at having been unable to come to the concert. She spoke to him about me in the most flattering terms, and said that my departure prevented her from issuing me an invitation to come to and also from hearing me at the palace on this occasion, but that it was her wish that on my return to London she should be informed of it. That really would be a launching-pad!

Once again, dinner and soirée this evening, dinner and soirée tomorrow, and finally I return home Monday evening... I lunched today at Sargent's house, in the midst of unfinished portraits.

154   GABRIEL FAURÉ to MARIE FAURÉ

London
23 March 1908

So the reception by the Queen and Empress Mother of Russia is over, and it has been very pleasant. I had brought along a little American singer,[26] whose father is American, mother Swiss, who was born in Florence and resembles a Japanese! In spite of all that, she sings my songs very well, and we served to their Majesties the good old favourites: *Les Berceaux*, *Le Secret*, the *Sérénade toscane*, *Après un rêve*, *Les roses d'Ispahan* and *Nell*.

Not invited: the male and female staff. The awful thing is: the Queen wants to visit *our* Conservatoire and go to some of the classes! Moreover she is deaf but not blind, and will no doubt be taken aback by our miserable conditions!

So there we are! Till tomorrow evening, for the finer details.

As in 1907 Fauré spent some time in Lausanne during the summer, working on *Pénélope*. He visited Germany in September, attending several concerts at a French Festival in Munich. Despite the heavy workload he had to sustain at the Conservatoire, Fauré was able to get away for a series of concerts in Berlin, London and Manchester from 20 November to 5 December. His host in Berlin was a Dr Frenkel, and Fauré travelled direct from Berlin to London.

155   GABRIEL FAURÉ to MARIE FAURÉ

Berlin
22 November 1908

My day yesterday: rehearsal at half-past two with a scratch quartet. The shifts change according to circumstances! At four o'clock, a reception with about 80 or 90 people and reciprocal introductions! Conversation: 'Do you speak German?' Reply; 'Scarcely French today, I'm so tired!' Names, titles, spheres of activity! I lost my presence of mind. The Ambassador was there too. Dinner on Wednesday at his house was changed to lunch today at one o'clock, because he had been recalled to Paris. Today just now, at ten o'clock, rehearsal for a soirée taking place this evening at Mme Steinthal's house: the *Pavane* danced and sung, *Madrigal*, songs, etc. At one o'clock lunch at the Embassy; at four re-rehearsal at Mme de Mendelssohn's (family of the composer and Jewish bankers – absolutely rolling in money) for songs which the mistress of the house will sing tomorrow evening in her home.

What a life! And all this is as hollow and empty in Berlin as in London and Paris! But it's an essential *element*!

I was able to get to bed yesterday evening at half-past ten and I slept passably well. As for my host, he is like a broody hen; and his attentions have been such that for the rest of my visit he has made me have a French valet for my sole personal use! This valet is flabbergasted at having so little to do!

156*   GABRIEL FAURÉ to MARIE FAURÉ

Berlin
27 November 1908

The concert could not have gone better. The Second Quartet was very well done, and the songs sung to perfection. I am quite sure that if I *have* had a very big success, I owe it mostly to the fact that for five or six days people have heard a lot of my music played by myself and that I have been received by them in different social settings. So I mustn't turn my nose up at this life of luxury, with all its variety and the number of people I have seen, and the life they've had me lead here. I shall now pack my trunk and will leave at ten o'clock to arrive in London at eight o'clock tomorrow evening – with no stops anywhere. I am very well and can only say once again that the way the concert went was *very*, *very* good and the reception extraordinarily warm.

I fear that Colonne does not play *Pelléas* well. He doesn't *understand* it!

157   GABRIEL FAURÉ to MARIE FAURÉ

London
30 November 1908

Always life at top speed here, as in Berlin. They were waiting for me at dinner in Lady de Grey's when I arrived on Saturday evening. What an end to my trip. And yesterday the day was taken up with rehearsals in the morning, a concert which I went to hear during the day while you were hearing Colonne's concert in Paris, and dinner at Schuster's followed by music in the evening. It was the daughter of old Mme Marchesi who sang several of my songs very well. And now I am leaving for Manchester, where I shall arrive to rehearse with the quartet for the evening concert. Four hours by rail! I return here tomorrow during the day.

158   GABRIEL FAURÉ to MARIE FAURÉ

London
1 December 1908

Here I am back from Manchester where yesterday evening I had a great success with the First Quartet, the sonata, some songs, the *Fantaisie* for flute and the impromptu for harp. All the artists (except the singer who is from London[27] and who will be giving a concert there on Saturday in which I am taking part) were from Manchester. They all played very well.

But what a black, smoky, foggy, dreadful city! Today London seems like Eden!

How can this life of being hustled between Berlin and here give me any feeling of repose, with last month's back-breaking examinations? It's a mystery! What is certain, however, is that I am very well and look well!

159 GABRIEL FAURÉ to MARIE FAURÉ

London
2 December 1908

After your white fog in Paris, we have here the dreadful black filthy fog in London. It's pitch black! Alas! I was dreading that performance of *Pelléas*. And how astonished – and hurt – Colonne would be if he were told that it's *not like that*! As far as musicians are concerned, interpreters are the reverse of the coin.

Yesterday evening at the home of an excellent pianist – she's become an amateur due to her marriage – I played my Ballade in its two-piano version and my First Quartet (again!) also on two pianos. This evening, in the home of a Member of Parliament where I shall be having dinner, there will not be any music – at least that's what they tell me. I feel certain that if we were to talk about politics in Europe it would be much more amusing, for a change!

In order to shower my music across the world I do not think of it any less comprehensively than I do of my family, and it really is as much – at the very least – for you all as it is for me that I am trying to establish my reputation!

Two momentous events occurred in 1909. The Société Nationale, under the presidency of Vincent d'Indy, had been a reactionary institute for some years, with a reputation as merely a vehicle for composers from the Schola Cantorum. As a result, a breakaway group, the Société Musicale Indépendante, was founded in early 1909, mainly on the initiatives of Ravel and Koechlin. Fauré accepted the presidency, despite continuing as a member of the parent body. This brought him some enemies, but Fauré's sole concern was a desire to see that modern music of all kinds was given an opportunity to be heard. Inevitably the two societies became rivals, although d'Indy and Fauré remained good friends until Fauré's death. Fauré himself encouraged both groups to perform his own music.

While in Barcelona in March, Fauré finally obtained a seat in the Institut, gaining 18 votes to Widor's 16. His father-in-law, now 84, and Saint-Saëns, who was 73 and made a special trip from Algeria to Paris, took it upon themselves to do the necessary canvassing, but even so the ballot had to be taken five times before the result was conclusive.

Fauré's many reforms at the Conservatoire included the appointment of Debussy to the Conseil Supérieur, an act to which Debussy responded very graciously.

160　CLAUDE DEBUSSY to GABRIEL FAURÉ

80 Avenue du Bois de Boulogne
[Paris]
14 February 1909

Dear master and friend, I hear with great pleasure that it is you to whom I owe an appointment which, by coming solely from Dujardin-Beaumetz, was something of a mystery to me.

Officially I could tell you of my devotion to the teaching side of the Conseil Supérieur at the Conservatoire de musique... I prefer to tell you rather more frankly that I shall be happy to be at your side at this same Conservatoire.

Believe, dear master and friend, in my respectfully devoted sentiments.

CLAUDE DEBUSSY

For the summer of 1909 Fauré returned to Switzerland, this time staying at Lugano in the Ticino. Its beautiful lakeside situation and close proximity to Trevano, where its castle was the scene for frequent musical performances which Fauré often attended, made it a blissful sojourn for Fauré. His host at Trevano was a M. Lombard, who had made his fortune in the United States. He directed concerts in his castle, and Fauré was invited to dine there twice per week. His *pied-à-terre* in Lugano was the Grand Hôtel Métropole et Monopole, where he arrived on 18 July.

161　GABRIEL FAURÉ to MARIE FAURÉ

Lugano
25 July 1909

I have started working a little, but this work yet again consists of getting some fodder ready for Heugel, that is to say sketching some songs for *La Chanson d'Eve*, which I shall complete quite easily in Paris in November and December. I owe him five pieces, and I prefer to get ahead of myself. I shall work better on *Pénélope* when I feel that I am a little further ahead with Heugel's work.

162　GABRIEL FAURÉ to MARIE FAURÉ

Lugano
26 July 1909

I'm continuing the song sketches, and have begun to orchestrate the prelude to *Pénélope*. Yesterday and the day before I worked fairly well, the weather helped enormously.

163   GABRIEL FAURÉ to MARIE FAURÉ

Lugano
5 August 1909

It's maddening to see the days going by so quickly and finding my work so little advanced. How long it is! I have no more than *one* page of the prelude to orchestrate. That will make up 28 pages of orchestra. But this was the tricky bit: having to find sonorities which were appropriate for the creation of dramatic atmosphere, having to think a great deal as a result, and having to start all over again on that which had already been completed. Yesterday and the day before I did not leave my work-table except for meals.

My Trevano neighbours have produced for me a regular season of music and dinners on Thursdays and Sundays. I'm going there this evening, and at the same time am invited for next Sunday. They have sent for my *orchestral music* for their next programmes.

164   GABRIEL FAURÉ to MARIE FAURÉ

Lugano
9 August 1909

I have continued this amusing orchestration job, following the completion of the prelude; that is to say, I have begun the first scene. I've done six pages. But this afternoon I am going to confront the text of the second act (composition) – I had only sketched out the beginning. I'm certainly not taking things easy. Besides, the weather is very hot and the best thing I could do would be to stay in the house.

Yesterday I had dinner in Trevano. Concert at four o'clock, a superb 45 kilometre trip in fantastically beautiful countryside from half-past five till eight; return to Trevano and dinner. Next Sunday, they're doing the *Pelléas* Suite, *Shylock*, the *Elegy* and a romance for violin (transcription for violin and orchestra of the third *Romance sans paroles* for piano).

165   GABRIEL FAURÉ to MARIE FAURÉ

Lugano
1 October 1909

Right – I really don't feel like any more work, and 'I'm closing down!' I shall quietly pack up my luggage, bit by bit; I shall go and have dinner tonight at Trevano, for farewells and to take some toys to the four younger children: Allain, Aïda, Loÿse and Zuleika!!! Not ordinary names, but very nice youngsters.

I have examined my work carefully; I believe that I have made my characters speak as they should do – in the second act, as well as the first. I haven't tried to impose my will on it in any way at all; I have simply allowed myself to be guided by the intrinsically simple action and the dignified mien of the character. I did the same thing for *Prométhée*.

Nevertheless at the piano it leaves a *terribly cold* impression, its general bearing seems to me formal and academic. It's only when I listen in my mind to what I've done that I feel some sort of satisfaction. I really ought to rely on someone else's critical judgement. But whose? Just at the moment I am totally confused. Perhaps when I have allowed all this to lie dormant for a fortnight or three weeks I shall feel somewhat better about it. The excessive polyphony, even though it is always quite justified, of Wagner, the chiaroscuro effects of Debussy, the vulgar and passionate writhings of Massenet, these are the only things which move or attract the public today. While the clear, *honest* music of Saint-Saëns, which attracts me more than anything, leaves this same public indifferent. And all this sends shivers up my spine! On the other hand, if I didn't get the *wind* up, if I were not suffering these doubts, I should not be an artist!

The inaugural concert of the Société Musicale Indépendante took place on 20 April 1910, a concert which included the first performances of *La Chanson d'Eve*, performed by Jeanne Raunay and the composer, and Ravel's *Ma Mère l'Oye* for piano duet. This concert is mentioned in the next letter, written at the country house of Ravel's friends, the Godebskis, whose young children, Mimi and Jean, were the dedicatees of *Ma Mère l'Oye*.

166 MAURICE RAVEL to GABRIEL FAURÉ

[Valvins, Seine-et-Marne]
La Grangette
21 April 1910

My dear Master, How I should have liked to express my happiness to you as strongly as I experienced it yesterday, after *La Chanson d'Eve*! I was much too moved, and in any case how could I, in the middle of that crowd? But you would have understood certainly. One experiences a sense of closeness, at wonderful moments such as these.

Another piece of good fortune awaited me after the concert; at the home of some good friends, I read *Comoedia* and what you say there about your pupils.[28] . . .

MAURICE RAVEL

Again Fauré left Paris during the summer in order to work on *Pénélope*. It was, unfortunately, an upsetting summer. His hearing difficulties increased and it was now obvious that the condition was serious and not responding to the various remedies which had been tried. In addition, the health of his father-in-law, to whom he was deeply attached, was causing serious anxiety to all concerned. (Emmanuel Fremiet was now almost 86 years old.) The 'professional anxieties' mentioned in Fremiet's last letter (171) to Fauré refer to the hostile reaction of some members of the Académie des Beaux Arts concerning his statue of the sculptor François Rude (1784–1855), which he had wished to see unveiled in the gardens of the Louvre. Rude had been

Fremiet's own master.

Fauré spent most of the summer at Lugano, but he also stayed for three weeks at Bad Ems in Germany in order to have treatment for a throat ailment. He went back to Lugano, and finally returned to Paris on 8 September. His 'distraction' from *Pénélope* this summer was the collection of Nine Preludes for piano, eventually published as op.103.

167 GABRIEL FAURÉ to MARIE FAURÉ

Lugano
23 July 1910

I am working continually on my preludes and am almost at the end of number five (the second one here). And again I have taken up the statutory dinners on Thursdays and Sundays at Trevano, along with the equally essential concert. My health seems to improve with the effects of the climate; but I still have some most unpleasant sensations of deafness at times. It comes and goes for no apparent reason!

168★ GABRIEL FAURÉ to MARIE FAURÉ

Lugano
27 July 1910

I have finished the fifth prelude (that means earnings of 1,200 francs) and have begun the sixth. The wretched thing is that when I try out my work on my wonderful Erard, the sounds in the middle register come to me from far away, although they are accurate; while the bass and upper registers only give me an unintelligible racket!

I wrote to Sébileau[29] yesterday to put him in the picture regarding this dreadful state of affairs, and to talk to him *about Ems*... I'll see what he says.

I am saddened by what you tell me of grandfather's state of mind. Do please keep me informed.

169 GABRIEL FAURÉ to MARIE FAURÉ

Lugano
2 August 1910

I have almost finished – there are only a few bars needed – the sixth prelude. In piano music there is no place for padding; you must pay cash, and this is what is always so interesting. It is possibly the most difficult medium if you want to be as satisfying as possible in it... and I'm making every effort. The only trouble is, the effort can't go any more quickly.

Fauré's rather rambling letter to Fremiet is typical of the somewhat
tautologous efforts which everyone makes when writing a difficult letter.
Fremiet's reply was evidently one of distress and anguish; this can be seen in
the awkward, and at times almost illegible handwriting.

170   GABRIEL FAURÉ to EMMANUEL FREMIET

[Lugano]
5 August 1910

My very dear father, Marie writes to me that you really are better, that
you look well, that you are finally coming to grips with what Chauffort
has so amusingly christened: foodphobia, and that the various purées no
longer cause you any upset. If you could only realize the extent to which
all of us are on tenterhooks over the least bit of every little detail which
concerns you; if you could only realize how much we are either
profoundly happy or profoundly unhappy, according to which line your
physical or spiritual health is taking, if you knew the real extent to which
all of us worship you – and this will never be to the extent you deserve,
as far as we are concerned – you would look after yourself fearlessly,
with conviction, and above all with the thought that we are quite unable
to enjoy anything ourselves unless you too can enjoy it.

That is what I should like, what all of us should like, to be able to say
to you ten times a day, in the hope of convincing you and of cheering
ourselves up in the most effective way possible. You do see that it's not
just for your sake that I'm asking a favour from you to take good care
of yourself, it is for all our sakes, all who have constant need of you, of
knowing you are there, of talking about what you have done, of what
you have said, right down to the very smallest detail.

And if you want me to tell you about my lofty deeds, I will confess
to you that for the time being they consist of working not too badly
and of looking after myself a great deal. This little rascal of a country is
dreadfully alluring and I am spoilt here right down to the Hotel
proprietors, who accede to my every wish. Quite apart from the
wonderful natural beauty, there is the delightful climate, there are even
the inhabitants who are a handsome breed and whose dealings with you
are invariably most courteous, there is everything which makes a stay
here the more pleasant the longer you remain.

I shall not find all this at Ems, where I am going for three weeks'
penance, to take care of my larynx; but perhaps I shall discover there a
magnificent tenor voice,[30] which will change me considerably and allow
me at least to come beneath your windows, to serenade you in fine
fashion! However, don't depend on it too much!

I do not speak to you of our fine young lads, for you are at least as
well-informed as I am on the subject. Something which has deeply
touched me is to see Philippe going away into the country to Mme
Clerc's house, just as I did myself so long ago, and finding there the same
welcome, so understanding and family-like in its affection.

As for Mr Laboratory-assistant,[31] you know he is going to make our name known throughout good old Belgium!

Farewell, dearest father, see you soon, and allow me to kiss you, as well as mother-in-law, very tenderly,

GABRIEL FAURÉ

171 EMMANUEL FREMIET to GABRIEL FAURÉ

[Prunay]
7 August 1910

My dear Gabriel, It's one thing to have an understanding daughter determined to see that everything is alright by reason of her love, it's quite another to see the truth of the matter. Eight weeks ago I just had a very acute intestinal sickness. I looked after myself as well as I could, and perhaps would have managed a period of convalescence, but I exchanged it for seven weeks' professional anxieties which have worried me very much, and which rather than aid my recovery have made me get weaker from one week to the next. I used to walk about, I am almost unable to do that any more, I can no longer get into a carriage, and I get back into bed during the day with as much pleasure as a dying man exhausted with fatigue.

And this is still not the worst part regarding my state of health. What is much more serious, I feel, is a distressing throat disorder, with a slight cough which exhausts me and each time makes me red in the face – I fear I am experiencing at the moment something more serious than this convalescence, which is degenerating into absurdity.

The doctors' ignorance, regarding this bad throat infection of mine, is laughable, in short I am in very bad voice, and every week it gets progressively worse; and it is hard to think about this when I see so well-expressed in your letter that tender affection which you have for me, it makes me feel much better and gives me the rare opportunity of responding from the heart to a letter as loving as yours.

God grant that I last until you come back, there you have the truth, wrung from this torment I am suffering night and day.

I kiss you most tenderly, my dear Gabriel
E. FREMIET

All of which does not prevent me from taking pleasure in the existence of my loved ones, as I turn over thoughts of them in my mind.

Fremiet's illness turned out to be his last and he died in the autumn. Fauré's sorrow was relieved by some invigorating concert tours in Russia and Finland

during November. He was exceptionally well received, and some indication
of his pride comes through in the letters he wrote to Marie Fauré. In these
letters Fauré referred to Helsingfors, the Swedish name for the Finnish capital.

His host in St Petersburg was the Russian pianist and conductor Alexander
Siloti (1863–1945), a pupil of Tchaikovsky and Liszt. He directed his own
orchestra in St Petersburg from 1903 until the Revolution in 1917,
introducing a considerable amount of new music, including works by Elgar.
After the Revolution he emigrated to England, but in 1922 went to live in
New York, where from 1924–1942 he taught at the Juilliard School of Music.

172   GABRIEL FAURÉ to MARIE FAURÉ

St Petersburg
11 November 1910

The trip went very well from the comfort point of view. I arrived here
at four o'clock. At the station I found M. Siloti and his wife, who most
cordially expressed their disappointment to me that the illness of one of
their children (a little pulmonary congestion, not too serious) prevented
their offering hospitality to me. So I am in a very good hotel, where I
have a bedroom and a sitting-room which has had a piano brought in.
Also at the station was the Capet Quartet who are also staying here.

Tomorrow morning I shall rehearse with the orchestra for the concert
in the evening, and on Sunday night the chamber music concert will
take place. I do not feel tired, and have not found the temperature at all
severe – it's thawing, in fact. Tomorrow I shall unpack my trunk and
shave off a venerable-looking three-day beard.

173   GABRIEL FAURÉ to MARIE FAURÉ

St Petersburg
12 November 1910

I dined, in a somewhat numbed state, yesterday evening at M. Wachaw-
ski's house, Russian style. This did not prevent me from just eating and
drinking whatever I wanted, without people trying to force things on
me. A sumptuous house on the banks of the Neva. A very private family
party. This morning I had the rehearsal of my orchestral suites for this
evening. Everything is going very well.

I am greatly coddled, very much the centre of attraction, and this
facilitates the inconvenience of not knowing or even reading Russian.
This business of language and style of writing makes Russia seem much
further away than it is. The city, although relatively modern, offers some
very fine sights. The river is superb. But I've been promised that some
wonderful sights will be impressed on my mind; in Moscow especially...
In spite of the mildness of the weather, I'm taking great care. The
Russians call this sort of weather 'bad weather'. They are sorry that I am
not seeing St Petersburg with 15° below, as they've had recently. My
imagination is re-creating it!

174★   GABRIEL FAURÉ to MARIE FAURÉ

St Petersburg
Sunday 13 November 1910

I am unable to write to you at great length today. I have left the reception, which was very fine, very flattering and very moving, which they have just arranged for me at the Conservatoire. It was superb, but I won't be able to tell you about it until tomorrow.

The concert yesterday went very well. But I had to have supper afterwards, which got me into bed at half-past two. I must repack my trunk, for I leave this very evening for Helsingfors. Everyone here is delightful to me.

175★   GABRIEL FAURÉ to MARIE FAURÉ

Helsingfors
14 November 1910

Yes, the reception they had for me yesterday at the Conservatoire, it was so heart-warming and brilliantly splendid, really moved me. What a pity that Dubois and Widor were not able to see it, from the outside! No doubt they would have found this welcome very excessive! . . . So imagine it! A large concert hall bedecked with shrubs and flowers! Fanfares of trumpets when I arrived, bouquets offered by beautiful young ladies, a charming speech by the Director [Glazunov], a very large crowd of guests and students, a nice concert of my works, a sumptuous buffet and a whole lot of young people who were shouting: Fauré! Fauré! fit to bring the house down! It's only in cold countries where such enthusiasm breaks out! But, joking aside, it was delightful and immensely flattering!

I spent the entire night on the railway. We have a chamber music concert this evening. Tomorrow I shall do nothing. I shall set off again for [St] Petersburg tomorrow evening, I shall spend the day there with the Silotis, who are delightful people, and will be in Moscow on Thursday morning.

176   GABRIEL FAURÉ to MARIE FAURÉ

Helsingfors
15 November 1910

It's not lacking cheek to give a programme consisting entirely of a quartet, sonata and quintet all by the same composer! However we were daring enough to do this yesterday evening before an extraordinarily sympathetic audience, which was warmer than others in its enthusiasm. The evening was really marvellous. We had the same programme at St Petersburg – except the sonata – with some additional songs well sung by Mme Kouznesoff, a professional who has sung at the Opéra-Comique in Paris, and is billed for next spring at the Opéra.

Today I'm having a complete rest: I got up at 10.30, and went on a

pleasant carriage excursion (covered, of course) beside the sea. The city
is charming: a whole district is made up of quaintly-styled villas with
roofs of green, blue, pink, all colours in fact, set up in vast parks
dominating the Baltic. Helsingfors is, in Northern climes, a summer city
like Dieppe or Trouville...

177   GABRIEL FAURÉ to MARIE FAURÉ

Moscow
Hôtel du Bazar Slave
18 November 1910

I travelled quite well for the *14 hour* trip from St Petersburg to Moscow,
and I must admit that I journey in a princely fashion and very comfortably,
in such a way that I don't get exhausted. As soon as I arrived this morning
I had an orchestral rehearsal; tomorrow morning I shall have a second
one for the evening concert. And tonight, there's a quartet concert. I
shall leave on Sunday evening, and on Wednesday morning will be in
Paris... I have seen many curious things on this trip; but I should never
have imagined anything like this: large altars with pictures of Saints, lit
up by lamps and wax candles in the *railway stations*! There you have a
fundamental trait which characterizes a whole nation.

As yet I have seen almost nothing of Moscow, and that little too
quickly; but it's the most unexpected sight you can imagine. Some friends
are coming now to take me for a drive...

As usual, once Fauré had returned to Paris his life was outwardly uneventful.
His duties at the Conservatoire, while they were time-consuming and
deprived him of the pleasures he used to have from direct contact with
students, nonetheless enabled him to further the careers of old friends and
gifted younger men.

The summers of 1911 and 1912 were much happier and much more
productive for Fauré than the correspondingly unhappy period in 1910. Again
Fauré returned to Lugano, working hard at *Pénélope*. In 1911 he rewrote a
certain amount of the music he had done two years previously.

178★   GABRIEL FAURÉ to MARIE FAURÉ

Lugano
6 August 1911

Our letters crossed and as it happened I was talking to you about
Pénélope. Our last summer was spoilt so much that I was scarcely able
to keep you informed on how little work I had done. At Ems, especially,
I didn't write a single note.

I have always, in my music, avoided *fillings*, I have a horror of them.
Now, I had allowed a few to get left behind in *Pénélope*, in places where

the libretto did not carry me along. I have therefore undertaken to correct all that, and I congratulate myself for doing it. But I have quite enough left to keep me busy for a week.

179★ GABRIEL FAURÉ to MARIE FAURÉ

Lugano
8 September 1911

You don't have to be angry with me if I seem to be a bit lax in writing. You know that I always have a fairly heavy correspondence because of the Conservatoire and that I do not get any *help* at all with this. And then my work this year is making me particularly irritable because time is slipping by and the dates and engagements are fixed and agreed. I cannot breach faith with Gunsbourg,[32] since *Pénélope* will be the work for the 1913 *season*. At the moment I am finishing the first act so that there will be no delay with the printing of the score.

180 GABRIEL FAURÉ to MARIE FAURÉ

Lugano
3 October 1911

I have just written at last 'end of act one!' The ink is still wet! What a pity I have other things to do apart from compose!

Letter 181 again demonstrates Fauré's keen desire to appoint to the Conservatoire teaching staff experienced musicians of considerable distinction. Composers as dissimilar as Debussy and Ravel were by this stage assisting the Conservatoire by sitting on the Conseil Supérieur and acting as examiners. Fauré arranged for d'Indy to be appointed a professor of orchestration in March 1912. D'Indy was still head of the Schola Cantorum, but he was nonetheless very happy at the prospect of his new appointment: his reputation for hard work and thoroughness was legendary. His letter refers to those people who were attempting to make mischief between himself and Fauré, but in an amusing way: it indicates that whatever reputation he may have had for severity and lack of a sense of humour was certainly not justified.

181★ VINCENT D'INDY to GABRIEL FAURÉ

[Boffres, near Paris]
Thursday 28 [March]

Dear friend, I received my appointment yesterday! It seems that it was not like 'over [illegible]'... I willingly submit and I could hardly be more pleased.

In short, I do thank you for your increasing support for me despite opposition.

So, I start on Monday, don't I? You can be sure I will be punctual –

nine o'clock on the dot.

On the desks I should like:

1 Overture *Egmont*....................Beethoven
2 Symphony in G Minor...............Mozart
3 Overture *Euryanthe*................Weber

Moreover I should very much like, if possible, to have for myself a copy of the register of the students present and to do the roll-call myself (if it is not contrary to the usual practice); it always inspires more respect than when you have it done by an underling.

Forgive these trivia, my dear friend, but since I still do not know whom I should get in touch with on this, I am letting them come your way; you won't be cross with me, I'm sure, although it is as clear as day that I am only accepting this class in order to replace you as Director of the Conservatoire and to throw you out at the appropriate moment!...

Good heavens, must we have journalists with nothing better to do! Another thing: more prolixity. In a concert on the instrumental and vocal *Lied* which we are giving at the Schola, we would like to put on a Romance for violin and orchestra which is in the catalogue of your works, but I do not happen to recall it?[33]...

So tell me frankly on Monday if it would be pleasant or unpleasant for you, since sometimes there are early works (I know this!) which one does not very much like seeing resurrected...

See you on Monday, I hope, and believe always in the very sincere friendship of one who does not shrink from any shady means of replacing you...

VINCENT D'INDY

Since there were now mounting pressures on Fauré regarding *Pénélope*, he took an additional working holiday at Easter in order to compose the third act. He travelled down to Hyères on the Côte d'Azur, between Toulon and St Tropez. As usual he wrote frequent letters to his wife, but letter 182 is to his elder son, now firmly established as a biologist; he was on holiday in Austria and Hungary.

182* GABRIEL FAURÉ to EMMANUEL FAURÉ-FREMIET

Hyères
Saturday 20 April 1912

My dear little one, Well, there you are in Magyar country, people, we're told, who have beautiful high boots, and moustaches waxed in Hungarian style! I hope you are having a good trip, but I am sure that the journey is beautiful, and moreover most interesting in every possible way. In Austria I know only Innsbruck, which left a wonderful impression on me and I still experience that wonderful journey through the Arlberg! But it seems that there are better things than that, there's the descent to Verona through the Brenner.

You will take that route another time. As for me, I was rather more modest yesterday – I went on the little Southern railway as far as St Tropez, and I must say, I've never seen anything more delightful than the scenery of this region: it is mountainous and maritime at one and the same time – and full of flowers! At this time of year when everything is in flower, it's wonderful.

And for *Pénélope*, the crucial moment of the bow draws near.[34] My work has progressed a great deal here. I've been able to think only of this, and as a result my state of mind is such that musical phrases which have to follow those on which work is being done take shape in advance almost without thinking about them. In truth, one really ought to have nothing else to do apart from that which one is destined for – when one is destined for something.

I am sending you this little note to Vienna *poste restante*... just in case, and I kiss you most tenderly, my dear little one.

Your papa
GABRIEL FAURÉ

I shall leave Hyères (Park Hotel) Sunday 28.

In May, Fauré moved to his final home at 32 Rue des Vignes in the Passy *arrondissement*. Again he returned to Lugano for his summer's work on *Pénélope*. The première at Monte Carlo Fauré regarded only as a dress rehearsal for Paris, where he could be sure of meticulous and careful preparation. Despite his worries his general attitude was one of serenity and quiet confidence in the value of his work. Letter 183 would have been a source of pleasure to him, as d'Indy was not the sort of man to mete out praise indiscriminately. The 'Government honour' was his election to *Officier* of the Légion d'Honneur; he had been a *Chevalier* since 1892.

183* VINCENT D'INDY to GABRIEL FAURÉ

Boffres
3 August 1912

Thank you, dear friend, for your kind postcard. It gives one pleasure to receive Government honours, because in the process one gets to receive letters from good friends with whom one never, so to speak, corresponds despite a friendship which is maintained on both sides.

What are you doing near the lakes? I think you must be working and we shall finally have from you the *dramatic* work for which we have been waiting for a long time – for let's see, the Man who has written *Lieder* as dramatic as yours ever since the early *Berceaux* up to *Spleen* and *La Bonne Chanson*, *this* Man must write a real drama, and a good one...

People say you are at work there... but newspapers!!... Well, I hope that it is true and that with the fine and lofy inspiration with which you are endowed you will not need to provide 'explanatory notes'... it will at least be a change for us, with these recent productions!

But I forgot that I am writing to the Director of the ... servatoire (for ladies) and that I should not be indulging in these familiarities as I used to do at the houses of friends ranging from Duparc to Chabrier.

Bah! I also know that he will excuse an old chum who loves him dearly and who has always retained the same sincere affection for him deep in his heart, despite the efforts which a good many people have made to persuade us quite unjustifiably that we detest each other ...

Always believe, dear friend, in this old affection of youth, which will never change, on my side at least, I can guarantee it to you.

Your old comrade
VINCENT D'INDY

184   GABRIEL FAURÉ to MARIE FAURÉ

Lugano
6 August 1912

It's me who must be excused for writing so little, but never have I been disturbed more than during this summer. The Minister himself writes to me personally, and direct to Lugano! Oh well! And my holidays? I am working feverishly. I'm counting the days. It's *already* 6 August! However I have filled my time in well this first couple of weeks, and I've not got on too badly. I now have to find some descriptive effects – the suitors who are attempting to stretch Ulysses's bow and are not succeeding in it – and I am not very gifted in this sort of thing! It gives me a great deal of difficulty. After this comes the battle and the closing finale. Meanwhile, I do a little orchestrating each day. But how swiftly each day goes by! It's terrible!

185   GABRIEL FAURÉ to MARIE FAURÉ

Lugano
18 August 1912

My work is difficult, I am near the end, but there is still a great deal to do, at least for the next fortnight still. I'm getting a bit flustered! When I have completed the composition, I shall begin the orchestration, which will seem a pleasure, a relief, a relaxation ...

186*   GABRIEL FAURÉ to EMMANUEL FAURÉ-FREMIET

Lugano
25 August 1912

My dear Emmanuel, I do thank you for keeping me informed, you give me much pleasure, and I am happy that your plans are not too reckless. With the bad weather which seems to be more or less the same everywhere, it is better to be careful and sensible. How I wish I could send you Lugano's climate!

I am for ever working like a lost soul on the finale of *Pénélope*. I should very much like it to be finished by 1 September, so that I can start on the orchestration, which again represents a considerable labour and a very long printing job. I must not make those unfortunate people mad or insane!

I kiss you very tenderly, my fine young man. All your little cards are delightful. No news yet on Philippe's return.

GABRIEL FAURÉ

187   GABRIEL FAURÉ to MARIE FAURÉ

Lugano
31 August 1912

At last, it's finished! It ends in tranquillity. Everyone is happy and sings *without shouting* 'Praise be to Zeus!'

I've found a copyist at last. He has copied everything I've done here; tomorrow he will copy the pages I have just finished, and I shall be able to send my manuscript to Paris in complete safety. Tomorrow I shall again revise the work I have done, and the first thing on the day after will be to go back to the orchestration. I must get on quickly in this respect because of the very long job of printing the orchestral score and all the separate instrumental parts!

188   GABRIEL FAURÉ to MARIE FAURÉ

Lugano
6 September 1912

I am quite well today. The fortnight in which I finished off the score has been very hard from the work point of view and in mental tension as well. I was really screwed to my table, and I could not rest my brain, not even at night!

Now it's just a matter of physical work. But *it's terrifying* what remains to be done! The fifty pages of orchestration which I had in hand was written two years ago here, when I was so worried about grandfather's illness! I just have to re-do them, they're worthless! I have already restarted this job and have 30 pages in front of me, completed. But just think, there will be a *thousand*, probably! Still 950 at least to write! And it's not just a question of putting pen to paper! Often I have to think for hours over four bars! I must face the prospect of going to ground in a sunny corner, from 1 December till 10 January, that is to say at a time when the Conservatoire will not need me very much. But so as to make sure that the Conservatoire does *not* need me, it must be known that I am not in Paris.

The work at Monte Carlo itself is short enough. A fortnight will suffice, for it's in Paris that the artists are prepared to tackle the final rehearsals. As for the date of the performance (of the *three* performances, for I am not being given more) it was fixed for the final days of February or the early days of March.

Carré[35] is full of enthusiasm. At my request he has engaged Alice Raveau for the role, very short in fact, of Euryclea, the old nurse. Bréval, Rousselière,[36] Raveau... it will cost him dear! He is treating me *admirably*.

For once, Fauré found it necessary to spend Christmas away from his family. He spent the period from mid-December until 12 January in Monte Carlo, consulting with Léon Jéhin, who was to conduct the première of *Pénélope* there. Fauré returned to the principality on 19 February in order to be on hand for the final preparations. The dress rehearsal of the opera took place on 2 March, the public première on 4 March. Saint-Saëns's comments (letter 196) refer to the second performance on 11 March.

189 GABRIEL FAURÉ to MARIE FAURÉ

Monte Carlo
30 December 1912

I'm living here in absolute solitude! The only people I know, people from the theatre, are respecting my work and my isolation almost to excess. On Christmas Day I hardly had to open my mouth to say good morning or good evening to anyone at all. You could almost say it's the Christmas and New Year of a deaf-mute!

Heugel has written to me that he will send today, Monday, the first act of *Pénélope* to Léon Jéhin, the conductor here. They'll then be able to read it in three or four days. And as the work has been rushed (this is Heugel speaking) the parts will be filled with mistakes.

190* GABRIEL FAURÉ to MARIE FAURÉ

Monte Carlo
Friday 10 January 1913

I had some difficulty in remembering whether I told you that I had changed something in *Pénélope*. It would be, possibly, some detail in the orchestration. I had hoped to do without the bass drum in the forte passages. It wasn't possible. But Wagner used it successfully. So why not me!

Speaking more generally Jéhin is, on the contrary, surprised that my very simple orchestration in the first act sounds so sonorous.

I shall leave on Sunday evening, and will arrive in Paris on Monday morning. I'll lunch near the Conservatoire.

191   GABRIEL FAURÉ to MARIE FAURÉ

Monte Carlo
Friday, 28 February 1913

Wednesday's rehearsal was more satisfactory. Meanwhile, many points which were to have been finalized should have brought the whole company together yesterday. Unfortunately it rained, and so those with delicate gullets stayed at home while we waited for them! So, a wasted day... Risler has spent three days here; he set off again yesterday, but his presence and appreciative remarks have been lovely.

This evening, *they've said*, we shall rehearse with the three stage-sets and the costumes. I shall believe it when I see it. Despite these annoyances I am very well, and sleep a great deal, even during the day time!

Risler said to me 'Your masterpiece will live, but it will take a long time to become established'. That, alas! is very probable; it is even a certainty when you think of the mediocrities which the public feeds on, or which *people feed it with*!

Fauré received a preliminary greeting regarding *Pénélope* from Cortot, who was in Poland at the time of the opera's first performance.

192   ALFRED CORTOT to GABRIEL FAURÉ

Grand Hotel
Lódź
28 February 1913

My dear Master, I should like this distant line to be handed over to you before the dress rehearsal of your cherished and admirable *Pénélope* and for it to convey to you a musician's tribute and the expression of his gratitude when you endow our art with a masterpiece which will take its place in our time.

I really envied – when I was a child and those great names of Wagner, Schumann and Chopin used to overwhelm me in a quasi-religious emotional state – those contemporaries who had been admitted to their friendship and intimacy. I no longer regret having come too late into a world all too old, I too shall have had in my lifetime the great musician, the great poet of sound. And I say to you: thank you, with my whole-hearted admiration, whole-hearted devotion and whole-hearted affection,

Yours
ALF. CORTOT

193★   GABRIEL FAURÉ to MARIE FAURÉ

Monte Carlo
Wednesday evening 5 March 1913

I truly missed you yesterday, for the work began to really take off. But, as Lalo says, one must regard this only as a rehearsal for Paris. Up there we shall be able to work more calmly and carefully. The scenery has resulted in some very heavy expenses; it is all most beautiful, and on this matter I can only congratulate myself.

This evening I'm dining at the Prince's residence. I am very tired because I feel *tense*, but I am very well.

194★   GABRIEL FAURÉ to CAMILLE SAINT-SAËNS

Monte Carlo
Hôtel du Helder
[6 March 1913]

My dear Camille, I am very sorry that I am obliged to return to Paris first thing tomorrow. The reason? Emmanuel's forthcoming marriage about which my wife gave me instructions to tell you many days ago. But I didn't know where to catch you! By the same post I ought to have asked your permission to dedicate *Pénélope* to you. Forgive me for having done so without waiting for you to give me your *authorization* in that respect. I have requested Jéhin to have a score reach you in Cannes. If you can come on Tuesday, please expect some fast-moving action as far as the performance is concerned. Rousselière and Mme Bréval are quite remarkable, though.

I come back to Emmanuel, who is marrying the daughter of Henneguy, his professor.[37] So he's now in a great scientific family more than ever.

I hope you won't delay your return to Paris; I shall be delighted to see you again; many affectionate good wishes.

GABRIEL FAURÉ

The Prince has shown extraordinary kindness towards me. He has awarded me his order of the Cross of *Grand-Officier*, which has pleased me; and he said to me that you were very fond of me, which made me even more pleased!

195★   CAMILLE SAINT-SAËNS to GABRIEL FAURÉ

Cannes
7 March 1913

My dear Gabriel, You give me the greatest pleasure by telling me that you have dedicated *Pénélope* to me. I was even a little moved...

After what you tell me, I see that Gunsbourg has expended all his attention on *Venise*;[38] but the essential thing is the musical performance and it must, inevitably, be good. I shall pass judgement on it on Tuesday and give you my impressions. You do not tell me when Emmanuel's marriage takes place, I should, however, like to know.

Every affection
C. SAINT-SAËNS
I have not yet had the score of *Pénélope*.

196★ CAMILLE SAINT-SAËNS to GABRIEL FAURÉ

Hôtel de Paris
Monte Carlo
12 March 1913

My dear Gabriel, The performance was very fine, the artists in very good voice; but is it their fault or that of the hall? You don't hear the words, when in that sort of piece one ought not to miss a single one. The brass are too noisy, but there it is certainly the hall which is guilty, you must not worry about that; the effect will be quite different elsewhere.

I found the suitors lacking in youth and distinction. For example I don't like the way in which Mr Fauchois has made a travesty of the *Odyssey*, with the suitors caressing the female servants in full view of Penelope! It is inadmissible, and there are many other things of the same kind. He has got the story about the bow completely wrong; he has confused *tightening* the bow and *drawing* it in order to shoot the arrow; they are two quite different things. One *tightens* the bow first in order to get it ready: one *draws* it afterwards in order to use it; in the same way that you cock a pistol and *shoot* afterwards. It is only one piece of stage business to change, an easy matter. But what nice ideas on your part! How I loved the dances in the first and third acts, the result of the 'shroud' being made visible through the sounds!

One final criticism, I do not see why Penelope should always drift around like a sleepwalker, ostensibly because she is missing her spouse. Penelope is an energetic character.

It seemed to me that the dance stopped too soon in the first act and the music called for more.

Your music, just like mine, is not conceived in terms of the piano and cannot be arranged for that instrument. It is tiresome as far as trying to get the work widely known is concerned, but as to that there is nothing you can do and I can hardly reproach you for it.

Every affection
C. SAINT-SAËNS

After the success of *Pénélope* at Monte Carlo, Fauré turned his attention to the forthcoming Paris production, which was to be conducted at the new Théatre des Champs Elysées by Louis Hasselmans (1878–1957). The brother of Marguerite Hasselmans, he had been a pupil of Godard and Massenet at the Conservatoire. From 1903–10 he was cellist in the Capet Quartet, but from 1905 was increasingly active as a conductor. Since there had been a number of minor annoyances at Monte Carlo which had made Fauré believe that the success of *Pénélope* there was a somewhat qualified one, he was particularly gratified by its triumphant reception at the Champs-Elysées on 10 May.

As usual, any new production brought the attendant problems of new singers. The most eminent was the Belgian tenor Ernest van Dyck (1861–1923) who had achieved considerable fame in both Paris and Bayreuth in numerous Wagnerian roles. In 1907 he had spent an artistically successful but financially disastrous season as manager at Covent Garden in London, where he revived *The Bartered Bride* and *Fidelio* as well as producing many Wagner operas.

Passages in Fauré's letters have already demonstrated that he particularly enjoyed doing the orchestration for this, his only completed opera. It is worth stressing this, since all too often Fauré has been censured for a supposed lack of interest in orchestration and even an inability to do the job properly. As Robert Orledge observes

> Fauré orchestrated about four fifths of Pénélope himself, only entrusting the parts that interested him least (Act 2 from the duet 'O mon hôte, à présent' to the end… and the end of Act 3) to Fernand Pecoud, a composer and violinist in the orchestra of the Concerts Hasselmans, as he ran short of time.[39]

Léon Jéhin had already remarked to Fauré at the beginning of the year that the simple style of his orchestration was nevertheless surprisingly sonorous, and Fauré must have relished the flattering remarks and letters received with a certain naïve pride.

197*   CAMILLE SAINT-SAËNS to GABRIEL FAURÉ

Rue de Courcelles 83b
[Paris]
10 May 1913

My dear friend, If you hear that I left yesterday before the end, don't be startled by it! I had colic, following an over-protracted milk-diet. I really *wanted* to see the scenery for the third act, and then I ran away, I was only just in time!

The scenery isn't as good as down there, [Monte Carlo] despite the pretty effects of the clouds as seen through the window. But how much better Muratore[40] is than his predecessor; it's the difference between a voice and an artist.

It's really a fine success, for which I congratulate you. What a pity it's the first!

I embrace you cordially,
C. SAINT-SAËNS

198★   VINCENT D'INDY to GABRIEL FAURÉ

[Boffres]

10 May [19]13

Dear friend, To congratulate you on your great and wonderful success yesterday is banal, to say how much this success has given pleasure to your old comrade is absolutely obvious.

But what he must say to you, this old comrade, is the extent to which he has been charmed by your music because it *is music* and not harmonic chi-chi, which seems to be what so much present-day fashion dictates.

Yes, I was absolutely delighted by the beautiful *musical* structure of the prelude, of the ravishing *musical* landscape of the second act and above all by the really dramatic aspects (which never cease to be *musical*) of the whole of the third, which is superb from one end to the other and left a really great impression on me.

I did not know where to find you, and I was obliged to leave soon after your final call, I would have embraced you most heartily, because it is always a pleasure to see someone who really writes *music*, at times such as these in which we live.

Believe in the real admiration of your old friend.

VINCENT D'INDY

And then, too, what a lovely orchestra, without celesta or muted trumpet!

199★   CAMILLE SAINT-SAËNS to GABRIEL FAURÉ

Rue de Courcelles 83b

[Paris]

12 June 1913

My dear Gabriel, I did enjoy the performance of *Pénélope* more yesterday, thanks to Mlle Féart, who is at last giving us a lively Penelope; if she were not made to cross the stage so slowly in the last act it would be perfect.

How much more theatrical is her appearance in Homer, when she appears at the door holding Ulysses's bow!

Regarding this famous bow, I saw with pleasure that you had taken note of my remarks.[41] I've said nothing about it so as to let you have all the glory.

One mistake: Ulysses's handsome costume at the end is too far-fetched.

Every affectionate good wish

C. SAINT-SAËNS

In the summer Fauré returned to Switzerland for his working holiday, where various problems over *Pénélope* were still occupying his thoughts. On 6 August (letter 202) he wrote to his wife about his discovery of Le Jardin clos by Van Lerberghe (1861–1907). The music for this song cycle was written in the early months of the First World War the following year, and published in 1915 as op.106.

The next two letters refer to the revival of *Pénélope* at the Champs Elysées in October. Fauré's fears that these performances would be marred by slipshod production on a shoestring budget proved to be well-founded. In fact the theatre went bankrupt, and *Pénélope* was withdrawn after seven performances.

200★   GABRIEL FAURÉ to MARIE FAURÉ

Lugano
25 July 1913

I discovered once more in the streets of Lausanne many memories of my early work on *Pénélope*. But here those impressions are reappearing in abundance. Poor *Pénélope*! I still see days of travail ahead for her, and the new production in October will certainly not take place without some worries. What a pity that Astruc[42] is not giving us a real excuse to show him that he's got it wrong, and take the piece back off him!

Alas! I do not as yet know what I am about to work on, although I have discovered on my table some manuscript paper from last year, my pens, scraper, etc.

And here I am with my 1870 decoration! And I'm sending you the little cardboard box with the autograph. You will notice that the Minister of War has signed it personally.

201   GABRIEL FAURÉ to MARIE FAURÉ

Lugano
5 August 1913

What is really ruining my holidays is this business of reviving *Pénélope*. In vain does Lalo say to me: Why worry? Your work exists and *that's* the main thing! It doesn't prevent a fresh performance in mediocre circumstances from having the most disastrous results. It will take place in October when Astruc brings the price of seats back to the normal level and will then bring *Pénélope* into contact with the real public. It's before this public that it will have to succeed.

I have begun to work on a piece which will be for piano, or which will not just be for piano. I don't really know yet.

202   GABRIEL FAURÉ to MARIE FAURÉ

Lugano
6 August 1913

I have just had a volume of poetry by Van Lerberghe, which one of his Belgian friends is lending me (for the work is out of print). Perhaps I'll find something to do in the said volume.

As for the piece I've started, it will only be the fiftieth, or more, of my piano pieces; with rare exceptions, pianists just let them pile up without playing them. After 20 years their turn will come!

203*   GABRIEL FAURÉ to MARIE FAURÉ

Lugano
Wednesday, 10 September 1913

My telegram telling you I would be in Lausanne (Hôtel Beausite) on Friday evening will make you think that I am *moody* and *always on the move*! By doing this I get nearer to Paris and I shall finally perhaps see some useful people for the open-air theatre – for the future! I do not have any new *news* from Paris, except a line from M. Heugel; I sent him a short orchestral ending so that the prelude to *Pénélope* can be played as a separate piece in the concert-hall.

204   GABRIEL FAURÉ to GABRIEL ASTRUC

Conservatoire National de Musique et de Déclamation
Cabinet du Directeur
Lausanne
Monday, [probably 15 September][43]

My dear friend, I arrived here feeling *very off colour* and the doctor immediately stuck me in bed. So do excuse my tone and handwriting. This is exactly what I telegraphed this morning to Messager and Broussan.[44]

> Hear that Muratore would very kindly sing Pénélope *several times if were to authorize. Count on your friendship: would value it a great deal and very much so for première. Regards.*

I thought the best thing I could do was to ask for as much as possible and stress my insistence on *première*.

Have you heard Lafitte? His voice is really very fine and he is a very good musician. He is short. But one must admit that the crafty Ulysses is not big. Rousselière is not big.

In any case I know you are involved in this business in a big way, and so I do thank you most sincerely. I was equally touched by your recalling my wish to see the rehearsals and early performances entrusted again to Louis Hasselmans. The day we talked of this, you were planning to divide the direction of the performances between him and Inghelbrecht.[45] But I thought that Inghelbrecht would doubtless be responsible for other productions and this would then increase his workload. If you are of the same opinion, allow me to ask you that Mathieu[46] should appeal to Hasselmans.

Mathieu is a very good musician and a very good and very experienced orchestral conductor in the opera-house. I noticed that he had followed the rehearsals for *Pénélope* with obvious assiduity and interest. You would oblige me by entrusting my work to him. I was going to put you in the picture regarding a letter from Georges Petit asking me for the role of Eurymachus, when I heard that you have given it to him, which is fine.

I hope to write to you more solidly tomorrow. It's only a slight indisposition and is being looked after most carefully. I certainly think I shall be back in Paris about the 24th at the latest, if not before.
Every good wish from your devoted

GABRIEL FAURÉ
The floor?... If you knew how much...

Fauré's earlier fears about this new production of *Pénélope* turned out to be justified. October saw seven performances of the opera, performances which became increasingly bad: Hasselmans and Muratore could take part in only the first four, while the smaller solo roles were eventually sung by different singers on different occasions, exchanging roles with one another. The final blow was the bankruptcy of the theatre in November, when Astruc was forced to close it down. A projected revival of *Pénélope* at the Opéra-Comique the following year was prevented by the outbreak of the First World War. The Opéra-Comique did revive the opera in 1919, and the Paris *Opéra* in 1943, both revivals being successful, but *Pénélope* has never really held the stage even in France. Its avoidance of all that the opera-going public enjoys – flamboyant effects, opulent orchestration and broad sweeps of melody – makes this neglect understandable if completely unjustified.

Notes

1 A spa, some 30 miles north-west of Béziers.

2 Victorien Sardou (1831–1908), French dramatist, most famous for his comedies. The première Fauré refers to was the French production of *Tosca*, whose libretto was adapted from Sardou by the Italian dramatist Luigi Illica (1857–1919). He also wrote *La Bohème* and *Madama Butterfly* for Puccini.

3 The Second Violin Sonata was composed in 1916–17. It is possible that Fauré is here referring to an early sketch of this work; more likely, these ideas were incorporated into the First Piano Quintet on which Fauré was now working in earnest. (*See* letter 119.)

4 Fauré is in error here. Schumann wrote his three String Quartets op.41 with extreme rapidity in 1842.

5 Pierre Waldeck-Rousseau (1846–1904), French statesman, best remembered for his legalization of the trade unions and his pacification of the Dreyfus affair. He suffered from ill health during his last two years, and his death was the result of an unsuccessful liver operation.

6 Fauré is alluding to the Russo-Japanese War which lasted from February 1904 to the middle of 1905; a peace treaty was signed between the two nations on 5 September 1905. The human carnage Fauré refers to was indeed horrific: on 25 August 1904 at the Battle of Liao-yang, the Japanese had triumphed against the Russians despite their inferior numbers; nevertheless in that one battle alone the Japanese lost 23,000 men.

7 Aristide Bruant (1851–1925), French singer and songwriter. He gained his greatest fame as a commentator on social injustices by his performances at the famous Chat Noir in Paris.

8 Saint-Saëns's second opera, first produced in Paris in 1877.

9 Opera by Bellini (1801–35), first produced in Milan in 1831.

10 Frederick (1831–88), the second German Emperor, King of Prussia and son-in-law of Queen Victoria. He died of throat cancer after a reign of only six months.

11 Probably the First String Quartet in E Minor, op.112, composed and published in 1899.

12 Evidently Fauré was making preliminary arrangements for his new contract with the firm of Henri Heugel, which officially began in January 1906.

13 Intense emaciation caused by malnutrition.

14 i.e. about the Directorship of the Conservatoire.

15 Maurice Rouvier (1842–1911), Prime Minister, who made such appointments.

16 Written in the right hand margin of the last page.

17 Octave Maus (1856–1919), Belgian art critic.

18 Philippe was referring to the cockcrow-like motif at bar 66 in the finale of the A Major Violin Sonata.

19 Camille Chevillard (1859–1923), conductor and composer, succeeded to the conductorship of his father-in-law's Concerts Lamoureux in 1899. In 1907 he was appointed Professor of Instrumental Ensemble Music at the Conservatoire.

20 Lucien Capet (1873–1928), violinist and composer who was to assume great importance towards the end of his life as an interpreter of Fauré's late chamber works. He was particularly famous for his performances of Beethoven's quartets.

21 Louis Niedermeyer's son-in-law, Gustave Lefèvre (1831–1910), who had obtained for Fauré his first organist's post at Rennes in 1866.

22 Probably of the Royal Academy, and therefore Sir Edward John Poynter (1836–1919). By this time Fauré was a good friend of Sargent, and doubtless Emmanuel Fremiet's work was of mutual interest to them. Poynter, though of British parentage, was born in Paris.

23 The Bechstein Hall, now the Wigmore Hall.

24 Mrs Carl Derenburg, about whom *The Times* critic wrote on 20 March that she 'played with the composer his version of his ballade for two pianos; and her part, which is very brilliant and prominent – the other being a mere accompaniment –

was exquisitely played. The composer accompanied throughout the concert in most artistic style.'

25 The Russian imperial family was on an official visit to England.

26 Miss Susan Metcalf. She married Pablo Casals in 1914.

27 Mrs George Swinton.

28 Ravel was alluding to an article in the journal in which Fauré as chairman of the new society expressed his confidence in a committee on which there were a number of faithful friends and former pupils.

29 Pierre Sébileau, who was caring for Fauré's health.

30 This reference to voice and throat trouble must have been distressingly ironic for Fremiet, as his reply indicates.

31 Fauré's elder son Emmanuel, who had already achieved fame as a biologist.

32 Raoul Gunsbourg (1859–1955), French composer and impresario of Romanian birth. He was director of several theatres and opera houses, and his direction of Berlioz's *La Prise de Troie* at Nice in 1891 marked its first production in France. From 1893 to 1950 he was director of the Monte Carlo Opera, where Fauré's *Pénélope* was to be staged. Gunsbourg composed operas himself which were orchestrated by Léon Jéhin, who was to conduct the first performance of *Pénélope*.

33 Since the orchestral version of the Romance for violin and piano, op.28 was not made until 1919, this may be either the *Berceuse,* op.16 or the slow movement of the Violin Concerto, op.14. Only the first two movements of this work were ever performed, and indeed Fauré left its finale uncompleted. He used some of the material from the slow movement in the Andante for violin and piano, op.75, which dates from 1897.

34 The point in the third act where the suitors try Ulysses's bow.

35 Albert Carré (1852–1938), director of the Opéra-Comique in Paris.

36 Charles Rousselière was taking the role of Ulysses, Lucienne Bréval that of Pénélope.

37 Louis-Félix Henneguy (1850–1928), French biologist and doctor. In 1900 he was appointed Professor of Embryology at the Collège de France where later Emmanuel also taught for many years.

38 Opera by Gunsbourg.

39 Orledge, op.cit., p.152.

40 Lucien Muratore (1876–1954) had taken over Rousselière's role as Ulysses. He had begun his career as an actor, appearing occasionally with Sarah Bernhardt, but achieved his greatest successes in Massenet's operas. In later life he taught singing, and became manager of the Opéra-Comique in Paris in 1943.

41 *See* letter 196.

42 Gabriel Astruc (1864–1938), director of the Théâtre des Champs Elysées.

43 From the previous letter we know that Fauré arrived in Lausanne on Friday 12 September. From the content of letter 204 Fauré must have written it on the following Monday.

44 Louis Broussan, co-director of the Paris Opéra.

45 Désiré-Emile Inghelbrecht (1880–1965) started his career as a violinist, but soon became famous as a conductor of French opera in general and of Mussorgsky's *Boris Godunov* in particular.

46 Emile Mathieu (1844–1932), Belgian conductor and composer and director of the Ghent Conservatoire from 1898 to 1924. He wrote operas, songs and a few instrumental pieces.

4

The Great War
1914–18

It has often been said that the outbreak of the Great War marked the end of an era. Music was affected no less than other aspects of civilization. Gargantuan orchestras of the size required for Stravinsky's *Le Sacre du Printemps*, which had received its première in Paris on 29 May 1913, were henceforth to be a luxury rather than a necessity, as most composers realized. Fauré's sympathies had always been directed towards the smaller forms, and so it is not surprising that the War should coincide with a resurgence of interest by Fauré in chamber music and songs. As usual, Fauré was only able to work uninterruptedly during his summer holidays. As ill luck would have it, he had chosen in 1914 to return to Bad Ems in Germany, scene of a visit in 1910 and made for the same reason. There was no hint early that summer of the catastrophe that was to overtake mankind.

205   GABRIEL FAURÉ to MARIE FAURÉ

Ems
21 July 1914

The weather here is sultry and threatening; my course of treatment tires me somewhat, but I feel much better than when I left. I have started to work. For the time being, it consists of a group of three or four songs; it's one way of breaking into a trot...

   I am working on some poems[1] by the same author as the 'La Chanson d'Eve', Van Lerberghe. I find nothing, alas! in today's French poets, nothing which calls for music.

206*   GABRIEL FAURÉ to MARIE FAURÉ

Ems
Tuesday, 28 July 1914

You must be dreadfully worried by the political turn of events, which seem very serious, and to me perhaps more serious as I am a long way from Paris. Here one lives in the midst of people – the Germans – who are always serious-minded and solemn. So one is unable to judge whether they are more serious-minded and solemn than usual, and whether the news worries them..

   I hope to bring back from here three new short songs. The rain is inspiring me!

207*   GABRIEL FAURÉ to MARIE FAURÉ

Ems
Wednesday 29 July 1914

Your feelings of panic reach me just when I was thinking that the only thing to do was wait until things become clearer. If I were to perceive the slightest signs of apprehension here, I should take the train immediately, I'd be able to travel through Switzerland to get back to Paris if the German frontier proved impossible to cross.

208*   GABRIEL FAURÉ to MARIE FAURÉ

Ems
Wednesday evening [29 July 1914]

I have decided to come home early to prevent your being bored to death with your dear mamma and to try and calm you down a little, if that is possible. Evidently the situation is *very grave*. I fear that Germany believes this is the right moment to stop the military build-up in Russia and France. On the other hand, it would be so horrendous to have hatched this *conspiracy* with Austria! But anything is possible!

Unfortunately, on his departure from Bad Ems, Fauré found the French frontier closed. German trains took him as far as St Louis, from where he was able to reach Basle partly on foot and partly by car. Only after reaching Geneva did Fauré, now in his seventieth year, feel himself to be safe. The next letter was written on the day Germany declared war on France.

209*   GABRIEL FAURÉ to MARIE FAURÉ

Geneva
[letter-card postmarked Annemasse]
3 August 1914

I have just spent three appalling days with my blasted luggage. It is now at Geneva railway station. I am at the Pension Sutterlin, rue de la Corraterie. But do not write there. Communications with Switzerland have been broken off. It will be via Annemasse that I shall have to try to get back. When the trains have completed the mobilization. I am distressed at being so far away from you.

210*   GABRIEL FAURÉ to MARIE FAURÉ

Geneva
7 August 1914

A reservist friend is leaving for Paris and he is volunteering to take charge of a letter. I have made several attempts to communicate with you, but I do not know whether my various telegrams and letters could reach you. Here they are announcing a few departures *soon* for travellers *without luggage*; unscheduled trains which will be absolutely packed, for there are more than two thousand French people stranded here. If things carry on as they are in Belgium, I would prefer not to chance this risky departure straight away. What I absolutely need is somehow to get your news again. The distance from the frontier to Annemasse is impossible for me to manage on foot. Tomorrow somebody from the house will go and fetch, I do hope with all my heart, some news of you all. I have again found some friends who could not be more obliging, and the pension to which fortune has led me is perfection itself in every possible way; and I am as well as I can expect, when you consider the emotional and anxious state I have been in since last Friday, the day of my hasty departure from Ems with all its trials and tribulations... I am attempting to work so as to be less inclined to get excited in this vacuum. Here, as in almost the whole of Switzerland, public morale is excellent and very much on our side. One's conversations in the street are extraordinary in this respect.

Eventually Fauré reached Paris, though he spent part of the autumn at Pau in south-western France, visiting his brother Fernand and niece Juliette. (His wife and mother-in-law were in Dax, some 50 miles away.) The *Taube,* literally 'pigeon', in the second paragraph of the next letter were German aeroplanes.

211 GABRIEL FAURÉ to JEANNE and EMMANUEL FAURÉ-FREMIET

Pau

15 October

My very dear children, We are being very lazy because we have very little to do and are using up our energy by waiting for some news.

These dirty *Taube* worry me: for both of you, as well as for Emmanuel who has to go to Val-de-Grâce every day. I hope that you are at least continuing to keep well. The weather is perfect here, life is peaceful, almost cheerful to all outward appearances. Are we really in the same country where so many areas have been devastated, where houses are being burnt down, and people shot or massacred! You have to think about it before you realize it.

Philippe was in Dax the day before yesterday. Grandma is well there, but I believe your mother is exhausted! And yet I prefer to see them remain over there, in peace, sheltered, as long as the Germans remain on our territory. Would that not be your advice too? At least in Dax they can enjoy relative peace and quiet. I have done a little work here, but only on the tiniest little things! And I think I shall return to the Conservatoire about the 24 or 25 October. There is no special reason to bring me back there since we shall not be having entrance examinations, as if this is some vague idea of a vague sort of duty! Poor Bourgeat[2] has had the excitement of hearing a bomb explode right in front of his house. As you can imagine, he has written four lengthy pages to me on this topic. It is true that if he had had it on his head he would have been unable to write anything to me at all! I hope from Le Croisic you hear only good news. Do not be lazy like us, write to us as often as you possibly can. We often see the Fernands and Juliette. My poor sister-in-law is really an excellent creature...

I kiss you most tenderly, both of you, do please look after yourselves, and I ask you to convey many many affectionate good wishes to your parents.

GABRIEL FAURÉ

My poor Emmanuel, I always see you pushing my trunk in front of you on the day of my departure! How hellish these journeys are!

The next letter has the year 1914 added by another hand, and is easily verifiable from the context.

212★ ANDRÉ MESSAGER to GABRIEL FAURÉ

11 Rue Grimaldi
Nice
28 November

My dear Gabriel, I read in the newspapers that there will be some examinations for admission to the Conservatoire quite soon; I come to place myself at your disposal for the examination board. I am only here to be close to my son who has been evacuated, ill, from the front; but he is recovering and will be setting off again, so that I am quite ready to return to Paris, and there I can do something useful. Last month before coming here, I tried to see you, but you had not yet returned; I heard through Gabriel Faure[3] that you had been unwell, I hope you are quite better now. And your sons? I hope you have no worries on that score. I read some fine poetry by one of them the other day in *Le Figaro*. I wish they could be near you once more!

Ah! My poor friend, how often my thoughts about you have taken me back to the other war, that of [18]70! Your departure as a light infantryman and Clignancourt and the Commune and all the rest of it! And to think that all that was only a joke compared with what we have been seeing during the last four months!

Well, I hope to have the pleasure of seeing you again soon: you are one of those rare beings who really miss me. So if you want me for the examinations have a line sent to me via Bourgeat, even a telegram. I can leave at any time.

Meanwhile, I clasp your hand with every affection.
Your old comrade and friend
ANDRÉ MESSAGER

Good heavens, how ridiculous our poor Camille is, with his need to be polemical and say such stupid things![4]

Despite the war, Fauré continued to direct the Conservatoire with his usual conscientiousness. He had been much impressed by Louis Vuillemin's *Gabriel Fauré et son oeuvre*, which had appeared early in 1914 and was the first book to be devoted wholly to Fauré. Like so many others, Vuillemin was now on active service, as the next letter indicates.

213   GABRIEL FAURÉ to MME LOUIS VUILLEMIN

Conservatoire National de Musique et de Déclamation
Le Directeur
14 February 1915

Dear friend, For so many days now I have been wanting to write to you. I have received from Louis some good letters, cheerful, teasing, full of hope and, as always, friendly in the extreme. But your husband's address, written in pencil, was so extraordinarily faint that I said to myself that I would let you thank him and send him my most affectionate good wishes. After what you have told me, there he is, suffering the consequences of an exceptionally hard life in a dreadful climate. I hope that the rest he is taking in the Midi will quickly prove to be to his benefit; but really I should prefer him to be left there and for a very long time. And I hope too that you will soon be able to rejoin him, if this has not happened already. Tell him how much we think of him, and how much we talk about him at every opportunity. Tell him from me that music is beginning to *revive* in Paris: I understand that a concert organized by Casella⁵ has resulted in two little first performances: an excellent trio by Ravel for piano, violin and cello, and a suite of eight songs, entitled *Le Jardin clos* which I composed recently, and which aspires to a rather different kind of reality from what is actually written, based on poems by the Belgian poet Van Lerberghe – one of which is dedicated to my dear interpreter Lucy Louis Vuillemin. And as soon as you can do so, give me some news of our fine sapper in the engineering corps. I hope that everyone in your midst is in good health. I beg you, dearest friend, to convey to everyone all my good wishes, and please accept the affectionate regard of your old friend

GABRIEL FAURÉ

We have had here successively and without let-up the entrance examination and the termly examinations, hence my delay in writing to you. You will forgive me, I hope, and give me some proof of this by letting me know very quickly.

For his working holiday in 1915 Fauré retired to St Raphaël, between St Tropez and Nice, to which he was to return two years later. Indeed he made a point of remaining in France throughout the war, rather than holidaying in Switzerland as he had sometimes done previously. Fauré spent seven weeks in

St Raphaël, engaged on several different tasks. He was preparing an edition of Schumann's piano music for his publisher, a labour of love as Schumann was one of his favourite composers. New editions were necessary as the war had made it difficult to obtain supplies of scores from Germany. He also wrote his Twelfth Barcarolle, op.106b and Twelfth Nocturne, op.107. It is not too fanciful to see in the latter his mental anguish regarding the war, an anguish that was to recur in the second Violin and first Cello Sonatas. His younger son, Philippe, was on active service throughout the war.

214   GABRIEL FAURÉ to MARIE FAURÉ

St Raphaël
1 August 1915

My trip has gone well despite the length of the journey. I had in my compartment some English officers, one of whom, a general, when he heard me coughing, offered me his seat so as to prevent my getting a continual draught. Here, hotels closed or converted into convalescent homes, but numerous pensions. I am very well set up at the villa 'Le Gui' [Mistletoe], where everything is comfortable. From my windows, a fine view over the sea immediately in front of me and to the right over the Maures mountains, which come straight down to the shore. It is a superb panorama. The only thing is that one's preoccupations, great and small, do not get left in abeyance. In fact could there be anything at all that would be a match for them! And yet the small population of this area seems scarcely affected. One is far from the combatants, far from important centres where incidents are being discussed; one enjoys life and one amuses onself at the sight (very curious and very funny, by the way) of a regiment of Senegalese, which is living here in a camp at the gates of St Raphaël: and at tall children superbly turned-out, who laugh, sing and dance all the time. I've only just arrived, and I have to prepare a long report for M. Dalimier[6] in which I shall try to get him back to a pile of projects whose only purpose is to twirl round and round *ad nauseam*!
    I have had 24 hours of extreme weariness.

215*   GABRIEL FAURÉ to MARIE FAURÉ

St Raphaël
9 August 1915

I am working on a nocturne for piano; moreover, I am continuing with the Schumann pieces, I've brought a heap of them here. But do I need to tell you that the news sickens me just as much as when I was in Paris, when we have this steadily deteriorating situation which I am hardly able to talk to anyone about?
    I've had a letter from Mme Croiza,[7] who talks of nothing but *Pénélope*! There are more serious things to sort out before one can start to think of that.

216   GABRIEL FAURÉ to MARIE FAURÉ

St Raphaël
19 August 1915

I have sent Durand some completed Schumann pieces, and I'm working now for myself.

Our Senegalese have left for the Dardanelles; some others, from Morocco, have replaced them. A pretty picture seen yesterday: on the stairs of a doorway, a Senegalese seated beside a nice youngster of ten or eleven who was teaching him to read. I stopped, and heard that dusky young chap repeating the syllables and trying hard to pronounce them properly!

217   GABRIEL FAURÉ to MARIE FAURÉ

St Raphaël
10 September 1915

'L'Oustalet dou Capelan', that means in Provençal, 'the little house of the priest', and it was in that house that Gounod spent the year 1866, composing *Roméo et Juliette*. In my walks around sunset, so beautiful here, I often go past this house where the garden is washed by the sea; and always with deep emotion I look at its high walls! Truly this panorama and this sky and light make work a cheerful business and almost easy.

218*   CAMILLE SAINT-SAËNS to GABRIEL FAURÉ

Rue de Courcelles, 83b
[Paris]
16 October 1915

My dear friend, I have just read the *Le Jardin Clos*. Despite its apparent simplicity it does not make for very easy reading; but how attractive and absorbing it is! I shall need time for it to sink in fully. Up to now it is No.1 which pleases me most but we shall see later on. Meanwhile, I congratulate you for writing accompaniments expressly written for the piano and not sumptuous orchestrations reduced for that instrument and unplayable, and for writing for the voice in both a vocal and literary manner. As for the words themselves, they are certainly pretty verses from the hand of a craftsman, but often very obscure: there are some things which I found impossible to understand. As Christ said: it is not the light which is lacking, it is your eyes at fault. I suppose, for my humble self, that this situation is analogous.

How pleasant it was to get together once again the other day! We'll make a fresh start on these little celebrations.

There is talk of important reforms at the Conservatoire.

I should like to see there a literary course, so that composers can learn to know, as you and I do, what the French language is all about and similarly for the poetry they are destined to set to music.

Toto corde tibi
CAMILLE SAINT-SAËNS

219★ CAMILLE SAINT-SAËNS to GABRIEL FAURÉ

Rue de Courcelles, 83b
[Paris]
27 December 1915

My dear friend, I am amusing myself by working at your second *Valse-Caprice* (in D flat); and it seems to me that there must be some mistakes in the passage beginning at the last bar of the last-but-one page and continuing on to the next page.

I have some worries over the chords in the left hand and the C flats or naturals in the right hand.[8]

Remove my doubts, as they say in *Le Cid*. I await with impatience, so I can learn it, your new *Barcarolle*[9] which Diémer has played me and which I found delightful.

On the other hand do not curse me if I confess to you that *Le Jardin Clos* is not taking me into its confidence and that the poetry is as inhospitable to me as the music.

> To this garden closed by thorns
> In a pitiless way
> I do prefer that which imparts its divine fragrance
> Les roses d'Ispahan.[10]   (original text on p. 208)

I was hoping to see you soon at the Académie, but you are so rarely there these days...

I advise you to look at the pieces for two pianos, *Noir et Blanc* [sic] which M. Debussy has just published. It's really unbelievable, and we must at all costs bar the door of the Institut against a man capable of such atrocities; they should be put next to the cubist pictures.

Every good wish
C. SAINT-SAËNS

The summer of 1916 saw Fauré at Evian on the southern French shore of Lac Léman, from where he could look across to Lausanne on the northern Swiss shore. This was to prove a profitable sojourn, as most of the large-scale Second Violin Sonata, op.108 was written there. The initial sketch of the middle movement was transformed into reality during the succeeding winter in Paris; it is notable for its reworking of the corresponding movement in the early discarded Symphony in D Minor of 1884. Fauré arrived at Evian on 9 August.

220 GABRIEL FAURÉ to MARIE FAURÉ

Evian
19 August 1916

Today I have a thankless little job to do. The casino has asked me to give myself a hearing, but I have accepted only on condition that the receipts go to the Red Cross. I shall play the [op.13] Sonata and accompany a big pile of songs. But they have put up a ridiculous poster in the streets: 'The famous composer will himself accompany his works!' It's idiotic.

221* GABRIEL FAURÉ to MARIE FAURÉ

Evian
22 August 1916

The little concert I spoke to you about has brought in 1500 francs for the Red Cross; I must congratulate myself all the more since, in spite of driving rain and the present shortage of carriages and cars, the hall was crammed full. As for the trouble it caused me, it was almost negligible.

I am working quietly, and the sonata has gained a few more pages.

222 GABRIEL FAURÉ to MARIE FAURÉ

Evian
3 September 1916

Yesterday I received a letter from M. Rouché,[11] director of the Opéra, telling me, *for certain*, that he will give *Prométhée* during the winter and that he has obtained Max's[12] co-operation. This pleases me very much, naturally, and I think that at the Opéra I shall find the right sort of material for the singing roles. I am continuing to work peacefully...

I still haven't been on the smallest trip, being content to come into town in the morning and return in the evening, around six o'clock, in search of the latest news: the three o'clock communiqué.

223 GABRIEL FAURÉ to MARIE FAURÉ

Evian
24 September 1916

Yesterday, I finished the *first* movement of the sonata. The finale is more than half done. So I haven't wasted my time here. Unfortunately, once I'm back in Paris, the entrance examinations will take up the whole day, and seeing that the second movement is hardly sketched as yet, I don't see myself at completion stage before January. We are having here beautiful autumn days with their distinctive colouring... Nevertheless, I must think about my departure.

224★   GABRIEL FAURÉ to MARIE FAURÉ

Evian
27 September 1916

I have decided to dedicate the second sonata to the Queen of the Belgians.[13] She is a violinist, and you know the sympathy she professes for my works. You will approve, I feel sure.

And every day, marvellous news about the war.

Although Emma Bardac's marriage to Debussy in 1908 must have, at the very least, caused some sort of estrangement between Fauré and Debussy, contact of a kind was maintained, possibly at Emma's instigation. The two composers said and wrote comparatively little about each other's music, and the relatively few surviving letters between them are always polite. Letter 225 replies to Fauré's request that Debussy perform some of his *Études*, which had been published in 1916, at a concert. Debussy's gracious letter conceals the fact that he had been suffering from cancer for some time; he was to die within a year.

225   CLAUDE DEBUSSY to GABRIEL FAURÉ

80 Avenue du Bois de Boulogne
[Paris]
29 April 1917

My hesitation in responding to your kind letter, dear Master and friend, stems from this lowliest of reasons: I can no longer play the piano sufficiently well to risk performing my 'Studies'... In public I am attacked by a particular kind of phobia: there are too many keys; I no longer have enough fingers; and all of a sudden I no longer know where the pedals are! It is sad and dreadfully distressing.

Do please believe that I am not trying to be in any way unhelpful, very much to the contrary, for I should have particularly liked to please you.

Forgive me, and believe in the devoted affection of your

CLAUDE DEBUSSY

In July 1917 Fauré returned to St Raphaël. His principal task was the composition of the First Cello Sonata op.109, whose anguished opening movement matches that of the Second Violin Sonata. The first two movements were completed in eight days, although the finale proved more troublesome. Fauré also revised some of the orchestration in *Pénélope*.

226★   GABRIEL FAURÉ to MARIE FAURÉ

St Raphaël
28 July 1917

I have just sent off to Durand the first two completed movements of the sonata for cello. Now here I am facing the finale, where I have not as yet found the first note! I hope it will not be too much to ask. But you can sense that I have not wasted my time over the last eight days.

In the succeeding letter, Léon Bourgeois (1851–1925) acted as a go-between. An eminent writer and politician who served with distinction in several high offices, including the Society of Nations, he was awarded the Nobel Peace Prize in 1920.

227 GABRIEL FAURÉ to MARIE FAURÉ

St Raphaël
2 August 1917

I have just written to the Queen of the Belgians, and here's why: M. Léon Bourgeois telephoned to the Conservatoire that he was returning from La Panne[14] with the President of the Republic[15] and that the Queen had instructed him to remind me that she was reckoning on my visiting La Panne now that I was on holiday. And M. Léon Bourgeois, hearing that I was a long way from Paris, insisted that I write to the Queen so that she would know that he had accomplished his mission. I have therefore written, apologising about the distance and offering to come in October with the first printed copy of the sonata which is dedicated to her.

Talking of sonatas, I have begun the finale without further delay. The finale of a sonata is to some extent dependent on the previous movements: these therefore can be engraved without too much worry. It is up to the finale to sustain the atmosphere which they have created.

228* GABRIEL FAURÉ to MARIE FAURÉ

St Raphaël
18 August 1917

The sonata is finished as from yesterday. The acknowledgement of my dispatch to Durand bears the date 28 July, and I can swear to you that at that time I did not know the first note of the finale! I have therefore composed much more rapidly than I dared hope. In fact, I have worked tremendously hard and without the slightest pause ever since I got here on 19 July, and I am very happy now to have to my credit two more sonatas. Among modern French or foreign sonatas for cello, there is only one of importance, that by Saint-Saëns, which is, moreover, one of his best works.[16] – Now I feel fickle! I do not know what to do! I haven't the slightest idea at all, unless I start on another piece.

229   GABRIEL FAURÉ to MARIE FAURÉ

St Raphaël
25 August 1917

Despite being bewitched by this marvellous region I should go up the
wall if I were not working. So, before undertaking a new composition
(which I do not just see at the moment), I shall work on a few areas of
the orchestration in *Pénélope* which did not completely satisfy me, and
this will give me something useful to do for a few days.

230   GABRIEL FAURÉ to MARIE FAURÉ

St Raphaël
12 September 1917

For some days the weather has been persistently stormy, though without
storms. My nerves are feeling the effects of this to some extent. But good
heavens, what irritations, what a mess we're in! What a government to
govern us, and there's a right old stew in Russia![17] Don't let us get too
alarmed, however. We've had the *Marne*!

Fauré suffered a serious bronchitic attack during the winter, and obtained a
two months' leave of absence from the Conservatoire to visit Nice in
February 1918. While there he started to sketch one of his finest but rarely
heard large-scale instrumental works, the *Fantaisie*, op.111 for piano and
orchestra, which was to be dedicated to Cortot.

231★   GABRIEL FAURÉ to MARIE FAURÉ

Nice
14 February 1918

What a happy spot this is, so beautiful under such a pure and luminous
sky. The only thing is, bearing in mind the times we live in, the worry
and anguish are as appalling here as elsewhere! The lively atmosphere in
Nice is quite a considerable one; but the town does not have, fortunately,
that somewhat shrill and extremely banal festival atmosphere of pre-war
winters. I prefer this side to its character.

   And our poor little Philippe has had to leave yesterday morning! What
a thorn in the flesh for you, and, as I don't have to tell you, for me as
well.

232   GABRIEL FAURÉ to MARIE FAURÉ

Nice
28 February 1918

I am now walking much more easily, I no longer cough and I sleep the
night through with uninterrupted slumber, something I did not do before
I was ill . . . I have received news from Philippe several times, brief news,

but good. Here the weather continues to be resplendent. Through the open windows sunshine fills my bedroom and illumines the manuscript paper spread out over my table. But up to now, and despite a little daily effort, this paper is still bare. This is actually beginning to annoy me.

233   GABRIEL FAURÉ to MARIE FAURÉ

Nice

3 March 1918

I feel real sorrow over the death of my brother Fernand, and I think sorrowfully of the one who now remains alone after so many happy and peaceful years. What a good man Fernand was and how distinguished his entire life. I was able to discover, in Pau, how he was surrounded with feelings of respect and affectionate consideration.

The war continued relentlessly and in March 1918 Marie Fauré was obliged, along with many others, to flee from Paris. The terrifying bombardment of the French capital began on 21 March, with the notorious 'Big Bertha' long-range gun claiming many lives and causing considerable damage. On 25 March, at the height of the German assault on Paris, Debussy died, having been bedridden for some weeks. Fauré's letter of condolence to Emma Debussy resulted in this reply; it must have been one of the most moving letters he ever received.

Here was the widow of the greatest French composer of the time writing to his older contemporary, who had been her lover and whom she forsook for Debussy. Fauré and Emma must have had many things on their minds at this time, not least perhaps *La Bonne Chanson*, which Fauré had originally written for Emma when she was his mistress. Emma's devotion to Debussy was, however, undeniable. Though dated only 'Friday' the letter, using black-edged notepaper, almost certainly dates from some time in April 1918.

234   MME EMMA DEBUSSY to GABRIEL FAURÉ

Friday

I thank you profoundly, my dear friend, for your affectionate feelings of respect over this terrible bereavement which has struck me.

I feel totally incapable of putting into words the cruel anguish which has taken hold of me since his decease and which will continue to grow.

I am trying to be brave by thinking of Chouchou[18] (how lovely she looks!) and also of all the beauty which he leaves behind and which in war-time one often forgets (at our house!!) But to think that I shall see him no more is a piercing stab wound which tortures me...

I have not replied to the telegrams which you have sent me, nor to so many other expressions of condolence from foreign countries, neutral or allied, in memory of the poor Master – it will be necessary to indulge me and forgive my unintentional forgetfulness – I can perhaps be excused.

Always believe, my dear friend, in my grateful affection.

EMMA CLAUDE DEBUSSY

He was so happy last summer to study *La Bonne Chanson*...

People were unaware of his kindness, his sincerity, and his loyal affection for 'the music'.

Fauré finally left Nice on 8 April for Toulouse. He spent two nights in Toulon on the way, arriving in Toulouse on 12 April.

235   GABRIEL FAURÉ to MARIE FAURÉ

Toulon
Wednesday, 10 April 1918

I have rediscovered in Toulon some friends of my youth in Rennes and also some old friends of my brother Albert. All these folk have made a fuss of me in the most charming way. I played in a little concert which was arranged in aid of Serbian tubercular patients who are being cared for in this area. I was offered a gigantic bouquet with an enormous ribbon on which was written in gold lettering: 'To M. Gabriel Fauré, the grateful Serbs'. I shall take the ribbon off.

Tomorrow evening I shall sleep in Avignon, and on Friday will be in Toulouse. It's really terrible, this dreadful battle! The news, sometimes extremely worrying, sometimes more reassuring, keeps us in a really distressing state of anguish.

Margot Fauré, mentioned in letter 236, was another of Fauré's nieces, a former director of an *école normale*, and now living in retirement at Foix.

236   GABRIEL FAURÉ to MARIE FAURÉ

Toulouse
Wednesday, 17 April 1918

Here I am again at Toulouse, with the dreadful weather from yesterday and the day before (icy rain and mud) having forced me to break my journey in Foix, alas! We left with Margot on Monday morning. Jean Fauré had hired a car which got us to Saverdun, where we had lunch, and drove us to Gailhac, and then to Pamiers, where we arrived in time for dinner and slept. But there, in spite of a most affectionate welcome from an innumerable quantity of cousins both male and female, the cold weather assailed me and I have been compelled to cover my back with a solution of iodine. Yesterday morning we were to have set off again for Ussat.[19] But since the weather continued to be as bad as it could possibly be, Margot was unwilling for me to continue on the journey. We therefore spent the day warming ourselves in front of very large fires of vine-shoots and logs, lunching well in Southern style, and in the evening we broke up. Today, by mischance, the weather is sunny... And I'm looking forward to arriving in Chateauroux the day after tomorrow!

Perhaps even more than usual at this period, Fauré and his wife each contrived to be in a place where the other was not. During most of May Marie Fauré remained at Chateauroux, some 50 miles south-west of Tours, while Fauré stayed in Paris, which was still being heavily bombed. He wrote on 22 May:

> Last night, quite a long raid – from 10.30 till one in the morning... The cannon bombarded us heavily, particularly between 11.30 pm and 12.30 a.m.

Fauré wrote to Marie solicitously on 29 May: 'You must be suffering greatly in your solitude'. Early in June in accordance with Fauré's suggestion in the next letter, Marie moved to Ussat-les-Bains.

237★ GABRIEL FAURÉ to MARIE FAURÉ

Paris
31 May 1918

Of Philippe, whom I think of unceasingly, I have no news. May God watch over him! Now let me talk to you about Foix, where I should prefer to know you were near Marguerite rather than be in the sorrowful loneliness of Chateauroux. There is a hotel of *quite recent* construction, nicely situated, near the house where we all lived near my mother, in 1887, and very close to Marguerite's house too.

As he had done two years previously, Fauré went to Evian for his summer holiday, where he continued to work on the *Fantaisie*. Although the orchestration was entrusted to Marcel Samuel-Rousseau (1882–1955), a minor composer who taught harmony at the Paris Conservatoire from 1919 to 1952, Fauré oversaw the final version and made a number of corrections and suggestions. Alfred Cortot also revised the solo part.

238★ GABRIEL FAURÉ to MARIE FAURÉ

Evian
6 July 1918

Paris is, at the moment, in the grip of a strain of influenza which attacks its victims on the sly, and it took hold of me on the day of my departure without my having the least recollection of having encouraged it in any way. The fact remains that I got into the train on Tuesday evening half-asleep, my eyes remained closed and I never said a word throughout the whole journey, at Bellegarde I obstinately refused to get out for the safe-arrivals ceremony, as soon as I got here I immediately went to bed; two days in bed, one day in my room and three days' diet have more or less put me on my feet completely. I have nothing worse than unsteady legs. The good Savoie air will do the rest... And now I only suffer from impatience: of getting your news and Philippe's.

It seems that at Bellegarde the whole coach knew who I was and was making sure my sleep was not disturbed by all those annoying people! A happy crown to my career!

239   GABRIEL FAURÉ to MARIE FAURÉ

Evian
26 July 1918

My strength returns a little more each day. Yesterday I was able to work for three hours up to dinner time. I am getting on with a *Fantaisie* for piano and orchestra.

240★   GABRIEL FAURÉ to MARIE FAURÉ

Evian
16 August 1918

I have no news of Philippe and I think you too will have had none. We are having some glorious times, but they are also very distressing, and if we could know what our little one is doing we should be happier. 73,000 prisoners and 1,700 guns! We have never had such success...

I am working without the least fatigue, without stopping, and fruitfully. Alas! It is only when I am far away from Paris that I work, and work *well*.

241★   GABRIEL FAURÉ to MARIE FAURÉ

Evian
13 September 1918

I do understand your strong desire to be back again in the Rue des Vignes, at home, along with all your things. But do not be hasty, although I do worry about what happens to the temperature in the Ariège as soon as the rain intervenes at this time of year. As for my work, I've got to the very end, and *endings* are always a thorny problem! You must take the requisite amount of time over them.

Gunsbourg, speaking to the Prince of Monaco (who was inspired, I'm sure, by Saint-Saëns!), has requested for next winter a small musical tableau for which Fauchois would work out a scenario; and it would consist of some of my previous pieces: *Pavane, Madrigal, Clair de lune*, etc., to which I would only need to add two or three little dances: minuet, gavotte... in short, a more comprehensive recreation of what happened at Madeleine Lemaire's house some ten or twelve years ago.[20] This will give me little trouble and I shall need to be in the Midi in February and March.

Fauré arrived back in Paris on 28 September and decided to stay at the Hotel Windsor, close to the Conservatoire, rather than at his own home. A week later he received news that his eldest brother Amand had suffered a stroke. Two weeks later he was dead. Gabriel was now the only surviving male of his generation in the family.

242★   GABRIEL FAURÉ to MARIE FAURÉ

Paris
17 October 1918

The events of these last few days have been so different from what we expected that one hesitates to believe them!... What changes, God in heaven! Can we finally breathe again? And think of other things than those which have been on our minds over the last four years?[21]

I am in the middle of examinations, and will be tied up with them until 11 December; another nightmare, though as nothing compared with everything else!... Cortot is in America. He got there on 9 October and will not be getting back until February. Only on his return will you be able to hear the *Fantaisie* for piano and orchestra. Since nobody could introduce it to the public as well as he, I want to wait until he has returned.[22]

And *Pénélope*?... When and where shall we hear it again? I'll say nothing about that, but it distresses me all the same! I've just had news from Amand's house. It is no more reassuring.

243★   GABRIEL FAURÉ to MARIE FAURÉ

Paris
Sunday, 20 October 1918

I have had a *Sunday* this morning! I had just got up, and was in the process of washing my face, when someone came to tell me that M. Carré, Director of the Opéra-Comique, was asking to be admitted despite the early hour. Perhaps you have read in the papers about Gheusi's[23] discharge and his replacement by Carré. This happened *last Wednesday*. So here we had, on Sunday morning, Carré in my hotel bedroom coming to ask me for *Pénélope*, with which he would like to inaugurate his new regime: with a *sensation*. Perfection itself; but we shall have to find two rare birds: Penelope and Ulysses, and there the difficulties begin... But it is not unpleasant for me to think that the Opéra-Comique needs *Pénélope*.

If you still plan on returning around the 26th, you will eventually get home at the end of the week. As for me, I think that from the health point of view it would be beneficial for me to remain at the hotel until the end of the examinations. Here I do not need to get up until eight o'clock, and I avoid, morning and evening, two rather worrying journeys bearing in mind this influenza season.

244★ GABRIEL FAURÉ to MARIE FAURÉ

Paris

24 October 1918

Amand's daughter came today. She told me that my brother had got progressively weaker since the attack, that he had been refusing all food these last weeks and that he had been carried off by a heart attack... Throughout these last few days I see going through my thoughts all my relations; my brother was, with our good Margot and myself, their last surviving relative.

You will see, I hope, *Pénélope* much sooner than I could have dared hope. Rousselière, that's the man who created the role of Ulysses at Monte Carlo so well, has been engaged, and Mme Croiza – *impossible* to find any other – will sing Penelope. Work will begin immediately. Carré would like to give my work around 15 December. Bearing in mind the present difficulties: influenza, etc., the usual delays, then Christmas and 1 January, it would be more realistic to think of 15 January. In the first few days of February I shall have to consider some sort of response over the concerts which I postponed last year in Bordeaux and Pau. From there I shall go on to Nice to do some work. I am therefore satisfied that the work on *Pénélope* will have to start as from now... I have asked Carré to try to re-engage the nurse I had at the Théatre Astruc, who looked just the part, so much vehemence and conviction!

Unfortunately Claire Croiza strained her voice during a performance of Massenet's *Werther* on 10 November, and for some rehearsals Fauré was obliged to substitute the young Germaine Lubin from the Opéra. As usual Fauré put a brave face on things: 'She is a young artist who will, I hope, save the situation'. In fact she became an acknowledged interpreter, and took the title role when it was revived at the Opéra in 1943. For the Opéra-Comique première on 20 January 1919 the original Penelope, Lucienne Bréval, appeared in the title role; Fauré appeared to be content. Sadly, as letter 250 makes clear, he was by this stage incapable of hearing music on a large scale.

Notes

1 *Le Jardin Clos*, op.106, published by Jacques Durand, to whom Fauré had transferred from Heugel in 1913.
2 Fernand Bourgeat, Conservatoire secretary.
3 Fauré's virtual namesake – without the accent – who published a book on the composer in 1945.
4 Saint-Saëns, now 81, had demanded the suppression of German music during the war, while his diatribes against the establishment of trade unions in France earned him a temporary ban on his own music.
5 Alfredo Casella (1883–1947), Italian composer who had been one of Fauré's composition students.
6 The under-secretary of State to the Académie des Beaux-Arts, and the son of one of Fauré's old friends from Rennes.
7 Claire Croiza (1882–1946), French mezzo-soprano who had a long and successful association with the Théatre de la Monnaie in Brussels. She had given the first

performance of *Le Jardin Clos* on 28 January 1915 with Fauré at a Casella Concert. (*See* letter 213.)

8 A key signature of five flats is to be understood.

9 The Twelfth, op.106b of which Louis Diémer (1843–1919) was the dedicatee. Diémer taught at the Conservatoire where his pupils included Cortot and Risler.

10 A poetic confession that with very few exceptions – this barcarolle and much of *Pénélope* are the obvious examples – Saint-Saëns preferred the music that Fauré had written in the nineteenth rather than the twentieth century.

11 Jacques Rouché (1862–1957), French administrator, appointed director of the Opéra in 1914, and elected to the Académie des Beaux Arts in 1924.

12 Max d'Ollone.

13 Elisabeth (1876–1965). She had studied the violin under Ysaÿe, Enesco and Thibaud, and was also a gifted painter and sculptress.

14 The French form of De Panne, a small town on the Belgian coast, two miles north of Adinkerke.

15 Raymond Poincaré (1860–1934). Queen Elisabeth had left the Royal Palace in Brussels on its conversion into a hospital, and was living at De Panne.

16 Saint-Saëns wrote two cello sonatas in 1872 and 1905; the former in C minor op.32 is certainly one of his finest chamber works.

17 After the abdication of Tsar Nicholas II in March 1917, internal strife within Russia was heightened with the return of the Bolshevik leaders from exile. Seizures of landowners' assets by the peasants led to various counter-measures by the Soviets, culminating in the formation of a Military Revolutionary Committee which was to order an uprising on 6 and 7 November 1917.

18 Chouchou, the Debussys' daughter, died the following year at the age of 14, due to improperly-treated diphtheria.

19 Small spa town, some 12 miles south of Foix, near the Spanish border.

20 Fauré's first intimation of the music for *Masques et Bergamasques*, produced at Monte Carlo in April 1919.

21 The end of the war was in sight, the armistice being signed on 11 November 1918.

22 In fact, Marguerite Hasselmans gave the first performance at Monte Carlo on 12 April 1919; Cortot performed it in Paris on 14 May.

23 Pierre Gheusi, who had been co-librettist with Victor Sardou of Saint-Saëns's opera *Les Barbares* (1901).

5
Indian summer
1919–24

245* GABRIEL FAURÉ to MARIE FAURÉ

Paris
22 January 1919

I am happy, happy to think that you were pleased. I was too. I did not want to appear. I have never liked that. I saw Carré *radiant* yesterday. Everybody has done their best.

Within a few days Fauré was off on a concert tour to south-western France, continuing on to Menton on the Riviera where he settled down to compose the overture to *Masques et Bergamasques*.

246 GABRIEL FAURÉ to MARIE FAURÉ

Toulouse
Monday 10 February 1919

It is fine but very cold, and I have decided against going to Foix; I am in a hurry to get settled in at Menton, in the warm... Yesterday, 20 programmes that they had me sign have brought in an extra 200 francs for the Red Cross at auction!

247 GABRIEL FAURÉ to MARIE FAURÉ

Hotel Balmoral
Menton
14 February 1919

Menton is charming: sea, rugged mountains and lush pastures. At the moment I have a little overture to write, then a gavotte and a minuet to add to the *Pavane*, the *Madrigal* and the *Clair de lune*, which will form a setting for a small scenario by Fauchois (very short judging from what he writes to me), which will be both sung and danced in the Monte Carlo theatre towards the end of March.

248★   GABRIEL FAURÉ to MARIE FAURÉ

Menton
12 March 1919

I have had nothing, or almost nothing, to do for Monte Carlo. This little tableau only joins together these older pieces (except a little overture), Pavane (sung and danced), *Madrigal, Clair de lune, Le plus doux chemin* (a song from the third volume, a volume which is still hardly known, for just as pianists play the same eight or ten pieces, so singers all sing the same songs), then *La Sicilienne* etc. It is therefore, as I told you, a re-working (enlarged by a small poem comprising three speaking characters) of what was done at Madeleine Lemaire's home a dozen or so years ago. Nevertheless, as everything has to be set up properly and in Monte Carlo they work in the *mornings* (rehearsing minor matters), I shall be going to get settled in there definitely at the Hôtel de la Terrasse as from Saturday.

249★   GABRIEL FAURÉ to MARIE FAURÉ

Monte Carlo
28 March 1919

If you know all about the performances of *Pénélope*, are you not surprised that the last two have been separated by a gap of ten complete days, and that the next, the one for the day after tomorrow, Sunday, will have been separated from the preceding one by a gap just as long, despite the undoubted crowds and success? That's how it is, alas! The result of these terrible subscription arrangements... When subscribers have heard a new work once, they no longer want to hear people talking about it! They want only to chew the cud, like calves, cows and oxen, over the same horrors: *Tosca, Manon, Vie de Bohème*! Novelties, they're only good for the general public on normal days! So much so that if the directors of the Opéra-Comique are not in favour of supporting a new work, they have this argument up their sleeve: the subscribers do not want it! I do not believe that this is the case with *Pénélope*. Therefore my dearest wish is to be played from time to time, even if it is only once a fortnight, but also to see my *Pénélope retained on the boards*... For the moment I am doing nothing! I am attempting to prepare some work for the holidays, but my brain absolutely refuses to be persuaded. It's all emptiness and nothingness. I believe that the mire into which events have dropped us accounts for this. I'm at least as fretful now as I was during the war!

250*   GABRIEL FAURÉ to MARIE FAURÉ

Monte Carlo
1 April 1919

I'm busy hanging on here so that people can keep themselves busy with my *little piece!* Gunsbourg's work has been hindered by artists' foibles or unforeseen difficulties. He has to get off the ground *this week*, two operas, an Italian *opera buffa*, and *Phryné*, by Saint-Saëns. I was hoping that on this occasion Saint-Saëns would be coming here, but unfortunately he isn't. And standing aside from all this, I continue to *search*, and still I find nothing!

I can confirm, even from what I remember long ago, that I have always had to put up with a defective circulation of the blood. All my life I have woken up feeling sluggish, and this would disappear only slowly. I was never any good at working in the morning, except for strictly routine jobs, choir-mastering, organ, etc. But for some years this has been the case for proportionally more and more time. It is for this reason that I forget my keys, my handkerchiefs.. that I *exasperate* you by not appearing to understand you *first time round, you* who are as wide-awake as a sparrow on its branch!

And I notice too that my ears are also more troublesome in the morning than later in the day. Undoubtedly the deplorable state of my hearing gets worse daily. I went to hear at the Opera here, on Saturday evening, a comic opera [*Falstaff*] by Verdi which I knew only from reading the score a long time ago. All I could hear were such discordantly intermingled sounds that I really thought I was going mad. This shows that with the spoken word being deaf is to hear very feebly, very indistinctly; but with music, I can confirm that I get an absurd phenomenon: low-sounding intervals get changed as they go lower, and the high-sounding intervals get changed as they get higher Can you imagine the result of this dichotomy? It is sheer hell. And this is exactly how, in the midst of these grotesque, distorted sounds, I hear *Pénélope!* What is least painful to hear is singing. But instrumental music is all chaos and pain...

I shall be lunching tomorrow at Roquebrune, at M. Hanotaux's[1] house.

251   GABRIEL FAURÉ to MARIE FAURÉ

Monte Carlo
Tuesday 8 April 1919

We have worked with great energy for 48 hours, at every moment throughout the day, and even in the evening. Perhaps this will produce a fairly pleasant tableau – spoken, sung, danced and pantomimed! (I do not know if the word exists.) I have just received a telegram from Albert Carré, telling me he will be arriving on Saturday. There will be only two performances: the first the day after tomorrow, Thursday, during the day; the second, Sunday. Carré will therefore be able to be present at the second. In short, I shall have achieved something down here, come what may. I have orchestrated an overture, composed and orchestrated three dances.

No, it is not the Midi which is bad for me, it's the accumulation of all these years...

252 GABRIEL FAURÉ to MARIE FAURÉ

Monte Carlo
Monday 14 April 1919

Carré is quite *entranced* by the tiny little piece. He will be coming soon to settle some details with me, as he wants to produce it *immediately* so that he can add it to the performances of *Pénélope* (performances have been suspended during a brief leave of absence granted to Rousselière).

This collection of the *Madrigal, Clair de lune, Pavane*, etc., all pieces with a somewhat evocative and melancholy – even somewhat nostalgic – character, I did fear that the *physical* performance might have harmed it. In fact it really is the impression given by Watteau, and of which Verlaine has given so good a definition:

> *Playing the lute and dancing and* quasi sorrowful *beneath their fantastic disguises!*
> (Jouant du luth et dansant et *quasi! Tristes* sous leurs déguisements fantasques)

Gunsbourg's production is a little heavy and too ostentatious. I think Carré will treat it more delicately. In any case, the two performances – there won't be any others – of Thursday and yesterday had a very great success. The little overture and dances which I composed and orchestrated here have been fun to do. Reynaldo Hahn says it is as if Mozart had *imitated* Fauré! It's a funny idea, but not in the least banal! The orchestra here is marvellous and, *not just because I was present*, many people applauded eagerly on hearing it. As far as I am able to judge, this is thanks to the conductor.

In the summer Fauré went to Annecy-le-Vieux, where he was able to stay in the villa rented by his friends, the Maillots. It was to Mme Fernand Maillot that Fauré was to dedicate his last and one of his greatest piano works, the Thirteenth Nocturne, written in 1921. Despite the natural beauty of his surroundings Fauré was to be troubled by the realization that his resignation from the Conservatoire in 1920 was inevitable due to his age and infirmity; worse, he had served for only 28 years which was two years too few for his entitlement to a pension.

253★ GABRIEL FAURÉ to MARIE FAURÉ

Annecy-le-Vieux
17 July 1919

I'm excellently set up here. The landscape is vast, and with a most relaxing air.

I spend my time saying to myself: make way for the young ones!

As long as my brain does not grow old all of a sudden, I must bless that fate which releases me from a very heavy burden of responsibility. I have never told you about the daily minor or major annoyances with which that institution is plagued! Dubois had enough of them after ten years, *I* shall have put up with them for fourteen. That is pretty good.

I am going to kick my heels for a few days, then get back to work. But I do not as yet have the slightest idea of what I shall do.

254* GABRIEL FAURÉ to MARIE FAURÉ

Annecy-le-Vieux
23 July 1919

What I cannot say to you too strongly is how much *I savour the prospect of my deliverance!*

I have sketched – very slowly, without straining myself – a song to a poem which M. Hanotaux had brought to my attention: just the thing to get me going.

255 GABRIEL FAURÉ to MARIE FAURÉ

Annecy-le-Vieux
2 August 1919

I am very well. I could be criticized for remaining *seated* to excess in my room. I am unable to walk across the fields and the town is too far away for me to saunter across there. I have finished one song, I am finishing a second and I have sketched a third.

256 CAMILLE CHEVILLARD to GABRIEL FAURÉ

Grand Hotel de Paris
Villard de Lans
5 August 1919

My dear Master and friend, I am not unaware of the fact that you have been one of the principal instigators of my nomination[2] and so I do thank you for this very much indeed.

We are in a beautiful region, but we are not greatly pleased with it here, since there is a shortage of good walks; apart from the superb one in the large gulleys which does deserve its reputation, there is not a great deal to do. Therefore we have decided to return to Chatou[3] soon. I think we shall return via Le Puy[4], which I have been wanting to see for a long time.

CAMILLE CHEVILLARD.

As my father used to say when talking about Beethoven, these are the phrases which one takes to the grave![5]

The next letter is to the French soprano Madeleine Grey (1897–1979), who was to make her début in Fauré's song cycle *Mirages*. She was later to become associated with the modern French repertory in general and Ravel's songs in particular.

257   GABRIEL FAURÉ to MADELEINE GREY

Hotel Savoie
Annecy-le-Vieux
Villa Dunand
10 August

Dear Friend, Your letter, so kind and so affectionate, was a lovely surprise and gave me great pleasure. I am happy to know you are experiencing such peace in that beautiful area near the mouth of the Rance [in Brittany]. Here, I myself also have before my eyes a wonderful, vast panorama, and as I am situated 500 metres above the level of the Vicomte, I enjoy pure, invigorating air, and I am working. I am even working at something you yourself will interpret particularly well. Unfortunately it is not a work with orchestra. But on this point, an idea has just occurred to me which you might refer to Chevillard – the old rascal! – but he is not such a rascal when he finds himself in the presence of a talented artist and a piece of music he appreciates. It concerns Gaîa's air in *Prométhée*, which Mlle Lapeyrette sang at the Opéra under Chevillard's direction. Write to him from me about this.

I have no news of Hettich.[6] I have informed him of my bitter disappointment concerning the recent nomination list for the Légion d'Honneur in which he did not appear, despite my ceaseless canvassing. The Lord knows, however, that he deserves that cross.

Beloved friend, beloved and fervent artist, *you will get there*, never fear. But, alas, look all around you and see how long everyone has *to toil* and *wait patiently*! – Give me your news once again, and accept these fond kisses from your old friend

GABRIEL FAURÉ
Now watch it, no *humbug*!

258★   GABRIEL FAURÉ to MARIE FAURÉ

Annecy-le-Vieux
14 August 1919

I wish you a happy birthday and I have just kissed you... I have just *completed* song number *three*. I am looking for a fourth after which I shall get on with another task but as yet I do not know what.

259 GABRIEL FAURÉ to MARIE FAURÉ

Annecy-le-Vieux
22 August 1919

I had already finished the *fourth* song three days ago. Since then, I have not started on anything.

The Conservatoire business is not sorting itself out too well. I mistakenly believed that I had been appointed Inspector of music schools in 1890, which would have allowed me to retire in 1920. My admission into the service of the Beaux Arts dates only from 1892. They are attempting to find a solution which will be in my best interests.

260 GABRIEL FAURÉ to MARIE FAURÉ

Annecy-le-Vieux
2 September 1919

I have begun a quintet.[7] But as yet there are only sketches. So for the moment I'm not speaking of it to anyone.

Robert Lortat[8] is in the area. He is grinding away at the *Fantaisie* for piano and orchestra which suits him *remarkably*. He will be playing it on 18 October (I believe the date is fixed) at the Société Nationale.

261 GABRIEL FAURÉ to MADELEINE GREY

[Paris]
Tuesday 11 November 1919

Dear friend, I have just written to Chevillard, (Villa Handel, Chatou, S[eine] et O[ise]) and I have urgently requested him to grant you an audition and ask you for Gaîa's air in the event of his considering it a possible item for one of the programmes this season. You can therefore write to him to confirm that you are entirely at his disposal.

Could you please keep free for me 24 November, a Monday, so you can come to sing at the Conservatoire at 4 my latest songs before the author of the poems and some four or five friends, one of whom is Jacques Durand? I do not know whether your copies are accurate regarding the latest corrections? Could you please let me know? Write to me on white paper. My sight has got worse since I have been unwell and I am not very good at reading your handwriting on dark blue paper! I am really longing to see you and hear you! Every affectionate wish,

GABRIEL FAURÉ
Rue des Vignes 32

262 GABRIEL FAURÉ to MADELEINE GREY

Conservatoire National de Musique et de Déclamation
Le Directeur   Rue des Vignes 32
                                                 [Paris]

[Tuesday 18 November 1919][9]

Dear friend, Chevillard writes to me (as yesterday) 'I await Mlle Grey today'. Tell me quickly what he said to you. – As for the *24th*, I have been asked to put it back two or three days. I have proposed Friday 28th. I shall let you know when I have got everything settled.

You are going to be asked by the Société Nationale to sing *Mirages* in a concert on 13 December (evening but I do not know if it is at the Conservatoire or the [Salle] Gaveau).

If you are able to accept, and this would give me great pleasure, you might also suggest the new songs by Georges Hüe.[10] No doubt it will be M. Samazeuilh[11] who will be writing to you. Speak to him about it.

So many things to do!!! I am really longing to go out, and I am really longing to kiss you all the more for your being so far away.

Your old friend
GABRIEL FAURÉ

In fact, the première of *Mirages* took place not on 13, but 27 December, due to Fauré's visit to Monte Carlo at the beginning of December. Philippe accompanied him. The precarious state of Fauré's health now required him to winter in the south on a regular basis. Nevertheless he returned to Paris for Christmas, and accompanied Madeleine Grey himself on 27 December. He evidently returned to Monte Carlo immediately, as the succeeding letters make clear.

263 GABRIEL FAURÉ to MADELEINE GREY

Monte Carlo
Hotel de la Terrasse
31 December 1919

Dear triumphant one! At the same time as your very kind letter – where very modestly you speak to me of the success of the composer and ignore the success of the interpreter – I received some more yesterday, which I fear I am unable to have you read! You have revealed, to people who are particularly difficult to satisfy, a voice, a talent and musical feeling remarkable *beyond all bounds* and quite unsuspected! Well done! I cannot tell you how happy I am to have been, for many of my friends, the occasion of so *dazzling* a revelation and how happy I am too to learn that people will hear you more than once this winter. – I know nothing any more definite yet regarding the Belgian tour, but I have high hopes that it will take place. I am mulling vaguely over a proposal to have you come to *Cannes* in *February*. What embarrasses me greatly is that I fear I am only able to guarantee your travel expenses! Certainly the trip is a beautiful one. You must tell me what you think about it.

I send you many many good wishes, and kiss you most warmly.

GABRIEL FAURÉ

Could your friend George[s] Hüe not be present at the rehearsal when you were singing Gaîa's air?

And how I regret my inability to be there myself. But I have been forbidden to return to Paris before March!

Though undated, letter 264 can be assigned to this period from the address and its contents. The letter demonstrates Fauré's wiliness in determining that prolonged absences from Paris did not necessarily result in ineffectiveness as Conservatoire Director, particularly if certain principles in which he believed were at stake.

Fauré's 'niece' Marie-Louise Boëllmann-Gigout was in fact the eldest child of Léon Boëllmann (1862–97) who had married the daughter of Gustave Lefèvre, son-in-law and successor of Louis Niedermeyer at the Ecole Niedermeyer. Eugène Gigout, one of Fauré's oldest friends and a fellow pupil of his at the Ecole, had also married a daughter of Louis Niedermeyer; he and his wife brought up Marie-Louise after the premature death of her parents. She called Gigout *parrain* as Fauré and Marianne Viardot had called Turgenev. Fauré often referred to Gigout as *parrain* when writing to her.

264* GABRIEL FAURÉ to EUGÈNE GIGOUT

Monte Carlo
Hotel de la Terrasse
[*c.* 1 January 1920]

My dear friend, I was most touched by your very affectionate thoughts and by the kind wishes of my dear niece. I embrace you both, proving to you my very real desire to be assured that you are enjoying the best possible health.

You will receive one of these days a visit from Lortat, who is in line to succeed Diémer, and you will give me a great and very personal pleasure by receiving him kindly and *voting* for him when the time – which is not far off, I believe – comes. Robert Lortat is not only a very brilliant virtuoso amongst those at present in the public eye, he is an *excellent musician*, who loves music and makes others love it. My absence from Paris makes my regret all the keener in that I am unable to vote for him when for so many reasons I find him superior to his rivals. But I am relying on my friends, and in particular on you, to counteract the inconvenience of my being so far away. You know what my prime objective has been in the Conservatoire: to obtain alongside virtuosity as much as possible in the way of musicianship. Lortat, among the numerous contenders (Risler is not putting himself forward) has by far the best qualifications for this result to be achieved. He applied last year, and applying again this year is Cortot. That gives you some idea of the confidence he inspires.

Once again, a Happy New Year, my dear friend, and every good wish to Marie-Louise and you.

Your old
GABRIEL FAURÉ

265 GABRIEL FAURÉ to MARIE FAURÉ

Monte Carlo
21 February 1920

On Monday I shall be at Tamaris,[12] where I hope I can find more peace than here. Refusing invitations on the pretext that I do not go out, people take advantage of this by coming to see me far too often; they really do come in droves...

What is driving me to distraction is the *future* as from *October*, despite assurances given me by the Director of the Beaux-Arts. I have no right to my pension until June 1922! To which he replies that the Council of State will use its good offices to ensure that it comes into effect at the end of 1920. But what proof do I have?

266* GABRIEL FAURÉ to MARIE FAURE

Tamaris
Grand Hotel
2 March 1920

As for *October*, I know nothing more... I am living on promises, assurances that *everything will be alright.*

I am extremely worried by it, and very upset. The only thing which is definite is that my directorship will finish on 30 September. They find me too old... and they have told me so quite categorically.

Give me a few details of your father's statue.[13] Do you know when it will be erected? Is there a final decision on this point?

Letter 267 is self-explanatory. Paul Léon was the Minister for Fine Arts, and it was due to his efforts that Fauré secured a pension, although in the end it was considerably smaller than he either expected or deserved.

267 PAUL LÉON to GABRIEL FAURÉ

Ministère de l'Instruction Publique et des Beaux Arts
Direction des Beaux Arts
Cabinet du Directeur

Republique Française
Palais Royal
25 March 1920

Dear Master and friend, I received your telegram yesterday telling me that you were bringing forward the date fixed for your return. I cannot stress too much the need for you not to undermine the felicitous results of this winter cure by travelling too soon. The inconveniences of a few months' absence are hardly worth a few days. You know only too well why it is necessary to consider the detrimental effects on the teaching of the Director's absence, but now the year is near its end, and control of the present administration up to the end of April would not present any troublesome consequences. I shall be most willing to approve up till then the appointment of the piano professor for the preparatory classes.

I hope to see you again after Easter completely restored to health. The summer starts to get rid of the symptoms of painful bronchitic attacks – and I am also relying on the distraction of the work which, I know, you have been courageously pursuing during these last months.

Please accept, dear master and friend, while looking forward to the great pleasure of seeing you again in our midst, my affectionate good wishes anew and my respectful devotion.

PAUL LÉON

I will not fail to support the application of M. le Bouchor for Montpellier. Your testimonial is, as far as I am concerned, the best recommendation possible.

Fauré suffered from an attack of fever towards the end of March, causing his general health to deteriorate still further. He decided to move on to Nice 'to await', as he said to his wife in a letter of 2 April, 'the real spring'. He returned to Paris towards the end of April, learning that he had been honoured further by the award of Grand Officier of the Légion d'Honneur. Doubtless this was an attempt to soften the blow caused by the inexorable need for his resignation, to say nothing of the vexatious correspondence necessitated by his pension prospects. For his summer retreat in 1920 Fauré chose Veyrier-du-Lac near Menthon-Saint-Bernard in the Haute Savoie. The knowledge that his administrative duties were almost at an end spurred on the composition of the second quintet, whose two central movements as well as half of the first were completed about 20 August. Fauré was visited by his sons and daughter-in-law during the summer. With Philippe he paid a visit to Nyon, the birthplace of his old teacher, Louis Niedermeyer.

268★ GABRIEL FAURÉ to MARIE-LOUISE BOËLLMANN

Veyrier-du-Lac
Haute Savoie
3 August 1920

Dear sweet niece, From my windows I can see everything over there, opposite and behind me, from where you could once see Veyrier-du-Lac. So it is in this lovely spot that I am enjoying my taste of freedom, now finally attained. For 50 years I have always been *on time* for one thing or another. So I will be able to do only what pleases me! But I hope uncle will not follow my example, for his pupils in the organ class need him. Also his departure would please other people rather too much;

I will not mention them by name but you can guess who they are!

If you are both remaining in Paris – and I would like you to for the whole holiday – climb up to Rue des Vignes from time to time. You know how much you and your uncle are always very welcome there!

Give me your news and let your little uncle kiss you most tenderly

GABRIEL FAURÉ

269 GABRIEL FAURÉ to MARIE FAURÉ

Veyrier-du-Lac
23 August 1920

My work is progressing. I have the *second* and *third* movements of the quintet ready, and I am in the middle of the first. The prospect of just having composition to keep me busy is infinitely pleasurable to me. But in this orderly state of mind, as Saint-Saëns says, difficulties are in no way ironed out with age! Nothing is a bed of roses!

Fauré's successor as Director of the Paris Conservatoire was Henri Rabaud (1873–1949). He was already famous for his dramatic works and as a conductor at both the Opéra and the Opéra-Comique. Rabaud held the post until 1941, and was succeeded by Claude Delvincourt (1888–1954).

270 HENRI RABAUD to GABRIEL FAURÉ

[Paris]
1 September 1920

My dear Master and friend, It is not without emotion that I read the two orders, one of which nominates you as Grand Officier of the Légion d'Honneur and honorary Director of the Conservatoire – and the other which calls on me to succeed you. On the first, I offer you my congratulations from the depths of my heart – and on the second, I do not forget, in reading it, that it is thanks to your kindly influence that this great honour has been offered to me by the Minister.

You can be assured, my dear Master, that I shall make every effort to walk as well as I can along the path you have trod, and that I shall have constantly in my mind first of all your example, and then the notion that each hour spent by me in the Conservatoire is henceforth for you an hour of leisure, permitting you to labour at those fine works which all your admirers await.

Include me among them, my dear Master, and also among those of your friends who have for you the most loyal affection.

HENRI RABAUD

In September Fauré, accompanied by Robert Lortat and his wife, visited Venice for a month; they stayed at the Hôtel Savoie et Iolanda.

271★ GABRIEL FAURÉ to MARIE FAURÉ

Venice
10 September 1920

So here I am, well set-up and refreshed by a journey which was not tiring, since I did it in stages. Here the weather is very fine, very hot. Fortunately the Adriatic breezes take care of all that.

I received your first despatch at the same time as a flood of letters and telegrams sent on by the Conservatoire. How shall I ever get round to replying! It's terrible! As far as postcards are concerned, brief replies. But there are so many proper letters, so many touching tributes from people whom I had forgotten or from people who might well have forgotten me.

272 GABRIEL FAURÉ to MARIE FAURÉ

Venice
16 September 1920

This morning the Director of the Conservatoire [here] came to offer me, most kindly, a visit to this establishment, which has been set up in one of the most vast, most imposing, most beautiful palaces of this extraordinary city. I am not familiar with the standard of teaching which the pupils receive there; but if the courtyards, staircases, ceilings, doors, all that profusion of ancient art which surrounds them, do not make artists out of them then they must be savages! The whole house is an enchantment...

I will not say that there is nothing ugly here, I will say that there is nothing here which is not beautiful, and of a beauty which is quite thrilling. And then, one is unable not to be continually moved by the thought that these *unchanging* settings possessed so much that is glorious and powerful and have witnessed the flowering of so many masterpieces!

Now that he was freed from his administrative duties Fauré was able to leave Paris whenever he wished, and in January 1921 he travelled south to Nice, where he completed the finale of the Second Piano Quintet at the beginning of February.

273★ GABRIEL FAURÉ to MARIE-LOUISE BOËLLMANN

Nice
22 January 1921

What a delightful Christmas! The container is lovely and the contents delicious, and I am smoking the contents while admiring the container!

How much pleasure you have given your old uncle and how he thanks you with all his heart.

How are you both? Here I am warming myself in the beautiful and beneficial rays of a sun which brightens my bedroom from eight o'clock in the morning. And in this warmth I am working a great deal and enjoying it. I do thank you once again, dear Marie-Louise, I kiss you and I send uncle my tenderest good wishes.

GABRIEL FAURÉ
Villa Mercèdes, Avenue Cernuschi, Le Ray, Nice

274* GABRIEL FAURÉ to EUGÈNE GIGOUT

Villa Mercedes
Avenue Cernuschi, Le Ray,
Nice
1 February 1921

My dear friend, Would you be able to send me here, as soon as you possibly can, a song by Niedermeyer entitled *Le 5 Mai*. You would do me a very big favour. But if the song is in a volume, and you feel you are unable to part with it, will you ask Marie-Louise from me to copy the words from it and send them to me?

Every good wish to you both, and please forgive this interruption.

GABRIEL FAURÉ

Having completed the Second Quintet in February, Fauré accepted a commission to compose a piece to commemorate the centenary of the death of Napoleon. He wrote it in short score, the arrangement for wind band being made by Guillaume Balay who conducted its première by the Garde Républicaine on 5 May 1921. Fauré later reworked this *Chant Funéraire* to form the noble slow movement of the Second Cello Sonata, op.117, which was completed in November.

275* GABRIEL FAURÉ to MARIE-LOUISE BOËLLMANN

Nice
26 February 1921

My dear Marie-Louise, You are right to describe me as a very ungrateful little-great-uncle! I have not yet thanked you for your parcel! I have to say, as my excuse, that I have been working tremendously, passionately, helped by the sunshine which gives me warmth through the window panes. I have completed my quintet, I have written a thirteenth barcarolle (not easy to play!) and I am in the throes of another composition. So you will forgive me, won't you?

I kiss and entrust you with many, many good wishes for uncle.

GABRIEL FAURÉ

And the lovely box of cigarettes is faithfully keeping me company.

276   GABRIEL FAURÉ to MARIE FAURÉ

Nice
4 March 1921

My composition for Napoleon is completed. I shall be asking the music director of the Garde Républicaine to arrange it for military band, since it is in that version that it will be performed at the Invalides on 5 May. That job is of a rather specialized kind, for which I do not have the training; it would take me an enormous amount of time, and in all probability I should not be successful.

There is the matter of the resumption of *Pénélope* for the beginning of April, when the tenor Fontaine is back in Paris. At the moment he is singing here, in the casino.

The next letter introduces a number of names.
Pierre de Bréville (1861–1949) was particularly famous for his songs and piano pieces. He had taught at the Schola Cantorum and the Conservatoire, and was a very active committee member in the Société Nationale.
    Gaston Poulet (1892–1974) was a French violinist and conductor. He founded his own quartet in 1912, set up a series of concerts which bore his name in 1927, directed the Bordeaux Conservatoire from 1932 to 1944, and during the 1939–45 war conducted the Concerts Colonne in Paris. He gave the first performance of Debussy's Violin Sonata with the composer in 1917.
    Marcel Labey (1875–1968) was a composer whose works include an opera, four symphonies and piano pieces, but he was best known as an administrator and conductor.
    André Tourret, Maurice Vieux and Gérard Hekking, along with Victor Gentil and Robert Lortat, gave the first performance of the Second Piano Quintet on 21 May at the Société Nationale. Vieux and Hekking were also to participate in the posthumous première of Fauré's String Quartet, op.121 in 1925.

277   GABRIEL FAURÉ to PIERRE DE BRÉVILLE

Villa Mercèdes
Avenue Cernuschi, Le Ray,
Nice
7 March 1921

My dear friend, I omitted to speak to you in my last letter of the likely date of performance of my second quintet at the Nationale.

When do you think it might take place, and with which quartet? I have kindly been permitted a hearing of the first three movements by the Poulet Quartet, but this would in no way inconvenience me unless he (Poulet) were to propose a number, as on a postmark, like the quartet you used recently and, I believe, have engaged for the forthcoming performance. As for the performance, I believe it might take place, *using the proofs*, towards the end of May.

I have seen your latest programmes as they've been going along. I think with sadness of the time it must take you, you and Labbey [*sic*], while Samazeuilh perhaps perpetrates 'a Summer Evening on the large river of Love' or the 'Sleep of the Guardian of the Night'.

Have you been satisfied with Tourret? His quartet includes a viola, Vieu[x], and a cellist Gérard Hekking, whom I appreciate enormously. In other words I do not think much of the Poulet Quartet. I only wish the whole business could be sorted out. A business contract for the season with Tourret would be sufficient to disentangle myself regarding the other quartet. Many kind regards, my best wishes for your health and work, from your very affectionately devoted

GABRIEL FAURÉ

278   GABRIEL FAURÉ to MARIE FAURÉ

Nice
9 March 1921

They are performing my *Requiem* at Cannes (in the church) on the Monday of Holy Week (21 March), but with restricted forces for the orchestra. All the same I shall go to hear it.

279   GABRIEL FAURÉ to MARIE FAURÉ

Nice
Saturday 19 March 1921

Here I am, embarked upon a *second* sonata for cello and piano some three or four days ago. Unfortunately, the last week will be encumbered with farewells from all kinds of people; my work will suffer because of it. On Monday I shall be going to Cannes for my *Requiem*; as for the other days, I see lunches springing up in the town! My ears are for ever getting worse, and my sight gets more and more dim! Ah! Old age!

280   GABRIEL FAURÉ to MARIE FAURÉ

Nice
Tuesday 22 March 1921

This Cannes *Requiem* did not go badly, the vocal side anyway. The instruments were insufficient in number. They settled me in an armchair, next to the lady-in-waiting of the Queen of Portugal and quite near the King,[14] a very young man with a very pleasant appearance, who spoke to me of what he had just heard, visibly moved and in the clearest and simplest language. He reminded me that I had been presented to him at the Elysée eight years ago. He really has a good memory!

I am happy at having begun a work which I can get on with at the Rue des Vignes.

The summer of 1921 was spent in the Ariège, at Ax-les-Thermes, where work continued on the Second Cello Sonata.

281   GABRIEL FAURÉ to MARIE FAURÉ

Ax-les-Thermes
17 July 1921

On the occasion of the prize-giving at the Conservatoire, Paul Léon spoke about me, from what Bourgeat passes on, 'about the 15 years of distinguished reputation which the genius, the talent, the charm of the great Gabriel Fauré had given to the Conservatoire'. And there was, says Bourgeat again, for several minutes, a never-ending and enthusiastic acclamation on the part of the professors, students and parents. The salvoes were repeated to such an extent that Paul Léon, smiling, could no longer continue! This gives me pleasure.

282   GABRIEL FAURÉ to MARIE FAURÉ

Ax-les-Thermes
6 September 1921

It's a small world! I am having great fun reading a book which traces the life of someone called Vadier, a distinguished member of the National Convention, deputy of Pamiers to the general Sûreté in the [Reign of] Terror, who had been baptised *one hundred years* before me over the same baptismal fonts in the Camp church, in Pamiers, and who died in exile in Brussels. But here is the spicy bit: amongst the papers from the end of his life is an epithalamium in verse dedicated to Mme Rude.[15] It is dated 1825. Moreover, this man had been frightening in the way he exerted his powers of authority. But if he and those like him had not been so terrible, would they have been successful in quelling a foreign invasion whose aim was rather to appropriate France than to reestablish the monarchy, and all the plots, all the internal revolts? They were abominable human beings, but they were convinced of their ideals, honourable for the most part, and useful for the new France.

What bores me is the fact that after a first month which has been ideal both for my health and my work, for the last month I have only been vegetating!

Letter 283 refers to one of two articles Fauré was writing for the *Revue Musicale*: an account of early days at the Ecole Niedermeyer which appeared the following October. This issue was also an act of homage to Fauré himself, since it included several pieces written on the musical spelling of Fauré's name by some of his former pupils.

283★ GABRIEL FAURÉ to EUGÈNE GIGOUT

32 Rue des Vignes
[Paris]
6 November 1921

My dear friend, Would you be able to tell me, if you were in a position to do so, under what conditions the pupils of the school in our young days participated in the offices at St Louis d'Antin and got to hear there Palestrina, Vittoria [*sic*], etc. etc? Was it not because this music used to annoy the clergy and the faithful of the parish that our collaboration at the offices came to an end?

Concerning old music I am preparing a little article and I have got to where I am talking about the school; and the information I am asking you for would be most useful for me.

My wife, who would really love to see Marie-Louise again, tells me to ask you if she has returned.

Both of us send you many, many best wishes.

Your old
GABRIEL FAURÉ

I have been unwell but I am now much better.

During the autumn Fauré completed the Second Cello Sonata and composed his last song cycle *L'Horizon Chimérique* op.118, consisting of four poems by Jean de la Ville de Mirmont (1886–1914). Fauré left Paris before Christmas for Nice, and on his arrival set to work on what was to be his thirteenth and last Nocturne in B Minor op.119. He completed it in ten days and dedicated it to Mme Fernand Maillot; it received its first performance in April 1922 by Blanche Selva (1884–1942). She had studied at the Paris Conservatoire, and at the Schola Cantorum under d'Indy, and achieved particular fame for her performances of modern French piano music.

Saint-Saëns died at the age of 86, while on holiday in Algiers, on 16 December 1921. Fauré was to commemorate his former teacher in a further article for the *Revue Musicale* in 1922.

284 GABRIEL FAURÉ to MARIE FAURÉ

Hôtel d'Europe
Nice
24 December 1921

As from the day before yesterday, Thursday, I have taken up once more the nocturne I began in Paris. I should like to make considerable progress with it before I get on with the article on Saint-Saëns, which will not be easy to do, given the more *avant-garde* nature of the *Revue Musicale*. I am thinking about it a great deal.

285★   GABRIEL FAURÉ to MARIE FAURÉ

Nice
2 January 1922

You made me very happy when you wrote to me that you kissed my manuscript paper, for on the 31st, in the evening, *I completed the Thirteenth Nocturne.*

As from yesterday I have been glued to my article on Saint-Saëns. I am attending to it as best I can, but I must try to avoid saying yet again everything which has been said in profusion these last few days, and this is not easy! The weather is ridiculously fine here. Nevertheless I go out very little and not for long. Just to go and have coffee outside after lunch.

286   GABRIEL FAURÉ to MARIE FAURÉ

Nice
20 January 1922

I haven't *hit upon it* yet! Durand is begging me to do a trio for piano, violin and cello. I shall think about it. I have been, it is true, somewhat distracted these last few days by the presence of Cortot, who has come to give a concert here: Schumann, Saint-Saëns, Liszt, Fauré.

Two days ago they entertained me at the Cercle Artistique, of which I have been elected Honorary President! A wonderful banquet – *exquisite* – and a lovely meeting.

287★   GABRIEL FAURÉ to MARIE FAURÉ

Nice
25 January 1922

M. Maillot has had an idea for a concert, which I wanted to keep to myself, before telling you about it, until it was a little less embryonic. There is going to be a concert, which would be held in the Sorbonne, in the second half of *May* and which would bring together my best interpreters, instrumentalists and singers. The intention is that this concert would be a sort of act of homage, and, at the same time, could bring in a very large financial return. This fine chap is putting his heart and soul into it, and all his energies.

Later Fauré left his hotel and went to stay in the Villa Frya on the Promenade des Anglais. This was the home of two friends, M. and Mme Grémy, who looked after his every comfort. Little concerts were organised for Fauré by his hosts; perhaps he was too tactful to tell them that by this stage such concerts would have been intolerably cacophonous to him.

288 GABRIEL FAURÉ to MARIE FAURÉ

Nice
4 March 1922

I am ashamed to confess that I am leading the life of a caretaker. I do nothing, and as yet have not discovered two musical notes worthy to be written since I got to Nice. Am I completely written out? Could this climate be a drain on me to this extent? I spend days in the house without the slightest wish to go out or work, I drift along in a smug and stupid way, though not without worrying about this weariness in my brain.

Our fine M. Maillot is going to endless trouble to organize this concert in my honour, which he plans for the month of May. He writes to me that it might take place at the Opéra-Comique on 6 May. There would be one part with absolute music, the orchestra of the Conservatoire Concerts Society and soloists such as Cortot, Capet, Lortat, Mme Croiza, etc., then the second act of *Pénélope*. He has set up an honorary committee consisting of the President of the Republic,[16] Barthou,[17] Léon Bérard,[18] Marshal Lyautey[19] and even more! I ask myself whether he is not dreaming! The Conservatoire pupils would sing the *Cantique de Racine*, one of my earliest works. It dates from the Ecole Niedermeyer.

289 GABRIEL FAURÉ to MARIE FAURÉ

Nice
17 March 1922

Mme Cortot writes that tomorrow evening in Brussels, her husband will play for Queen Elisabeth in her palace the sonata which I dedicated to her in 1917. This ill-fated sonata is still only very very rarely played! What a lot of time is needed for music to become known! Recently I was congratulated on my Ballade in the belief that it was one of my most recent works. Now it dates from 1881 and was given its first performance in the Salle Pleyel in 1885, *37 years* ago! And it's actually about this Ballade that a critic has written that I was *imitating* Debussy in a sensitive manner! Debussy in 1881 was 18! I don't think he could already have been imitated at that age!

290★ GABRIEL FAURÉ to MARIE FAURÉ

Nice
Wednesday 19 April 1922

I was wondering, yesterday evening, if you have been listening to *Pénélope*? I see that there is to be a performance next Saturday as well. From various quarters people have been talking to me and eulogizing over the first night, and I have just received a telegram telling me that last night was excellent.

Alas! The anguish of seeing, and at the same time hearing only bits of the singing; and of nothing, or very nearly so, from the orchestra being able to get through to me. Can you imagine that with my poor ears there are times when I should be unable to tell *whereabouts I was in the music* . . . I have *never played, neither for myself nor for anyone else*, a single note of *Pénélope* since its inception, which was in Lausanne, in 1907, if I am not mistaken. All this because even at that time my hearing was faulty, and when my fingers were hitting certain notes, it was *other notes* which *I heard*! It was Cortot who arranged for my score to be heard by Lucienne Bréval in Lugano, then by Gunsbourg, and then by Carré and Heugel! I doubt that any of my colleagues have experienced the latter pleasure!

My hosts strenuously object to my being allowed to go out. So I shall remain here for eight or ten days more, after which I shall return *straight through* to Paris.

The special number of the *Revue Musicale* to which Fauré refers in the next letter was to appear on 1 October 1922. Notwithstanding his physical infirmities, Fauré's letter shows that he was taking great care and trouble over his own contribution to this issue.

291★   GABRIEL FAURÉ to MARIE-LOUISE BOËLLMANN

[Paris]
6 May 1922

Dear Marie-Louise, The *Revue*, in which my little article appeared on Saint-Saëns, is preparing, with the co-operation of some of my former pupils, a number which will be devoted to me. For the said number I have been asked to write a few pages on a topic of my own choice. I should like *to tell the story*, as far as I possibly can, of the Ecole Niedermeyer. Will you be a sweetheart of a little niece and ask uncle to lend me (if he has them) the book for which Saint-Saëns wrote a preface, and the book by *Alfred* Niedermeyer, plus all the information he could conceivably possess on the subject of the school's foundation and the way it worked? And then bring me all that? – How happy you would make me! They are spurring me on for the article and I feel I am in an *inflammable* state that beggars description!!

Every affectionate good wish to uncle and you.
GABRIEL FAURÉ

Among other things I remember that there was a little polemic with our great Widor and uncle, I think, concerning Bach and organ registration which Widor, *alone*, practised and introduced into France! Does uncle remember this? . . .

Louis Aguettant, author of a book on Fauré published in 1924, sent Fauré the next letter, typical of many he received in June 1922. The Fauré Festival, an act of homage which gave Fauré enormous pleasure, took place at the

Sorbonne in June. In addition to the performers mentioned in Fauré's letter of 4 March, Charles Panzéra gave a second performance of the cycle *L'Horizon Chimérique* which, like the Second Cello Sonata, had had its première at the Société Nationale on 13 May. The evening, which was indeed attended by the President of France, marked the culmination of Fauré's public acclamations.

292   LOUIS AGUETTANT to GABRIEL FAURÉ

Lyons
20 June 1922

Dear Master, Distance prevents me from taking part in the celebration of national homage which this evening is an expression of the universal acclaim given to your work by the musicians of France – at a time when they are meeting together in your midst – in any event, a word can indicate to you my growing enthusiasm for your genius, which never ceases to revitalize itself in the process of transcendence. The Second Sonata for piano and violin, the marvellous Second Quintet, *La nymphée*,[20] le *Jardin nocturne* and *La Danseuse*[21] after *La Chanson d'Eve*, what prodigious treasures of an inexhaustible spring! And how can I express my gratitude to the Master, so universally loved, who charms my finest hours?

My young wife, 'A Fauréan', and as much one as I am myself (*La Bonne Chanson* was the music of our betrothal), would not forgive me if I did not say it here. We live in your work; it is the very breath of our happiness. Allow me therefore, dear Master, to offer you here, with our heartiest and very own good wishes, this token of affectionate and respectful admiration.

L. AGUETTANT M. AGUETTANT
39 Rue des Farges (Lyons)

The Spanish cellist Pablo Casals (1876–1973) was only one of many young performers who were increasingly attracted to the music of Fauré, and especially the late chamber works.

293   PABLO CASALS to GABRIEL FAURÉ

Hotel Majestic
Avenue Kléber
Place de l'Etoile
Paris
4 July 1922

My dear Master and friend, I am really touched by your visit, which I unfortunately missed, and by your words of affection – I cannot tell you how much the homage you were given has filled me with joy – it was the long-overdue outpouring of a crowd of people who have benefited so much from your genius, and who understand you and love you – I feel happy for the privilege of having contributed to this moving and unique demonstration.[22]

Would you be kind enough to send me your two sonatas for cello, which I do not yet know! I am setting off again for London but I shall be returning to Paris, Hôtel Majestic, in a few days.

Yours affectionately, and with deep admiration.

PABLO CASALS

That summer Fauré went to Argèles in the Pyrenees – not too far away from Cauterets where he had gone to take the waters in 1877 while engaged to Marianne Viardot. He remained at the Hôtel de France for a month, and then continued to Annecy-le-Vieux where he again stayed with the Maillots.

294   GABRIEL FAURÉ to MARIE FAURÉ

Argèles
14 July, 1922

What a mysterious find Reynaldo Hahn has made of a manuscript copy of *Le Papillon et la Fleur*! He does not tell me how or where he found it but he did think, in sending it to me, that it would awaken very old memories. It is, in effect, my very first song, composed in the dining-hall of the school, among the smells from the kitchen ... and my first interpreter was Saint-Saëns. It was also in connection with this first song that my name found itself in Victor Hugo's correspondence over the permission which was needed before it could be published! What an encounter between minor and major personalities, between things great and small! The peerless poet concerned with the most miniscule composer's rights!

295   GABRIEL FAURÉ to MARIE FAURÉ

Annecy-le-Vieux
20 August 1922

I have still not got back to music, but I am busy with an article on the Ecole Niedermeyer (the one long ago), for the *Revue Musicale*'s October issue. I am well, but I do feel the heaviness of age weighing upon me. This weariness gets distressingly worse. There's nothing you can do!

296   GABRIEL FAURÉ to MARIE FAURÉ

Annecy-le-Vieux
26 September 1922

I have undertaken a trio for clarinet (or violin), cello and piano. I began the trio here a month ago, and a large-scale movement is *finished*. My misfortune is that I am unable to work for long periods of time. My worst ailment is a *perpetual tiredness*.

The 'large-scale movement' of the trio was the central Andantino. Unusually, Fauré remained in Paris during the winter of 1922–3, working on the two outer movements of the trio.

From this time onwards, Fauré became physically weaker and increasingly prone to attacks of bronchitis and breathlessness. His creative faculties alone remained unimpaired. After the successful première of the Piano Trio on 12 May 1923 at the Société Nationale, one further major work remained to be written.

Fauré must have been proud to receive letter 297, surely one of the most remarkable documents ever sent by a monarch to a composer.

297 QUEEN ELISABETH OF THE BELGIANS to GABRIEL FAURÉ

Brussels
24 June 1923

Dear Master, I have heard your fine trio which has moved me deeply. This work is so great and full of the charm of poetry and I was enveloped by that inexpressible exaltation which emanates from your compositions.

How I regretted that you were not by my side at this time!

The artists who interpreted your Trio so well played 'my sonata' to me again – its dedication by the great, beloved Master is a precious thing to me.

Believe me,

Your affectionate
ELISABETH

The Société Nationale performance of the Piano Trio was followed by another one in Paris on 29 June in the famous collaboration of Alfred Cortot, Jacques Thibaud and Pablo Casals. This combination of virtuosi was to become a 'trio institution' over the years. Soon after this performance Fauré spent the remainder of the summer with the Maillots at Annecy-le-Vieux. Working almost in secret, he finally confided to his wife on 9 September that he had begun a string quartet. It was fated to be his swansong.

298★ GABRIEL FAURÉ to MARIE FAURÉ

Annecy-le-Vieux
3 July 1923

I am happy over what you wrote to me about the trio. I hope you will have the opportunity to hear it again next winter; alas! it will not be by last Friday's wonderful interpreters!

What I really want is to be able to continue working. Here my intellectual capabilities remain as undistinguished as my physical strength, and this grieves me deeply.

299★   GABRIEL FAURÉ to MARIE FAURÉ

Annecy-le-Vieux
6 August 1923

I do not think I have ever seen nature looking so beautiful, so resplendent.
In the evening, around six o'clock, there is here a lighting effect, which
spreads over an immense area and is deeply moving in its beauty. Why
is it necessary to live in cities, in noise and for a good third of the year
in darkness!

As I wrote to you, they are preparing in Annecy, for a performance
to be given in Annecy-le-Vieux on the 25th, some excerpts (almost all)
of my *Requiem*. But I do not have to concern myself with it. All the
tiredness has left my old self! How is Mab?[23]

300   GABRIEL FAURÉ to MARIE FAURÉ

Annecy-le-Vieux
26 August 1923

Philippe came yesterday to hear the *Requiem* and he was surprised, as I
was myself, at the results they got. Coming out of the church I had my
little ovation, including the little country girl who offered me a
bouquet... just as they do for M. Poincaré!

In the evening, inside the house, a cold supper for 58 people(!), garden
illuminated, fireworks and dancing until two o'clock in the morning.
But I was in my bed at half past ten, and all that *branle* dancing from
down below did not disturb my sleep: such are the advantages of deafness!

301★   GABRIEL FAURÉ to MARIE FAURÉ

Annecy-le-Vieux
9 September 1923

I have undertaken a quartet for strings, without *piano*. This is a genre
which Beethoven in particular made famous, and causes all those who
are not Beethoven to be *terrified* of it! Saint-Saëns was always afraid,
and only attempted it towards the end of his life. He did not succeed
there as he did in other kinds of composition.[24] So you can well imagine
I am frightened too. I have spoken of this to no one. I shall say nothing
about it as long as I am nowhere near my objective: the end. When I
am asked: 'Are you working?' I reply shamelessly 'No!' So keep this to
yourself.

At the moment we are having those marvellous autumn days – so
heavenly because of the warmth, nature's colours, and the attractiveness
of everything one sees.

302★ GABRIEL FAURÉ to MARIE FAURÉ

Annecy-le-Vieux
13 September 1923

Yesterday evening I put the *full stop* to the first movement of the quartet which I spoke to you about in my last letter.[25] This done, and with all the *fuss* over my impending departure, I feel certain that I shall not carry on with it until I have settled down with you, *rue des Vignes*.

On his return to Paris, Fauré wrote most of the first movement of the quartet, using material from his early unpublished Violin Concerto of some 45 years before. For much of the winter and spring he was confined to bed owing to the weakness of his legs. Despite his increasing infirmity Fauré intended to travel to the south for the summer as usual. Three days before his departure he wrote a letter of condolence to the son of Théodore Dubois, who had died on 11 June. The scandal over the 'Affaire Ravel' which had occasioned Dubois's resignation from the directorship of the Conservatoire and Fauré's appointment as his replacement in 1905, along with a professional rivalry from 1870–1905, had ensured that their earlier friendship had cooled considerably.

303 GABRIEL FAURÉ to M. DUBOIS

17 June 1924

Dear M. Dubois, The very indifferent state of my health has not permitted me as yet to tell you how much I have been affected by your bereavement. Please forgive me, and rest assured that I shall retain most faithfully the memory of your dear father whom I loved and admired.

Your very devoted
GABRIEL FAURÉ

Fauré, accompanied by Philippe, left Paris on 20 June; their first destination was Divonne-les-Bains, where Fauré once again returned to the string quartet, the last movement of which was still to be written. Eventually he made a start on it. On 24 July Fernand Maillot came to fetch him for the short trip by car to Annecy-le-Vieux for Fauré's last stay there. He managed to complete the quartet at Annecy on 11 September.

304 GABRIEL FAURÉ to MARIE FAURÉ

Divonne-les-Bains
23 June 1924

The hotel is so vast and so comfortable that I can exercise my feeble legs with small walks in the very wide, long corridors. If I were able to begin a little bit of work again, I should be delighted to spend three or four weeks here in the wonderful air, in the healthy-looking green of the trees and fields, and in this calmness – *unimaginable* calmness!

305   GABRIEL FAURÉ to MARIE FAURÉ

Divonne
Friday 18 July 1924

I shall leave for Annecy next Thursday. My room with terrace was secured a long time ago for the 24th, and as the hotel is absolutely full not only were they unable to give me equivalent accommodation, but they had nothing even that was more or less pleasant. I am sorry about this . . .

I have *finally begun to work again*, but *I hardly dare* say it!

306   GABRIEL FAURÉ to MARIE FAURÉ

Annecy-le-Vieux
Friday 25 July 1924

My little transfer yesterday was accomplished very well. M. Maillot's car is an excellent vehicle, very smooth; the roads are excellent and, in two and a quarter hours, we went from Divonne to Annecy via Geneva.

I am happy at being able to take up the reins again after the inactivity of the whole of last winter.

307   GABRIEL FAURÉ to MARIE FAURÉ

Annecy-le-Vieux
3 August 1924

I am working regularly, but I can progress only extremely slowly. And then my time, these last few days, has been poisoned by the wretched bind of having letters to write. This is not the last of them.

308★   GABRIEL FAURÉ to MARIE FAURÉ

Annecy-le-Vieux
13 August 1924

I wish you a happy birthday. Days go by. In two days we shall be on the final stretch. Up to now I have not suffered any indisposition, not even the slightest, and I am working a little each day, something which did not happen during the entire winter in Paris.

309   GABRIEL FAURÉ to MARIE FAURÉ

Annecy-le-Vieux
9 September 1924

Time goes quickly. I shall return to Paris on Monday 29 September, that is to say in *three weeks*. As for my work, I can say that it is reaching its conclusion. With the movement I am finishing off, this quartet would be self-sufficient; it would be like my trio in three movements; but as I am not in a hurry to introduce it to the public, perhaps I shall insert a fourth movement somewhere. I am thinking about it, but I have not yet decided. The main thing is that, such as it is, it is sufficient.

310 GABRIEL FAURÉ to MARIE FAURÉ

Annecy-le-Vieux
12 September 1924

I finished that finale yesterday evening. So therefore the quartet is completed, unless I decide to have a little fourth movement which might have a place between the first and second. But since it is in no way a necessity I shall not tire myself by searching for it, at least not at the moment.

During September Fauré suffered a serious attack of broncho-pneumonia and was forced to take to his bed permanently. It was evidently impossible for him to return to Paris on 29 September, though in an effort to lessen his wife's anxiety the next letters shows a somewhat deceitful optimism as to the true state of his health.

311* GABRIEL FAURÉ to MARIE FAURÉ

Annecy-le-Vieux
8 October 1924

As far as I am concerned, my health improves from hour to hour. Only my legs remain extremely weak. And then there is the *terrible deterioration of my eyesight*! I am really longing to see you again ... I am not speaking to you about Mab! I think that from this poor old body you will hardly get anything other than fatigue and sorrow. For all living things this sorrowful time, ever present, complicates their existence. Only the young can laugh a little. And again!

During his final days at Annecy, Emmanuel and Philippe came to join their father. Fauré's last letter, the most touching and sympathetic he ever wrote to his wife, is a shrewd appraisal of the many drawbacks and advantages which Marie Fauré had experienced as the wife of a composer who, unfortunately for her, had always composed more easily outside the home than within it. It is almost as though the prospect of his approaching death made him finally realize how neglected Marie must have felt for much of her married life.

312* GABRIEL FAURÉ to MARIE FAURÉ

Annecy-le-Vieux
14 October 1924

At the moment I am well, very well, just as well as when I left Paris. I have gracefully submitted to every precaution and I felt their effects admirably until I had this little bout of fatigue which was caused by the end of the quartet. I have a very good appetite, I am happy with the lovely weather these last few days, happy with everything, and I should like everyone to be happy all around me, and everywhere! You can see that I am not bringing back any melancholy thoughts!

During my quiet stay here, you can imagine how I relived that celebration of 14 June:[26] the simple, noble glorification – without the formal hubbub – but so moving even so, of your dear father! Will you look all around you, and even perhaps beyond yourself, and say whether any other woman but you has been able to take delight in such joy during her life? And if you will permit me to slip alongside your father – and you *will* permit me to, I'm sure – can you say what daughter, what wife too, could hear people speaking on the same day of the pure beauty of her father's works, of his career which was so nobly disinterested, and of the pure beauty of the works of her husband and of his career which was no less disinterested? Your life has been a sad one, and perhaps what you missed most of all was your inability ever to achieve your desire to be someone yourself! But does there not remain this profound happiness, to which you can add that of having brought up our sons? In these troubled times, *which are so tainted with unscrupulousness and ambition*, does all that count for nothing? I do hope that you will understand me, and that these lines will display themselves to you in all their sincerity! Do not see anything here, do not look for anything here which is no more than the truth, pure and simple.

In Paris I shall begin each day by giving you, so that you can consign them to the *flames*, all my sketches, all my drafts, everything of which I am determined that *nothing shall exist after me*. It was a big worry I felt when I was ill. You will help me satisfy it. Look after yourself, and see you on Saturday.

I kiss you from the depths of my heart.

Fauré finally returned to Paris four days later, accompanied by his sons. He died on 4 November in his eightieth year; Marie Fauré died in 1926, Philippe in 1954, and Emmanuel in 1971. Fauré's last words to them, the day before his death, had been:

I have done what I could… so may God be my judge![27]

Few can doubt that what Fauré did was in every sense a major contribution to French music. It is unlikely that Fauré's music *in toto* will ever be as popular or as well known as that of Debussy or Ravel, whether in France or elsewhere. Fauré's music never imposes itself by brute force and thus it will be always to a minority that his work will appeal. Even so, he remains a great if underrated figure in the history of music.

Notes

1 Gabriel Hanotaux's wife was to be the dedicatee of *Mirages*, op.113 which Fauré was to compose in July and August 1919. The poems were the work of Baronne Renée de Brimont, to whose work Fauré was introduced by Hanotaux.

2 Chevillard, who was holidaying at Villard de Lans, some 20 miles south-west of

Grenoble, had just been awarded the Légion d'Honneur to which Fauré refers in connection with Hettich in letter 257.

3 *Département* of Seine et Oise, near Paris.

4 The beautiful and historic town situated in the Haute Loire region, south-west of Lyons.

5 The example is from the second subject of Fauré's Piano Quartet, op.45.

6 A.L. Hettich, for whom Fauré had written a *Vocalise-étude*, which in 1907 Hettich had published in a collection of similar pieces.

7 The Second Piano Quintet, op.115. Dedicated to Paul Dukas, Fauré worked on it for nearly 18 months, completing it in February 1921.

8 Lortat (1885–1938) had trained at the Paris Conservatoire, winning the Diémer Prize in 1909. He gave recitals with Jacques Thibaud.

9 Added in pencil by another hand.

10 Georges Hüe (1858–1948), French composer best known for his operas.

11 Gustave Samazeuilh (1877–1967), French critic, translator and composer, who studied at the Schola Cantorum with Chausson and d'Indy.

12 Town nine miles from Toulon.

13 *Fremiet au travail* (Fremiet at work), sculpted by Henri Gréber (1854–1941). He is remembered particularly for his *Narcisse* (1908) in the Luxembourg gardens in Paris.

14 King Manuel II (1889–1932) had been overthrown in 1910 by the Republican movement in Portugal. He went to live at Twickenham and was a popular figure in England. His queen was Augusta Victoria, daughter of Prince Wilhelm of Hohenzollern, whom he married in 1913.

15 *Née* Sophie Fremiet; she married the sculptor François Rude (1784–1855). They were Marie Fauré's great-aunt and -uncle.

16 Alexandre Millerand (1859–1943).

17 Louis Barthou (1862–1934), a Minister who held posts involving both defence and home affairs.

18 Léon Bérard (1876–1960), Minister of Public Education.

19 Louis Hubert Gonzalve Lyautey (1854–1934), Maréchal of France.

20 *Dans la Nymphée* from *Le Jardin clos*.

21 *Jardin nocturne* and *La Danseuse* from *Mirages*.

22 Casals had performed Fauré's *Elégie*, op.24 at the Sorbonne Festival.

23 The Faurés' small dog.

24 Saint-Saëns's two quartets op.112 and op.153 were written in 1899 and 1918.

25 Fauré alludes here to the first movement to be completed, which was the central Andante. The first movement was undertaken on his return to Paris.

26 On that date a statue of Emmanuel Fremiet had been unveiled in the Jardin des Plantes in Paris. (*See* note 13.)

27 P. Fauré-Fremiet, *Gabriel Fauré*, p. 130.

——'Original French texts'——

Letter 11

O toi dont les doigts parfumés
pressent avec un rhythme
harmonieux les touches d'ivoire!
Ta mère pleine de grâce, qui habite
près du soleil au pied
des montagnes bleues m'a envoyé un
pâté dont les flancs jaunes
renferment mille délices
Un pâté semblable à la robe d'or
glorieux empereur de la Chine,
de la robe qui recouvre le sein du fils
du ciel, le sien qui
couvre les divines pensées.
Lundi, la robe d'or s'ouvrira et les
divines pensées
s'exhaleront; mais si ton regard
manquait à cette radieuse
éclosion
le pâté serait semblable au papillon
qui sort du cocon par un
jour de pluie, privé du regard du
soleil,
et mes joues pendraient sur mon sein,
fanées par la tristesse,
comme une pivoine oubliée dans une
vase sans eau.

Letter 23

Pleurez torrents, pleurez rochers,
pleurez fontaine,
Source de Mauhourat pleurez,
Le maît de chapell' d' la Madeleine
Va vous ravir l'aspect d'son nez!

Letter 219

Combien à ce jardin fermé par des
      épines
      Impitoyablement
Je préfère celui que parfument,
      divines,
      Les Roses d'Ispahan.

List of letters

each grouped under the relevant source

Lettres intimes
1 None
2 36, 62–6, 70–1, 73–4, 77–84, 86, 88–91, 93–104, 106
3 107, 108–28, 130–5, 137–41, 145–50, 152–9, 161–5, 167–9, 172–80, 184–5, 187–91, 193, 200–3
4 205–10, 214–7, 220–4, 226–33, 235–44
5 245–55, 258–60, 265–6, 269, 271–2, 276, 278–82, 284–90, 294–6, 298–302, 304–12

Fauré archives (now Bibliothèque Nationale)
1 1, 7–10, 12–27, 29–34
2 35, 43–8, 51, 53–60, 72, 75
3 136, 142–4, 160, 166, 170–1, 181, 183, 192, 198
4 212, 225, 234
5 256, 267, 270, 292–3, 297

Bibliothèque Nationale
1 28
2 40, 68–9, 76, 87, 105
3 204
4 213
5 257, 261–4, 268, 273–5, 277, 283, 291, 303

Correspondance Saint-Saëns – Fauré
1 2–6, 11
2 38–9, 41, 49–50, 52, 61, 67, 85, 92
3 129, 194–7, 199
4 218–9
5 None

Association des amis de Gabriel Fauré
1 None
2 37, 42
3 151, 182, 186
4 211
5 None

Index of letters

General Index

Names of persons appear below only if they occur in the body of the text; for names of the various correspondents, see index of letters. Towns and cities are listed with the exception of Paris. Only titles of works by Fauré occur in the index, headed alphabetically under Fauré, Gabriel.